ALSO BY JOHN DeMONT

*Citizens Irving: K.C. Irving and His Legacy*
*Coal Black Heart: The Story of Coal and Lives It Ruled*
*The Last Best Place: Lost in the Heart of Nova Scotia*
*A Good Day's Work: In Pursuit of a Disappearing Canada*

—

# THE LONG WAY
# HOME

—

# The Long Way Home

---

A PERSONAL HISTORY
*of* NOVA SCOTIA

---

## John DeMont

McCLELLAND & STEWART

Library and Archives Canada Cataloguing in Publication
is available upon request

ISBN: 978-0-7710-2511-2
ebook ISBN: 978-0-7710-2513-6

Published simultaneously in the United States of America by
McClelland & Stewart, a division of Penguin Random House Canada,
a Penguin Random House Company

Library of Congress Control Number is available upon request

Book design by Jennifer Griffiths
Jacket photograph: Sambro Island Gas House which housed the fuel oil
for Sambro Island Lighthouse, built in 1758 and is the oldest operating
lighthouse in North America © shaunl / Getty Images
Typeset in Sabon LT Pro by M&S, Toronto

Printed and bound in the USA

Quotation on page ix © 1949 Robertson Davies and used by
permission of the author's estate and The Cooke Agency.

Grateful acknowledgement is made to *Maclean's* magazine for permission
to reprint previously published material:

"A Cape Breton Farewell," John DeMont (January 31, 2000)
"One Last whistle," John DeMont (August 6, 2001)
"The Last Best Place," John DeMont (June 19, 1995)

McClelland & Stewart,
a division of Penguin Random House Canada Limited,
a Penguin Random House Company
www.penguinrandomhouse.ca

1  2  3  4  5     21  20  19  18  17

To Lisa, Belle and Sam

Before dinner, I observed, everybody seemed to want to talk about the Good Old Days. I am, generally speaking, better at this than anybody else, for I am not bothered by details of chronology, and tend to regard as my own, reminiscences which have been imparted to me by the Ancients of my tribe.

*The Table Talk of Samuel Marchbanks,*
ROBERTSON DAVIES

The author patrolling the lawless streets of Halifax

# Up in the Old Cemetery

*Walking Among Ghosts—The Ambiance of History—A Fine Specimen of Manhood—*
*Geography and Fate—Portentous Signs—Hard Slogging—The Great Migration*
*—The First Peoples—The Men in the White Robes—Human Narrative*
*—Melancholic Beauty—Forever in Flames*
*—Time, Take Me by the Hand*

I can't recall the moment when I first understood that I was on this earth. I do remember, though, when I first realized where I lived—the place I have now lived most of my life, and where I fully expect to be buried. It was dark. No one seemed to be around—which does not necessarily mean it was late, since it has long been my experience that no matter where you roam in the province of Nova Scotia it is usually mostly empty.

What was I doing out there on the loose at the age of six or seven? Everything and everyone I knew—friends, school, the fields where I played and the church where I worshipped—was bound up in a few city blocks in Halifax, the provincial capital. My parents were as on the case as any, but parents were parents in those be-back-when-the-street-lights-go-on days. It is possible that I was like a puppy that had crept tentatively outside when somebody left the door open. I really cannot say. I just know that it thrills me to think about this burst of freedom all these years later, so I must have felt much the same way then, crossing a wide avenue that was said to run halfway to the border of New Brunswick, the next province west.

I would have been moving quickly, for that is how I did everything in those days. The air was sultry. If fog was coming it was still a ways off. But the street lights, houses and occasional car all had a magnified brightness. Sounds—the rustling of trees, the buzz of an electrical transformer—expanded to fill the air. Time, which for me at that age unspooled at a languid pace, had slowed to a crawl, as it does when something special is happening. Wind rocked the chain on the gate to the Camp Hill Cemetery, although that could have just been my senses vibrating, for I was—and remain—a believer in things unseen and entities and eminences floating in the air. Stories just drifted into my head then, as they did to any kid with a fanciful mind. You saw something and you imposed a narrative, not because you felt it was fantasy but because you thought that it must be true.

I had no inkling then that people who had done things lay buried there: privateers, soldiers and merchants, enemies of Confederation and near-prime ministers. Folks who at one point started banks and breweries, shipping empires, the modern-day oil business and other necessities of life. Heroic figures who, because of a moment's actions, lived on long after they had fed the worms, and figures whose shameful deeds meant their names too would endure. Heralding the working life that would follow, I just walked right up to the wrought-iron fence and peered in. I tried to be quiet, since people seemed to be breathing in there. It would be another fifteen years before I attended my first funeral, so it is possible that by then I'd never actually been inside a cemetery and, therefore, could have been in search of spirits. I was looking for something; I do know that.

From where I stood I would have seen obelisks and squat gravestones that, if I'd been inside the gate and could have walked right up to them, I would have noted were covered in lichens and the grime of time, the inscriptions so worn away as to be indecipherable. It is possible that I heard voices—from the bloody scalpings and the terrible explosion, from the massing troops and warships, from the sirs and ladies carried through the muddy streets in gilded carriages, from the strutting pirates and the unfortunates who arrived here from the Highlands, the slums of London and the torched loyalist settlements of the Thirteen Colonies—rising like a collective moan. But I think I would have remembered. What I do certainly recollect is a pleasurable feeling that, half a century later, I recognize as the ache of nostalgia, even though at such an age I had nothing to be really nostalgic about.

The sensation cannot have lasted long. There was a noise. I turned, I'm sure without looking, and hightailed it, running as fast as I could, staying under the street lights all the way home, which was really only two city blocks but seemed like so much farther. I have no inkling of what happened next. Whether my absenteeism had repercussions or whether I just slipped back into bed without anyone noticing that I'd gone AWOL, I cannot rightly say. As I recount it now it all sounds like a dream, doesn't it? And I would have considered that maybe I made the whole thing up. Except for the desire to return to some hazy previous time. I remember it still. It's really never left.

I was born in the spring of 1956 in a hospital a few blocks from where I wandered that night. But genes have memory, so Nova Scotia and I go way back. My people are come-from-aways; unless your veins carry Mi'kmaq blood, that's true of everybody in this province. We have been striving folk from the start, working in the mills and mines, going to war, leaving the countryside for jobs that kept our faces clean in the glittering mecca of Halifax, vamoosing without a backward glance to parts unknown, sometimes just staying put. I've done my best to shake Nova Scotia. I've lived in Ottawa twice, and in Toronto and Calgary. But the tidal pull of the place has always been deep and emotional, beyond logic. Once, my wife and I were *this* close to heading somewhere exotic and far away. Then, good jobs opened up in Halifax and that was that, because, for better or worse, it seems I will have no other place.

Like most kids who grew up here, what I first learned about Nova Scotia I learned in a classroom, seated at a little wooden desk with iron legs and a top that lifted open, revealing the scribblers, pencils, rulers, scissors and rubber-stoppered glue bottles stored inside. My memory is that the cover of the history text then used in Nova Scotia's elementary schools was adorned with the province's coat of arms, which, along with reminders of its Scottish roots, featured a Mi'kmaq man, a mythical unicorn and a bare arm and laurel sprig, meant to represent the conquest of hardships to be met here. I must have liked what I read in there, because it stuck with me. New information got added in the formative years that followed, even though I wasn't much of a reader as a kid. But I watched our two channels of Canadian television. I'd hear some folk song or some old relative talking.

History really just seemed to be in the ether in this place where ambiance was everywhere: the fog, the air, the silence, the buildings that seemed to hide more than they revealed, the broody nature of the people, myself included. There was something else, too. If you paid attention, the past was here and now in this province, where it retained a power over human lives and destinies, unlike in other places I've lived and got to know. Looking at time in a linear A-to-B fashion didn't even make sense here, a place where once-upon-a-time and the present are so intertwined that they seem inseparable, existing in some new dimension.

This book began as an attempt make something of that old feeling of walking among ghosts, of being haunted by history that took place before I was even born and being transplanted back endlessly into a past that may or may not have existed. To get to the bottom of what I think I know about this place and how I feel about it. To understand, I suppose, how Nova Scotia somehow finally became Nova Scotia and, by extension, how I became me.

It was, by and large, a sweet idea because for a long, long time writers have been rambling around this province and making notes about what they think and see, who they meet and whatever adventures befall them. One of them is buried up in the old cemetery, on the southern side, under the shade of a hydrangea tree. Joseph Howe was just twenty-three at the moment I have in mind, which may sound young to own a newspaper, but not if you had already been in the business for a decade, if you were already a poet of sorts and knew the trade of the printer as well as that of the post-office clerk. Not if, with a partner, you had already bought one paper and, disposing of that, recently become the editor and sole proprietor of a weekly broadsheet called the *Novascotian*.

Howe's trio of half-brothers from his father's first marriage were said to be "fine specimens of manhood, tall, well-built, splendid in appearance." Howe was not. There's a photograph of him from what I assume to be the days when he was a spent force: he sits slumped supine in his chair. His hair—which one historian described as standing straight up as if "electrified by the energy within"—is as tangled as his eyebrows. His head, as disproportionately large as an Easter Island statue, seems to sit directly atop his shoulders. Yet it was said, of an earlier point in Howe's life, that "when his face glowed with the inspiration that burning thoughts and words impart, and his great, deep chest swelled and broadened, he looked positively nobly and kingly."

That is the man I choose to picture setting out in 1828, along one of Nova Scotia's two "great roads," which only meant that they were sturdy enough to carry stagecoaches drawn by four horses, such as the one in which Howe rode. He was, even then, a man who loved women and parties. Who, after a day on the political stump, would pull off his jacket and dance with the young folk into the wee hours. Who could hold his own with a visiting earl or talk animal husbandry at the kitchen table of a farmer out in the borderlands. Who could not write other than to mark an X to sign his name. A man who, after a long day's work at the printing shop, would, on warm summer evenings, sometimes trot down to a waterfront market slip, hurl his clothes to the ground and plunge into the harbour for a starlit swim, thereby raising his esteem in my eyes.

Howe's mission on this trip, as befitting a man who described himself as possessing a "restless, agitating uncertainty," was multidimensional: to keep creditors at bay—he was perpetually in debt because of bad business decisions and his willingness to front loans to credit-unworthy friends—and keep his business and household afloat by collecting what he could from existing subscribers to the *Novascotian* and finding new readers wherever he could; but also to take the temperature of the province, and then write a series of sketches in his paper about what he had learned.

Gingerly I walk in his footsteps; every scribbler does here. I've been cognitively aware of him since my junior high basketball team was pummelled by some tough kids from a school carrying his name, which also adorns streets and public buildings around Halifax. Joe

Howe's statue stands heroically on the lawn of the provincial legislature. His very words about the journalist's trade—"When I sit down in solitude to the labours of my profession, the only questions I ask myself are: What is right? What is just? What is for the public good?"—makes every reporter here bow their head unworthily.

When I began working on this book I was a columnist at the paper that brought Nova Scotians the news that the *Titanic* had sunk, but, from the looks of things, might not be telling them anything for much longer. While there was still time, I was supposed to mull the big and small questions about this province. Whenever possible I was supposed to slam my car into drive, exit the Halifax city limits in a cloud of dust and have a look around like a latter-day Joe Howe. I was supposed to cup my chin in my hand and consider the past and, with furrowed brow, ponder the future of a place that, depending upon your perspective, seemed as imperilled as the paper for which I worked.

Time was of the essence: the contraction of newspapers and magazines and the slimming down of television and radio stations, along with the ascent of a type of media that demands that the world somehow be contained in 140 characters, means the days are numbered for ink slingers with the licence to see things for themselves, to draw their own conclusions and, rightly or wrongly, tell their own version of events. But all we can do is what we can do.

A few things, after all this time here, I do know: it's easy to see how our geography made us who we are. How jutting out into the Atlantic, being perched on the periphery of the country and hanging off the very edge of the continent as we are, allowed this small stretch of land to catch all sorts of traffic from so many faraway places, some of which arrived intentionally, some of which just washed up here. We've been a bit player in the big story. We've been the battlefield of warring empires and the great prize in the conflict for a continent. We've seen some good days. We've had some wealth. We know this because we can still glimpse hints of it, outside of Halifax in just a few bricks left over from a wall, or an old B and B gussied up for the tourist trade. These at one time were the homes of industrialists, we're told. Great heroes at one point trod those floors, it is our understanding, stared into fires over the rims of their grog cups and contemplated their next decision.

Those were different days. Halifax—with its greater concentration of PhDs per capita than anywhere in the country, its navy, universities and government—was just dandy. But it had evolved into an independent city-state. The outlying areas, the countryside, are where the teeth-gnashing was loudest. The day I walked into the *Chronicle Herald* newsroom in 2011, a paper mill that had long been the economic lifeblood of the proud town of Liverpool closed for good. The malaise was deeper than the slump in newsprint markets. Anybody could see that the troubled rural economy was causing things to unravel. One day in Berwick, the "apple capital of Nova Scotia," a couple of twenty-year-olds doused a local homeless man with gasoline while he slept in a bus shelter, flicked on a cigarette lighter and set him aflame. At the other end of the province, where for generations my people had been punching in at the coal pit and steel mill, I discovered that the only shift change at J.A. Douglas McCurdy Sydney Airport was when the latest rotation out of the Fort McMurray oil sands disembarked from an airplane and the next crew bound for Alberta filed on. My dad and uncles, perhaps in that over-romanticized way that I have inherited, used to talk about the lovable oddballs who once roamed the streets of Glace Bay when they were growing up in the tough coal town. I thought about that one afternoon a few blocks from the old Demont hacienda as I passed a knot of hard-looking young guys who, to a person, fixed me with empty thousand-mile stares.

The portentous signs were everywhere. In Yarmouth, a boom-town during the Great Age of Sail, the best hope for the future seemed to be a heavily subsidized ferry that brought tourists for a few months a year. One day I pulled into New Glasgow, which Howe called "a thriving little village" and which, a century ago, was hailed by Prime Minister Wilfrid Laurier as soon to be "the Birmingham of the Country." There, in the downtown of a place where good people live, I walked along one of the main streets and started totalling up the "For Rent" signs until I just stopped counting.

I wasn't the only person who noticed. One day, the smart president of a tiny Baptist university in a pretty little town unveiled a report on the state of things in this province entitled "Now or Never: An urgent call to action for Nova Scotians," which laid out, as bluntly as he dared, the extent of the province's economic and demographic woes. There was nothing in it that expert panels around here hadn't been saying for a long time. I waited, we all did, hoping to hear about a new way forward. The problems were deep, the news noncommittal. Nova Scotia, compared to just about anywhere else in the world, was a great place, there's no denying that. But it is hard slogging here. It always has been. That, as much as anything, is the story, even if it is only one part of the story.


The first humans, we now know, came here by foot across a land bridge from Siberia to Alaska at a time of lower sea levels during the last Ice Age, then lurched down the continent through an ice-free corridor east of the Rocky Mountains. Oral history and archaeological evidence indicate that around ten thousand years ago a people who would become known as Mi'kmaq inhabited the coastal areas of Quebec's Gaspé peninsula and the Maritime provinces east of the Saint John River. The Mi'kmaq have an old story, passed down from generation to generation, about how a young woman once dreamed that she saw a small island floating in towards the land. The island held some bare trees and a few men, including one dressed in garb made of white rabbit skins. When told of her dream, Mi'kmaq wise men were baffled. But the next day at dawn, they saw a small island near the shore. There appeared to be trees on the island and bears climbing among their bare branches. Alarmed, the Mi'kmaq grabbed their bows, pulled back the strings on their arrows, and then stopped when they discovered that the shapes in the trees were actually men. The strange humans lowered an even stranger canoe into the water, jumped in and paddled towards shore. One of the men was dressed in a white robe. He approached the Mi'kmaq making signs of peace and goodwill, raising his hand, in a pointing gesture, towards the heavens.

This is mostly a book about what has happened to this place after the men in the white robes arrived. What has occurred since then is every bit as complicated and multidimensional as one might imagine: the overwhelming of the First Peoples and the arrival of a mélange of pioneers who carved out pockets of the wilderness; the random acts, unexplained mysteries and conspiratorial plottings; the mixture of shameful achievements and noble failures; the rapture and misery, the twists of destiny and the hard-heartedness of fate.

It is no inspiring, forever-onward-and-upward-yarn of a place and its people, either, for Nova Scotia has never been straightforward. The province's motto, *Munit haec et altera vincit* (One defends and the other conquers), acknowledges as much. So does the way the rest of world sees us—for a long time as a place of new starts, even a promised land, but more recently as a locale of shimmering geography, filled with people in out-of-step industries with last-century skill sets—which is so at odds with how we see ourselves: as a place forever on the cusp of something big. A place that still has much to teach the world about how to live even as it struggles, as it always has, to find a way forward.

The human narrative that explains this place and its people far better than mere events—its biography rather than its history—is, in my own stumbling way, what I went searching for and what this book is about. It is a tricky story to tell for a number of reasons. This has always been, by and large, an empty place. It seems forever in flames and yet, for long periods of time, not much seemed to happen. Economically, it would be hard to argue that Nova Scotia has really worked out. Yet around here we're always reminded of how great parts of this province have been from time to time, and how great— with the right circumstances and a little luck—they could be again. There's also a poetry to this small place that I've never quite been able to put my finger on, other than to say that it is as beautiful as it is melancholic and, impossible as this might seem, that is heightened by the hardships and perpetual disappointments faced by those who call Nova Scotia home.

It's an old thing I try to do here. The notion goes straight back to the days of Joseph Howe. I have tried to boil things down. I have sifted through ruins, because everyone who walked here before has left their mark on this land. I have considered the legends, which tell of a Nova Scotia that never was, but somehow must have been. I have contemplated the past, even though it is never really past. I have tried to give you a sense of how we got where we are and what, for a person who lived here, it was like. Consequently, I have had to make choices, which means some things and people get less coverage than they deserve and others more than they might seem to merit. Someday it will be somebody else's province and somebody else's story, but for now this is my explanation of Nova Scotia. And so I would direct you to a line I'm fond of from a poet named Ilya Kaminsky: *Time, my twin, take me by the hand through the streets of your city.* Then I would ask, well, are you ready? Shall we?

Actors recreate a gathering of the
Order of Good Cheer at Port Royal.

# Creation Song

Behind the paper where I worked in the smallish twenty-first-century Nova Scotia city of Halifax, there's a little side street adjacent to some raised railway tracks where trains run with less and less regularity. Back there, if you looked hard enough through the trees and scrub, you could see a camouflage-green pup tent with a tarp across the entrance held in place by some chewed-up blue twine. I would periodically go sniff around back there, in theory looking for something to write about, but really just curious to meet the occupant, most likely a victim of globalism, PTSD or just plain bad luck, but who I prayed was there of his own volition, not because he had run out of places to shelter. Since I was brought up to give people their space, I never picked my way up the little incline and flipped open the makeshift flap to introduce myself. I just stood outside, politely asking if there was anyone in there. Nobody ever said anything, even though I had the sneaking feeling that the durable person who laid their head there was perhaps somewhere nearby watching me.

Then, one day, I discovered that the tent was just gone, as if the occupant had been some figment of my imagination. It made me feel bad not to have done something to get him in out of the cold, to show him the sociability of God-fearing people with mortgages, Netflix accounts and acid reflux. But I would be lying if I did not say that I also savoured the notion that he/she was out there, somewhere, travelling light and free, living by their skill and wits, as unconstrained as an old-time Mi'kmaq warrior.

I was due somewhere else that day and rain threatened. But I left the Halifax environs distracted, my mind making an abrupt leap to years earlier, when I lived in Toronto, childless, without a mortgage or even a car, in those days when the disposable income and personal freedom curves briefly intersected. Back then my pals and I had a ritual. Every so often we would head to some fine eatery. We would peruse the menu and ask the waiters pensive questions about the wine list. Then, assuming that the day's deadlines had all been met, or at least pushed off far enough into the foreseeable future, we would do our part to stimulate Ontario's food and beverage industry.

Legends were forged during the epic luncheons, which could backfire if you returned to your magazine's office and discovered that you had four hours to write three thousand words about a failed trust company whose name you could no longer pronounce. Since we were blessed with a sense of occasion, one of us would invariably sit up straight in those glittering rooms and look ceiling-wards, as if in search of some heavenly place. He would say slowly, in a tone deeper than his own natural speaking voice, "To the Order," and then we would clink and glug.

It was a little joke we had. But the truth is that I was taken by l'Ordre de Bon Temps, the Order of Good Cheer, long before I actually knew what it meant. Inside some Halifax classroom, I enjoyed the rhythm of the words. Even a child can grasp the basic concept of good versus bad cheer. Sooner or later I saw some artist's rendering of the seventeenth-century Frenchmen with their doublets and breeches, their buckled shoes and frilly collars. In single file they paraded into the hall of Port Royal—our Plymouth Rock, where the story of the white people in this place began—to eat and drink and somehow enjoy themselves in the face of the dread that has to haunt every explorer in lands where any number of unseen terrors lurk outside in the dark.

To my kid's eyes it looked like a high old time. And since the Order of Good Cheer was my first and most enduring memory of Nova Scotian history, I thought it a logical place to begin this book. A story, after all, has to start somewhere. Mine opens the moment a fellow named Pierre du Bosc-Douyn, who went by du Boullay, walked into the hall where those great feasts were held. Like the other men who had settled there, he had come on a whim, from a place far away. Chances of it working out, he had to know, were slim. But in my mind, du Boullay's free, questing spirit was so directly linked to that of the restless soul in the woods in back of the newspaper, it is as if they were connected across half a millennium by the world's most durable fishing line. At least, so it seemed to me, pushing west in the gathering rain, in search of a creation story.

I know from the scant information available that du Boullay was no François Addenin. He could not, like the skilful bodyguard of the governor of the new French territory of Acadia, down mallards and geese on the fly or, from forty yards out, splatter the guts of partridges and of birds for which they had no name. But du Boullay was still a senior captain in the regiment of Jean de Biencourt, Sieur de Poutrincourt, the commandant of the habitation of Port Royal. As such he was a member of l'Ordre de Bon Temps, the dining club that had been struck to raise morale after the disastrous winter before. They took turns being responsible for the feast, each trying to outdo the other in the bounty they found in the harbour and forests. When it was his turn, du Boullay could look down the barrel of his musket, resting on its fork in the snowy woods around the habitation, and turn deer, bear, rabbits and wildcat into fare for the banquet. The cook then did his part, transforming the tender flesh of the stag into good pasties, fashioning something worthy of la Rue aux Ours, that Paris street of gastronomic marvels, from the delicate flesh of the beaver tail, even making a toothsome sauce to enhance the taste of the sturgeons that the Mi'kmaq had brought him.

Du Boullay is not singled out in any artist's renderings that I've seen. But I know in my heart that he marched into the great hall of the fort—napkin on his shoulder, wand of office in his hand, the collar of l'Ordre, which was said to be worth more than four crowns, around his neck—with the other founding members, who also arrived with spirits high and cheeks ruddy. My admiration for them shines through the ages because, like our modern-day hermit, they would have been weary men who had seen and experienced much. Men who were still trying to forget the carnage of the Wars of Religion, which pitted the aristocratic houses of France against each other, claiming millions of lives in the process. They wanted escape from a country where the economy was so blighted that even the king was poor. ("My shirts are all torn, my doublet has gone through at the elbow," Henri IV wrote when ascending the French throne, "and my soup-pot is often upside down.") Their health, in some cases, would never fully recover from the ailment that they called land sickness, and we would know as scurvy, which at first made their gums swell and their teeth fall out, but later left them bedridden and wracked with body-shaking convulsions.

My research has taught me that the small band of Frenchmen in the habitation that winter included nobles with élan, restless adventurers and men of the lower classes on the rise. Port Royal was an outpost of empire, a tool for their monarch's bid to expand France's reach into North America and the riches of its fur trade. The men in the banquet room—their mouths gaping and toothless, their beards wild, their hair stiff with grease, their scent gamey—fit that mould. Maybe, like wandering, lordless samurai in a Kurosawa movie, they craved motion and action. Perhaps, like a twenty-first-century man who would rather take to the woods in a tent than exist side by side with the rest of us, they never felt quite right in their former lives. It is possible that they only needed a purpose—adventure, riches, the greater glory of *mère* France—which they found in this unknown land that the mapmakers called La Cadie, l'Acadie or, in English, Acadia.

My understanding is that when the Order convened, a dozen or so dignitaries normally sat at the table of honour in the dining hall's gloom. It would have been easy, just by body language, to identify the habitation's leader. Sieur de Poutrincourt's sister was a lady-in-waiting to Mary, Queen of Scots. Two of his older brothers were lost to the Wars of Religion, in which Poutrincourt, a Catholic, fought hard against Henri IV until the monarch converted to Catholicism. At nearly fifty, this fourth son of an old and noble family, this big-spirited humanist who composed secular and sacred musical works in his free time, hoped to find peace for his wife and children in l'Acadie, where he wanted to create a paradise in the New World.

Poutrincourt's presence as governor of Port Royal was at the behest of another founding member of the Order: Pierre Dugua, Sieur de Mons, a resolute Huguenot nobleman who had earned King Henri's gratitude for his courage in the monarch's service during the Wars of Religion. Dugua was said to be good company, an affable, calm and generous *sieur* to whom the king had granted a charter "to people and inhabit the lands, shores, and countries of Acadia, and other surrounding areas, stretching from the fortieth parallel to the forty-sixth, and there to establish our authority, and otherwise to there settle and maintain himself in such a way that our subjects will henceforth be able to be received, to frequent, to dwell there, and to trade with the savage inhabitants of the said places."

I guffaw like Kramer when I think of the sensation the Sieur de Mons must have created when he arrived back in France in the winter of 1604 in the hope of rallying support for the enterprise. He brought with him a red thirty-foot canoe that his sailors paddled past the Louvre, to the delight of the young French dauphin. The holds of his ship held a baby moose, a caribou, a muskrat and a live hummingbird, along with other wonders of the New World. An impression was important: the court of Versailles was a place of intrigues at the turn of the seventeenth century, and de Mons had powerful enemies—his mercantile rivals, who connived against his Acadian monopoly.

In the Port Royal hall, even through the swirling mists of time, two diners in particular stood out. Marc Lescarbot was a figure of note back in Paris, where he practised law and counted writers and nobles among his circle. When the wine flowed, as it often did at Port Royal, Lescarbot—who, during long winter nights, would retire to his rooms to write and read in Latin, Greek, Hebrew, Italian and French—made reference to some ancient wrong at the hands of unscrupulous judges in Paris and disappointments that perhaps could never be righted. He was induced to come to Acadia, he later wrote, "by his desire to flee a corrupt world and to examine this world with his own eyes." In any event, he wrote a poem, "Adieu à la France," and at Poutrincourt's invitation joined the expedition.

Back in Paris, Lescarbot would publish a book with a long, rambling title: *Nova Francia: or the description of that part of New France, which is one continent with Virginia: described in the three late voyages and plantation made by Monsieur de Monts, Monsieur du Pont-Gravé, and Monsieur de Poutrincourt, into the countries called by the French men La Cadie, lying to the Southwest of Cape Breton: Together with an excellent severall treatie of all the commodities of the said countries, and maners of the natural inhabitants of the same.* It was a mix of travelogue and anthropological study and is said to be one of the first great books of the history of Canada. In 2015 a copy of this exceedingly rare, 406-year-old manuscript fetched $285,000.

In it he called Samuel de Champlain, the other figure of note at the Order's head table that evening, a man of "good courage" and an individual of "reckoning." The understatement makes sense. De Mons's cartographer was a fleeting presence at Port Royal. Often, Champlain was far away. If he wasn't exploring the "great river of Canada," which meant the St. Lawrence, or retracing the travels of the great Jacques Cartier, he was "discoursing" with the savages. L'Ordre de Bon Temps, the continent's first social club, was his idea.

But that is not why I have long been haunted by Champlain. I was taken with him from the moment I heard his name for the same reason that, as a kid, I was obsessed with Robin Hood movies and every one of Muhammad Ali's fights. Because they had courage and flair, as well as an other-worldly level of skill. More than anything, I have not been able to get Champlain out of my head for all these years because of this: he was the first genuinely heroic person I had ever heard of with a connection to the place where I lived. He was touched by splendour and by extension; therefore, so was I.

What do you need to know about him? That Champlain was a soldier who fought in Europe, the Caribbean and North America "until he bore the scars of wounds on his face and body, and witnessed atrocities beyond imagining," according to his biographer David Fischer. In a thirty-four-year career at sea, he made at least twenty-seven Atlantic crossings and hundreds of other voyages. Experts, Fischer said, marvelled at his mapmaking excellence, particularly with the crude instruments at his command in the early seventeenth century. He wrote more and better than any major explorer of North America during this period. He set the standard among explorers for good relations with the native peoples of the New World. He was the "Father of New France."

Is it fair that I don't feel the same way towards him as I do to the other wanderers who came before him? Giovanni Caboto was a flat-earther thought to have been born in Genoa, Italy. Based on the paintings I have seen, John Cabot, as he came to be known, had a nose like a swan's beak and a beard woven into a pair of stalactites. Like his more-famous contemporary Christopher Columbus, he thought that sailing west from Europe was the quickest route to Asia; people cared about such things in the Middle Ages, when merchants felt a pressing need for new trade routes to the east. Under the auspices of King Henry VII, Cabot left Bristol in the spring of 1497 on a fast, able ship with a small crew. They travelled west and north, believing it was a shorter route to Asia than Columbus's along the Trade Winds. Fifty days into the voyage, Cabot landed on the east coast of North America. Precisely where is a mystery: some historians think he may have alighted at Newfoundland, Labrador or even Maine. Others believe that Cabot disembarked at Cape Breton Island, perhaps even mainland Nova Scotia. In any event, thinking that he had made land in Asia, he claimed it for England's king.

I've only once been on a vessel in the middle of the Atlantic Ocean: a container ship making its way from Halifax to the French island of St. Pierre, off the south coast of Newfoundland. I went in December. It gets worse: I did so mainly for the food, which was supposed to have been provided by full-fledged French chefs—St. Pierre, as it remains today, a possession of France—and the wines, which were from Bordeaux and Burgundy. Except that seasickness kept me in my bunk for thirty-six straight hours. On the way back I bought a ticket on a rickety turboprop that only set down on the St. Pierre airport when the fog managed to lift. A phobic flyer, I preferred death by plane crash to another day and a half of delirium-inducing nausea.

So I have a respect for those ancient ocean explorers that goes beyond what appears in the history books. My pulse beats a little quicker when I think about some Viking adventurer at the bow of his longship, squinting through the spume for the first view of terra firma, or, centuries before Cabot lived, an Orkney prince, supposedly on the run with the treasure of the Knights Templar, peering through the fog at the forests of spruce, the barrens and beaches and sharp, prehistoric edges of the land. When I was a kid reading textbooks, it seemed that so many of the Europeans who showed up around here back then did so largely by mistake, or because they were guided by some crazy notion. They got lost and sailed completely off course. They came out of a bank of fog, and *Jesus Christ*, there was some rocky shore that took the ship down and ensured that those who were left eventually had to dine on each other as they waited for another misguided explorer to happen by.

A few of them knew what they were doing. Before Cabot made his brief appearance, Basque fishermen, searching for cod for the many fasting days in the Catholic calendar, routinely dried their catches on the Canso Islands on the Atlantic Ocean side of this province. (Champlain had great admiration for a Basque whaler he encountered there named Captain Savalette, who had crossed the Atlantic eighty-three times by 1565, the year Champlain was born.) Then Henri IV, the first of France's Bourbon monarchs, finally began thinking about New France and its rich fur trade, which changed everything. As his banner carrier, the king chose Troilus de Mesgoùez, Marquis de La Roche-Helgomarche, a chevalier, a captain and a counsellor of state whose first flotilla got no farther than the French coast before sinking. When the fleet finally left the European shores, La Roche's crew was mostly made up of vagabonds and vagrants. They were bound for a crescent-shaped spit of land in the Atlantic Ocean where, years before, a Portuguese explorer named João Álvares Fagundes may have established a settlement.

There was no need for niceties on this place, which had been known as Sable Island but was rechristened the Île de Bourbon by La Roche. He settled his people on its north side, then promptly vanished. Every spring for the next few years one of his ships would return with supplies for the deportees. One year, the usual shipload of fish and wine failed to arrive. The colonists took it badly, slaughtering the commandant and the storeskeeper, and then, in a fit of bloodlust, butchering everyone else in a position of authority. Just eleven men boarded La Roche's supply ship for the return voyage that spring. Back in France, they were presented to Henri IV who, if appalled by their behaviour, did not show it. "Instead of their being hanged for their misdeeds," an indignant La Roche later wrote, "they have been given money, although they have themselves admitted to the murders."


I try not to get too bogged down in that grim story because it is conceivable that, at the precise moment La Roche was putting quill to paper with those aggrieved words, *La Bonne Renommée,* 120 tons when fully loaded, and the 100-foot-long *Don de Dieu* were drawing provisions in a pair of Norman seaports. Aboard those ships were straight-up noblemen, as well as "gentlemen adventurers" not of noble birth. There were mariners with long experience at sea. There were housewrights, master carpenters, master miners, blacksmiths and others who worked with their hands. There were, in addition to surgeons and apothecaries, skilled and semiskilled men and boys, some of whom were paupers and convicts who had been told to choose between the ship and the scaffold. Aboard the ships were Swiss soldiers, the leading mercenaries of their day, along to keep order, and men of the cloth, Protestant and Catholic, there to minister to spiritual needs, and a "*naigre*" of African origin who "spoke the languages of Acadia."

At the helm of the whole enterprise was de Mons, the leader of the expedition as well as the instrument of Henri IV's forward-ho foreign policy. I am not precisely sure when the misguided view that de Mons was an ancestor took hold among my people. I am just happy to say that it did, because even a fictional connection makes it easier for me to imagine the pair of ships, flying the naval ensign of France and the royal standard of Henri IV, leaving Normandy in April 1604, bound for the New France fishing harbour of Canso. The Atlantic waves were so high that one nearly carried a carpenter over the side. Nearer the New World the ships ran into ice floes that forced them to veer far enough to the south that only agile navigation stopped the expedition from going aground on Sable Island. A week later they dropped anchor in a long bay by a headland, where they stayed a few days, before heading southwest along the coast.

One of my favourite parts of the story of the early colonization of Nova Scotia is how, as the Frenchmen sailed along, they named places into existence: at one harbour they discovered a French vessel violating de Mons's monopoly by trading furs with the Indians. So the place became Port au Rossignol, named after the ship's captain they imprisoned. Another bay, where a sheep went overboard, was christened Port au Mouton. Champlain, commanding a small barque, stopped at one place he called Isle aux Cormorans, after the birds he found there, and another that he named Cap Fourchu because it resembled the tines of a fork. In a small shallop used to cross shallow waters, Champlain and de Mons turned the southernmost point of Acadia. Then they made their way around the great bay to a river, which they may have christened Saint-Jean because they arrived there on the feast day of St. John the Baptist.

Nearby was a wooded island that looked easy to fortify, an important consideration when colonists feared death not just from Indians in the woods but also from European rivals from the sea. There looked to be good farmland and plenty of timber and water. The river appeared to teem with fish. To the Frenchmen's dismay, the moment they started building their quarters, clouds of biting blackflies descended from the sky and mosquitoes coated their skin. The first snow fell in the first week of October. A cruel wind forever howled. Temperatures plummeted, freezing not just the river, isolating them from the mainland, but also their wine, cider and drinking water, which had to be hacked out of an icy block. The firewood ran out. Soon, all they had to eat were dried provisions and salt meat.

Before long the scurvy set in, an event Champlain described this way:

> There developed in the mouths of those who had it, large pieces of excess fungus flesh which caused a great rot. This increased to such a degree that they could hardly eat anything except in very liquid form. Their teeth barely held in place, and could be removed with the fingers without causing pain. This excess flesh was often cut away, which caused them to bleed extensively from the mouth. Afterwards, severe pain developed in the arms and legs, which became swollen and very hard and covered with spots like fleabites. They could not walk due to the tightness of the nerves. Consequently, they had almost no strength and suffered unbearable pain. They also had severe cramps in the loins, stomach and bowels, together with a very bad cough and shortness of breath.

There was, wrote Champlain. "no remedy with which to cure these symptoms." Consequently, of the seventy-nine colonists who wintered on Ste. Croix Island, nearly half were dead by late March, when the river thawed and the Indians arrived with fresh meat. It is not unreasonable to speculate that at about this moment de Mons and Champlain might have recalled the place across the bay where they had put down anchor months earlier. At the time, Champlain declared it "one of the most beautiful harbours I have seen on all of these coasts." That sounds about right, for when the weather permitted, that is precisely where they went.

Whenever I go to Port Royal these days it involves driving through a sweet little colonial town, past artists' studios and people who look like they make their own honey. It's easy to find a reason to linger in the nearby town of Annapolis Royal, which Howe found decaying and dull with only "the weekly visits of the Steam Boat, and the passing and the repassing of the Stages" breaking the monotony, but where I find lots to look at, from the great harbour to the ample old buildings that have seen so much. I like to drive a little farther, past the continent's only tidal power generating plant and homes owned by folks who once fished for a living but now put pens in the water and farm Atlantic salmon like they are chickens in a Texas feedlot. Just before the government-sanctioned-and-paid-for re-creation of Port Royal, I like to pull off to the side of the road, park and get out. Then I turn my back to the water and try to see what they would have seen after sailing from the bay through a narrow passageway, which somewhere along the way someone described as a gut, before entering the sheltered basin.

Aspens, oaks and maples ran right down to the water then, as they do today. When the Frenchmen climbed ashore they stepped through briars, cranberries, nettles and rhubarb. I like to think of them standing there for the first time—the modern-day busts make Champlain look like Douglas Fairbanks Jr., while Dugua resembles José Ferrer playing Cyrano de Bergerac—with the glint of purpose in their eye. They were determined to learn from their mistakes. They chose a location "under shelter from the Northwest wind," Champlain wrote, "which we dreaded having been much harassed by it." The design was meant to assuage the settler's "habitual sense of insecurity," which Fischer says was inspired by the incessant warring most of them experienced back in Europe.

The reconstructed settlement still feels tight and compact today—the roofs steeply pitched, the palisade formidable, the chimneys tall and well made. The chapel, kitchen, blacksmith shop and gentlemen's quarters form a box around a central courtyard. But Lord, it is tiny, with battlements low enough that LeBron James could dunk over them and a footprint that would cover just half a hockey rink. It was no paradise, underscored by the big cross meant to symbolize the graves of the colonists who didn't survive that first winter. Provisions had been slow to arrive from France; soon the wine and other supplies gave out. Despair set in—how could it not for the newcomers, surrounded everywhere by dark, vast forest and pernicious wilderness in which lived *les sauvages*? Did they redouble their prayers to their Christian God? As conditions worsened, did anyone slip out of the habitation in the middle of the night, fill their pockets with stones and wade out into the bay?

All we know for certain is this: at some point Champlain and some of the other leaders made the last-ditch decision to crowd all but two of the colonists onto a pair of small barques and make for Canso, where, they hoped, there would be help. Starvation was near when, on the horizon, a sail appeared. Soon, Fischer wrote, they heard the voice of de Mons's secretary, who told them that a supply ship had landed, carrying with it provisions, colonists and a new governor, Poutrincourt, with a head full of new ideas.

I like the enterprising sound of this man who had fields cleared and ordered the construction of a water-powered grain mill. Poutrincourt introduced cattle, pigs, pigeons, poultry and a solitary sheep to the settlement. Under his direction the men planted orchards. For a few hours every day they took on communal tasks, digging ditches and moats outside the palisades and a well inside the habitation, before returning to their own gardens.

That September, Poutrincourt and Champlain took a barque and headed south along the present-day New England coast. Several crew members died during a bloody scrimmage with First Peoples near the present-day town of Chatham, Massachusetts. When the Frenchmen made their return to Port Royal, something strange awaited. Staged completely on water, *Le Théâtre de Neptune en la Nouvelle-France,* written by Lescarbot especially for the occasion, is said to be the first theatrical performance in North America. Neptune was there, perhaps played by Lescarbot himself. Some Frenchmen were dressed as tritons—all characters who had gathered there, so the storyline went, to welcome the colony's leaders back from some fictitious and dangerous expedition. It sounds to me like a real humdinger: the performance featured a trumpet call and a song, performed in four parts, called "Vray Neptune." Musical scholars have since speculated that Lescarbot "borrowed" the melody from a French folk song. The slender text, in any event, was "replete with neo-classical allusions," according to the *Cambridge Guide to Theatre.* A version of the play was performed in 1954 at the Toronto Arts and Letters Club. But in 2006, the four-hundredth anniversary of the "reception"—as the dramatic sub-genre was known—somebody gave the text a close read and decided the "imperialist sentiments" it expressed were no longer right for public consumption, and cancelled its re-enactment.

Today we only really make a big deal in Nova Scotia about that first performance, when it gets re-created on big anniversaries. But when I look out on the water and think about that kooky first performance, it moves me. I've chosen to write about these men because of the historical significance of what they did, but also because in them was the towering spirit of the day. They had seen bad times. More lay ahead. But that day, however briefly, the gloom must have lifted. The first gathering of l'Ordre de Bon Temps followed soon after. Port Royal's one and only great winter had begun.

———

Twenty minutes from Port Royal, on the banks of the Bear River, is a fanciful village that is home to an endearing collection of artists and artisans, folks who have been around there for a long time, and aging hippies who could have some information on where the grow-ops back in the woods are. On the outskirts of town, a narrow road winds past riverfront houses mounted on stilts until it starts to rise. There must be a thousand Reservation Roads across this continent. On either side of the site of the one in Bear River, Mi'kmaq people have lived for as long as anyone living or dead can remember.

For now, the population of the Bear River First Nation is around six hundred souls. There is a great range of opinions on how many Mi'kmaq—who called themselves L'nu'k, meaning "the people," but who were also called Gaspesians, Souriquois, Acadians and Tarrantines in some historical sources—lived when the first Europeans arrived. Estimates run as low as six thousand and as high as a hundred thousand in a territory that encompasses all of present-day Nova Scotia, Prince Edward Island and New Brunswick as well as much of Quebec's Gaspé Peninsula. The great Mi'kmaq grand chief Membertou once told a French priest that before his people began to appear in these parts, the Mi'kmaq were "as thickly planted there as the hairs upon his head." That was before the Basque fishermen arrived and Jacques Cartier passed by, even before an English ship approached a shallop in the Bay of Fundy and discovered it to be crewed by Indigenous sailors, including one "apparelled with a waistcoat and breeches of blacke serdge, made after our sea-fashion, hose and shoes on his feet."

The Mi'kmaq they met moved around, spending most of their year along the coast, where the fish, eels and seabirds that made up the bulk of their diet were easily accessible and, when the weather turned cold, making their way inland, where they lived in camps and hunted larger mammals like bear and moose but also smaller game like beaver, porcupine and even squirrels, which they dried and smoked to preserve. They knew no fear, crossing the waters in large canoes and, as hunters and traders, ranging as far north as Newfoundland and as far south as southern New England. Their ability to move quickly through forests and along rivers made them feared warriors to their enemies. But it was said that they fought only to avenge the death of a band member or to win glory—until they faced the real-life manifestation of the Doctrine of Discovery, the European notion that condoned expansion into newly discovered lands where the native people did not worship the Christian God.

A French priest said of the Mi'kmaq at the time, "You do not encounter a big-bellied, hunchbacked or deformed person among them." Such perfect specimens of humanity were they that when a Mi'kmaq encountered a white person with some defect—"such as the one-eyed, squint-eyed and flat-nosed"—they would laugh at them, but only gently behind their backs. Each and every one of them, noted another French priest, possessed "a sound mind and common sense beyond what is supposed in France." All of which squared with Lescarbot's view that the First Peoples of La Cadie, whom he greatly admired, "have courage, fidelity, generosity, humanity and their hospitality is so innate and praiseworthy that they receive among them every man who is not an enemy. They are not simpletons like many people over here; they speak with much judgment and good sense."

It is no surprise, then, that the Mi'kmaq found ingenious ways to use what Mother Earth offered them. Their wide-bottomed birch-bark canoes were things of wonder—able to shoot through rapids, manoeuvre through shallow streams and, with their square-rigged sails and high gunnels, to withstand the open Atlantic Ocean. They were sturdy enough to hold a family of six and everything they owned, but light enough for a single person to lug.

Birchbark, which was waterproof as well as portable, was used not only to cover their wigwams, but also to fashion "callers," which looked like megaphones and were used by skilled hunters to imitate the call of the moose. With animal sinew and bone needles, they sewed together deer and moose hides to make clothes, which they decorated with dyed porcupine quills and painted with pigments made from a mixture that could include red and yellow ochre, charcoal, ground shell and fish roes and bird's-egg yolks.

The Mi'kmaq ingeniously made tools and equipment from everything they could find. For precise carving they used sharp beaver teeth. Bone points were used to make harpoons. Copper was turned into fish hooks. Mi'kmaq stuck stakes into stream-beds and then interspersed branches between them until they were dense enough to trap eels or fish. Their snowshoes were framed in ash loops and bound with sinew and leather bindings.

The Mi'kmaq also knew how to have a good time. They shot dice and ran, wrestled and turned ball games into competitions. Every Mi'kmaq adult smoked a tobacco made from bark, leaves and a native tobacco plant. During feasts, long and detailed genealogies were recited to preserve traditions from father to son, to keep alive the history of their ancestors and immortalize their fine actions and greatest moments. They spoke, but did not write, a still-extant Algonquin-rooted language that is particularly rich and descriptive, and told stories, some of which lasted several days.

Glooscap, a giant warrior hero whom the Great Spirit endowed with supernatural powers, figures in many of them. At the dawn of civilization, he lay on his back, head to the rising sun, feet to the setting of the sun, left hand to the south, right hand to the north. He lay there, according to the legends, for a very long time until the first Mi'kmaq was born from the foam of the sea.

Like many Aboriginal nations, the Mi'kmaq believed that all life was created by a Supreme Being, the ultimate Creator, whom they called Kji-Niskam, or Great Spirit. They also believed that everything on Mother Earth had a spirit. Their entire philosophy, religion and way of life were built around the notion that life and death and every person and thing are connected. To this day, when Mi'kmaq people pray or dance, they do so in a circle. It was thought that some among them, called the *puoinaq*—had a direct line to the Great Sprit. With the help of sweetgrass, drums and rattles, the *puoinaq* possessed the ability to intercede in the spirit world where they used their extraordinary powers to see the future, communicate with the environment around them and interpret dreams.

I heard drumming, so deep and resonant it sounded to be coming from the bottom of a thousand-foot well, when I entered the band office of the Bear River First Nation. If I had called ahead I would have learned that today was the annual band council meeting, upstairs in the grand hall. The offices were empty. But the door was open, so I walked in and nosed around a little, eyeballing the pandemic response plan and the mission statement hanging on the wall, the government directive on how to avoid Lyme disease, the deer antlers and the hoopy dream catcher meant to filter out the bad visions.

I picked up a copy of the *Mi'kmaq Maliseet Nations News*, sat down and flipped through the pages, reading a letter to the editor in which an eighty-five-year-old elder from Sipekne'katik—which in Mi'kmaq means "where the wild potatoes grow" and is geographically located smack dab in the middle of Nova Scotia—justifiably groused about some white person being appointed director of

Indigenous education at Halifax's Saint Mary's University, which had granted the same elder an honorary degree. I looked at a picture of six Mi'kmaq warriors chosen to represent the province in the upcoming Canadian Field Lacrosse Championships. I ran a finger across the page and read the obituary of a woman named Freda Mae Bernard, age seventy-three, of Eskasoni, who was the great-great-great-granddaugher of one Mi'kmaq grand chief and the great-granddaughter of another.

Eventually I opened the office door and followed the sound upstairs to a big room where a bunch of people were sitting around, talking. I stood outside for a minute, and when it seemed like that could go on for a long time, I walked back downstairs into the office, sat down again for a little while more, and eventually took my leave.

Back in Halifax, I sent an email to Danny Paul, the Mi'kmaq historian who told me it was all but impossible to trace a person's lineage, even a person as revered as Membertou, to a single geographical point four centuries after their death. Through the electronically transferred words, I imagined I could hear Paul's exasperation. Membertou, who would become the first Mi'kmaq to be baptized in the Christian church, let the Europeans in the door—and we all know how that turned out.

Even so, in modern Nova Scotia there are lots of statues of Membertou, who, it was said, one day simply materialized from the woods to stand before the French settlers and came to enjoy a place of special honour in the banquet room at Port Royal. Everything about him had the whiff of legend. "The greatest, most renowned and most formidable savage within the memory of man," is how a grudging Jesuit priest described him around that time. "Of splendid physique, taller and larger-limbed than is usual among them; bearded like a Frenchman, although scarcely any of the others have hair upon the chin; grave and reserved; feeling a proper sense of dignity for his position as commander."

Lescarbot said that Membertou had to have been at least a century old, since he had known Jacques Cartier, and looked fit enough to live fifty years more. As *sagamo*, he didn't quite have the authority of King Henri back in France, but he had sufficient powers to lead his people into battle and render legal judgments. The young were under his command; married men paid him tribute. Although Membertou couldn't impose taxes upon his people, he was entitled to beaver skins and his share of the yield from hunting and fishing without having to take part in either. As medicine man he was capable of curing the sick and prophesizing their death or recovery. When some Penobscot Indians from the modern-day state of Maine killed a Mi'kmaq warrior, Membertou took harsh revenge, roving the coast of Maine, raiding the Penobscot villages.

One day in 1607 he told the Frenchmen that he had seen a sail out on the water. When the Europeans looked, they saw nothing, but since Membertou's eyesight was fabled, a barque was sent out. Once it was determined that the ship was friendly, sixteen small cannons were fired to salute the visitors. There was nothing jubilant about the news they carried: de Mons's trading company had failed. He had lost his trade monopoly and there was no more money to fund the habitation. Lescarbot laid the blame squarely on the shoulders of "the Hollanders," along with a "traitorous Frenchman named La Jeunesse." There was also some bad business with beavers and other furs, the less said about which the better.

Poutrincourt, who wasn't done yet, headed to France to make a case to inherit de Mons's monopoly over Acadia. Three years later he returned with his son Biencourt and a Roman Catholic priest who was quick to baptize Membertou and twenty members of his family before a member of the Jesuit order—loathed by Poutrincourt but beloved back in France by Henri IV—sprayed them with holy water. I will spare you the details of the wrangling this news triggered back in the French court, other than to say that a powerful ally of the Jesuits, the wife of the governor of Paris and the first lady-in-waiting to the queen, supported the order's desire to found missions in North America. And that a year later, when a resentful Biencourt set out with three dozen new settlers for Port Royal, a pair of Jesuit priests were also onboard.

Another of the pleasures of writing about the early days of this province is the way that chance and coincidence so often drive the storyline forward. The rancour was deep between Poutrincourt and the Jesuits. But could a Hardy have imagined a scenario in which the missionaries, spurned by the French and loathed by the Indians, would just give up on the evangelizing and try to found a new colony in the wilderness of what would become Maine? By rights, that could have been the last time anyone ever heard of these people. Except one day a warship carrying men and guns men from Jamestown, the first permanent English colony in the Americas, appeared in the nearby waters. In command of the vessel was Captain Samuel Argall, recently appointed admiral of Virginia with the singular mission of expelling the French from all territory claimed by England. Argall's place in history was already ensured: a few months earlier he had sailed up the Potomac River and kidnapped an Indian chieftain's daughter named Pocahontas. Now he and his men took the partially built French settlement in modern-day Mount Desert, Maine, with barely a struggle.

Among the French prisoners transported to Jamestown was one Father Pierre Biard, long a thorn in Poutrincourt's side. His role in what happened next is conjecture. Biard always maintained that some unidentified Indian *sagamo* guided the English to Port Royal. Poutrincourt later told a French admiralty court that the Jesuit clergyman led Argall's ships there. We do know this: Biard was aboard when the Virginian raiders arrived at Port Royal by moonlight at a time of year when most inhabitants were on work detail. With no opposition, Argall's men rounded up the settlement's livestock and herded it onto the English ships. Records show that a mill and some barns escaped destruction, as did most of the planted fields. The rest was a smouldering ruin when the settlers returned.

I think about the colonists; I can't help myself. Because there must have been a moment when they sat in the Port Royal hall, faces ablaze in the firelight, waiting to be fed like the members of some millennial housing commune and thinking that what they had there, what they had managed to carve out of that wilderness, was something, it really was. So, what I wonder is whether those men, when they went about what remained of their lives, ever cast their minds back to those nights and this place and what had happened here. I think about Poutrincourt, Champlain and de Mons, all of whom dispersed after Argall's raid left the settlement uninhabitable. Most of all I think about du Boullay, from whom, to my knowledge, history never heard again after he left Port Royal. There is no way of knowing whether, on his deathbed, the memory of l'Acadie washed over him as the memories of his life dissolved one by one. It would be nice to think that it did, I said to myself four centuries later, standing just where he might have stood. Then I got in my car and drove away.

Ruins, like these remains from Halifax's 1882 poor house fire,
are "extant fragments of some lost and noble poem."

# Ruins

This book is about a small place—just over twenty thousand square miles in total, less than four hundred miles tip to tip—yet it is still hard to get everywhere here. My atlas of Nova Scotia is twenty-five years old, but since not much has changed in the past quarter century I see no reason to replace it. Lots of the nine thousand names on the maps aren't really places at all in any traditional sense: they're hillocks, brooks, gullies or ponds that people use to orient themselves to the landscape. They're singular landmarks—the Barrens, the Big Grassy, the Churn, the Guzzle, the Tittle—that may mean nothing to anyone but the folks who lived there. They're reminders of what was and, I suppose, could be again.

Those names would have just been gibberish to the first men: Europeans may have called a sweet little harbour on the southwestern tip of the province Yarmouth, but Mi'kmaq referred to the place as Malikiaq, which translates into "winding and turning every which way." They had known Canso as Qamso'q—in the words of the settlers, "across a body of water"—for as long as historical documents show or anyone can remember, just as they referred to Tidnish ("at the small paddle place") long before the Europeans arrived. Place names weren't just names to the First Peoples; they told them where to hunt and fish—Kopitek, "place of beavers," which the white folk know as Aylesford, and E'se'katik, "at the place of clams," known on most modern maps as Lunenburg. They told them where to avoid. (Scatarie Island, which the Mi'kmaq refer to as Askataliank, which means "troubling.") They could even tell them where to go for a good time. (Weskewinaq, the modern-day town of Digby, which in their tongue means "cheerful place.")

Before that, the geography of this place had no name at all. Nothing did in the days when the plates of the earth's crust—floating as they still do on a softer, hotter layer of rock—migrated, making oceans open and close and continents collide. The last great merger occurred before dinosaurs or mammals roamed the earth, when an ocean of unimaginable size closed, creating a supercontinent. Nova Scotia sat near the equator, next to what would become North Africa and the Cornwall coast of England, before beginning its slow, inch-by-inch migration northward. Volcanoes and erosion did their thing with the various parts of the province. The earth's surface cracked and faults formed. Glaciers had their way with the land. At times, parts of where I now stand were sea bottoms, swamps, deserts, rainforests, inland lakes and mile-high glaciers.

Once, near the top end of the province, I was walking past some layers of geological strata, the bones of the earth, which had been knocked askew and hauled into the open. The cliffs slanted downward, at times almost on a ninety-degree angle from left to right. Since I am not a man of science, they reminded me of the Statue of Liberty poking up through the sand in the final scene of *Planet of the Apes*. Luckily, that day I was with a geologist who possessed a poet's heart. He told me that as we moved from west to east, we were travelling through layers of ancient time, and I've never really been the same since.

Now I look to see the old story unfolding before my eyes as I drive around this place: the elevated coastal cliffs made up of cover from the Paleozoic Era, pierced by change-resistant granite backbone. The valleys carved out by volcanic action in later, Triassic times. It thrills me, in the nerdiest possible way, to drive down some stretch of this province where I've never been before—past places that the Europeans, for some reason, called Doanes Cove, Blackberry Island and Coffinscroft—and think of the thin layer of humanity's story atop the fathomless eons of deep geologic time, to imagine history issuing from geography.

I happen to know that in the 1920s, two cars jostled their way south from the settlement of Barrington, Nova Scotia, in the same direction I am now driving. It's picturesque country, but empty enough that Howe skipped it altogether on his rambles. Just south of a nice swimming spot, they came to a series of dunes. They parked and walked west along a rock bluff that extended a hundred yards or so before it slanted down to the south side of the beach. According to a newspaper account written by Father Clarence J. d'Entremont, a local priest who was part of the delegation, they could see foundations of walls that periodically disappeared and then reappeared, always running in the same straight line. The whole structure, they estimated, was 160 feet long and the walls three feet thick. The priest's uncle, H. Leander d'Entremont, who was also present, would later write that the group had seen enough to declare once and for all that no matter what anyone else thought, this was the one, true, real location of Charles La Tour's fort.

Why, when there is so much to tell about this province, am I telling you this? Because whenever possible I like my understanding of things to arise from personal experience. The government of Canada took a stab at identifying where the fort was, placing a cairn and plaque commemorating the fort at the aforementioned Port La Tour. Other historians threw up their hands in confusion, or because they just didn't see the point in getting all bent out of shape about it. H. Leander d'Entremont was interested enough to write a small book in 1931, arguing the case for the second location. Since I have to accept *someone's* word, I choose to take his, because he cared enough to be obsessed by the idea long after most people had stopped caring.

These days, it's parkland around there. Leaving the parking lot, I become all discombobulated and head in the wrong direction, past a couple of moms keeping a casual eye on children playing in the sand and on through some marshlands traversable only because the tide was out, before I got my bearings. West of the beach, some neat homes stand along a bluff atop a low cliff, reinforced by large boulders held in place by industrial wire. That could have been where d'Entremont meant. Or he could have meant nearer again, where you have to shorten your stride to make it up the dunes of fine-grained sand. It's wild and overgrown now—in some parts the brush only shin high, in others the vegetation thick enough to leave it dark underneath. To my practised eye it has the look of a long-ago nooky spot, where excitement tended to intervene in young rural lives. But I don't see anything that even charitably could be called a ruin.

That is disappointing, since I like ruins. Ruins were why I was in this place I'd never been before, at the end of a road that hugged the water and looped, climbed and veered. In Nova Scotia, conquerors, immigrants, religious faiths, industrial eras and artistic movements have left their traces all over the place. We seek them out, or at least

I do, because we need reference points amid the vanishing empires and the disappearing horizons, in the vast, ill-defined landscape that is history. I have searched for these markers where I can find them, even in a place called Sand Hills Park, which is too small to show up in my government-sanctioned atlas.

Hoping to find a few foundations, maybe just an indentation in the ground to show I was in the right place, I keep looking around, using my hands to push aside brush to see what is underneath and the toe of my boot to slide rocks around. From there I can hear the song of what might have been a piping plover or Atlantic brant, since I know they are common around the salt marshes in these parts, although I have no idea what either of them actually sound like. Besides my own manmade commotion, the only other noise is the heave of undertow on the rocky beach.

You could let your thoughts wander here, on a summer day in the early years of the twenty-first century, which is what I did. I've already told you how constant squabbling between the Jesuits and Poutrincourt's adherents split the colony asunder. And how the English freebooter Samuel Argall and his raiders sailed up and down the Atlantic coast, burning and plundering all the French settlements they could find, including Port Royal. His actions were propelled by events far away and long ago. When William the Conqueror's claim to the English crown was ignored, he assembled an army and fleet on the French coast and invaded England. The Norman Conquest happened in 1066, but for the next eight centuries England and France would be at it with pike and sword, broadaxe and musket in a rivalry that played out in Europe, Africa, and the East and West Indies, but nowhere more than in North America. England's claims on this continent went back to Cabot's voyages. France maintained that Verrazano's voyage settled once and for all the question of who had arrived first. But as the great historian Francis Parkman wrote, "each resented the claims of each other and each snatched such fragments of the prize as she could reach and kept them as she could." In the midst of this epic tug of war, at the epicentre of this century-and-a-half-long conflict for continental supremacy, was the place known then as l'Acadie.

My sense is that this would have come as a revelation if you were a Frenchman returning to the smouldering ruins of Port Royal in 1613. Some of them, travelling by foot, made for Canso—where the codfish caught on the Grand Banks off what would be known as Newfoundland were cleaned, salted and dried for transportation—where they found passage back to Europe. Some of the Port Royal colonists travelled overland and somehow reached the struggling French settlements on the St. Lawrence. Poutrincourt's son Biencourt stayed behind. With him were a couple of dozen men, including his second-in-command, Charles La Tour. They spent some time rebuilding Port Royal. Then they sent word back to Paris that they intended to follow the fur trade, the lifeblood of New France.

To do so, La Tour would later tell the king, they lived a roving existence like "people of the country," by which he meant the Mi'kmaq, pretty much the sole inhabitants here at that time, who went bare-chested in summer and fur-clad in winter, slept in wigwams and ate the bounty of forests and seashores. La Tour and his men explored the coasts and river systems in their company. They learned to use Mi'kmaq tools and weapons to track bear and moose on land and paddle birchbark canoes over the roiling rivers and bays. "With great toil" they learned to speak the tongues of the different tribes. La Tour took a Mi'kmaq wife. Together they had three daughters, two of whom returned to France, where who knows what adventures awaited them.

One of the things I like about La Tour is that he was resourceful as well as swashbuckling. As the heir apparent when Biencourt died, he relocated the two dozen men who then constituted the entire European population of Acadia to headquarters somewhere southwest of Port Royal. Where exactly is a matter of some dispute. Names changed—at various points this settlement was called Port Lomeron, Cap Nègre, Cap de Sable, Port La Tour and Fort Saint-Louis—and so did locations. That this place existed, rather than where it stood, is what mattered. Call it what you will, locate it precisely where you may, the point is that during a critical period in history this bedraggled little settlement was all France had to show for its vast ambitions in North America.

When I hit the road in this province, which is pretty much as often as I can, my eye is peeled for decaying ruins because they are lovely, in an imperfect way, and because old things being reclaimed by the past make an impression. There is pleasure to be had in ruins, say the Japanese, who have a whole aesthetic and world view, *wabi-sabi*, built around the acceptance of the transience and imperfection that can be found in the peeling paint on an old doorway, or the lopsided bowl used in a tea ceremony. We cherish the crumbling barn in the woods for the same reason we cherish the Parthenon in Athens, the British novelist and essayist Rose Macaulay has written, because they are "extant fragments of some lost and noble poem," because they remind us that even the proud and powerful fall and all things eventually yield to time and eternity. They tell us that on this spot a moment of great drama unfolded. Yeah, this one right here, covered with scrub, with the gulls climbing and diving overhead.

The man Biencourt left in charge of l'Acadie was no foppish squire. La Tour had been living in the wilds of Acadia for sixteen years, the last six of them as a roving fur trader, when his father figure died. The times were precarious: the colonization of Virginia began in 1607. Thirteen years later the *Mayflower* arrived. La Tour would have known something else: a year after that, the English monarch issued a charter allowing one of his courtiers to establish a colony to be known as New Scotland. It was to be on the lands occupied by the present-day Nova Scotia and New Brunswick, part of Maine, and Quebec's Gaspé, which La Tour would have understood, with a start, to mean Acadia.

Who can blame him for writing to Cardinal Richelieu, the power behind the French throne, pleading for help? By now the on-again, off-again hostilities between France and England had erupted in full-out war back in Europe. La Tour told the cardinal that he would defend Acadia against the English to the best of his abilities with his allies, the hundred families of the "people of the country," his "little band of resolute Frenchmen" and his three modest ships. If worse came to worst he had no qualms whatsoever about returning to the woods to harass the English. But more troops and ships would surely help matters.

Carrying La Tour's request to Versailles was his father, Claude, a flimflammer, a mountebank, a seventeenth-century clip artist. After Argall's sacking of Port Royal, the elder La Tour had resumed his peripatetic ways, eventually returning to France, where his financial affairs were up and mostly down; at least once the elder La Tour was jailed for debts and had to be rescued by influential friends. But he had a knack for marrying well and, if the moment demanded, he could talk himself out of a corner. In Versailles he made the case for his son compellingly enough that Richelieu turned the request over to the newly formed Company of 100 Associates, which the cardinal had established to colonize and govern New France. Under its aegis, the following spring four heavily provisioned ships, carrying four hundred settlers, left for the young settlement of Quebec and Charles La Tour's Nova Scotia "stronghold."

They took their time, reaching the Grand Banks of Newfoundland and laying a cross at Anticosti Island before setting sail for the St. Lawrence River. There, in a way that illustrates how the whole era more closely resembled a drug war in the Bronx than historic empire-building, their English enemies waited. Quebec, under Champlain's command, was under siege. The French ships tried to sneak up the mist-shrouded St. Lawrence, but were intercepted and captured by the English. Critical provisions never reached Charles La Tour's settlement. Neither did his father, who returned to England a prisoner.

Not for long, though. A year later a boatload of Scots arrived in the Annapolis Basin and began building a fort a bit upriver from the now-abandoned French habitation of Port Royal. In command was a minor Scottish nobleman, Sir William Alexander the Younger, who was seeing Acadia for the first time. His aide-de-camp was a familiar face. Such was the allure of Claude La Tour that even before his prison ship had made it to England he had charmed the ship's commander, who would make the proper introductions for him in the English court. In no time at all, La Tour had friends in the highest circles in the land. He also had a new wife, a lady-in-waiting to the English queen, who was probably also a relative of a Scottish nobleman named Sir William Alexander the Elder, whom I think you should now meet.

Sir William Alexander of Menstrie, Viscount of Sterling, Earl of Devon and Lord Alexander of Tullibody was a scholar, courtier and poet, a debt collector for the crown, enough of a favourite of monarchs to be chosen by King James as a collaborator in translating the psalms of King David and enough of a screw-up that he died with creditors surrounding his deathbed in London. For our purposes the relevant facts are these: Alexander the Elder was the most loyal of Scots, a man who, when knighted, was made master of requests for Scotland, the sole purpose of which was to act as a buffer between his needy countrymen and the English court. Later he became a member of the Scottish Privy Council, the royal court's highest advisory authority on Scottish affairs.

You have to remember the time—the early seventeenth century—and the country, an England anxious to expand overseas. According to historian D.C. Harvey this patriotic Scot "began to dream of making a name for himself by diverting the constant stream of Scottish manhood from the continental wars into a colony that should bear the name of Scotland." Alexander the Elder never did lay eyes on New Scotland, which is how he came to think of the land the French called l'Acadie. That did not stop him from writing a forty-seven-page pamphlet laying out its splendours and potential as breathlessly as some modern-day junior ad copywriter in the Nova Scotia Department of Tourism. In fevered prose he extolled the place's "very faire meadowes," its roses "white and red," its "very good, fat Earth," its rich grains, and its abundance of fowls and fishes. In that pamphlet—entitled *An Encouragement to Colonies*—he invited his Scot countrymen to settle in this new country where successful commerce might be pursued by the merchant, where the sportsman might find a paradise, and the Christian ample scope for missionary enterprise. "Where," argued the author of the tragedy *Julius Caesar* and the sonnet sequence *Aurora,* "was euer Ambition baited with greater hopes than here, or where euer had Vertue fo large a field to reape the fruites of Glory." In Nova Scotia, Latin for New Scotland, Alexander declared "a great Man . . . may build a Towne of his owne, giuing it what forme or name hee will" that in the end would allow him to "leaue a faire inheritance to his pofteritie who fhall claime vnto him as the Author of their nobilitie there, rather than any Anceftours that had preceded him."

My head pounds when I read that. But it seemed to be to the taste of the monarch, who soon announced the creation of a new species of nobleman: knights baronet of Nova Scotia, the only requirement for which seems to have been the willingness to financially support six settlers in this new place for two years. At first, uptake on this titles-for-money scheme was disappointing. Somehow, somewhere the money was found. In the spring of 1629, with France and England again at war, Sir William's namesake son left with a fleet of four ships, bound for New Scotland. Not much is known about the mainland settlement that William Junior built, other than that it was downriver from the ruins of Port Royal, that it was small and that its first winter was hard indeed. When the bad weather broke, only thirty of the seventy settlers were still alive. Every day, they scanned the horizon for the pair of supply-laden ships that had sailed from England in early spring. I imagine their anger would have been deep if they understood that the ships, on the final leg of the voyage, made a little detour. At the fortress where resided Charles La Tour and the sum total of French might, the ships anchored. From one of them a boat was lowered into the water. Into it climbed an unexpected man.

In Nova Scotia, where geography is small but time is large, stories can double back on themselves, the themes repeating, the timeless old questions new again. Like a conspiracy theorist living in a room lined with aluminum foil, you must recognize the patterns. I say this by way of introducing a story that has been told and retold so many times, with so many dramatic flourishes that I think the best approach is to stick to the just-the-facts-ma'am version and leave it at that.

Claude La Tour, nearly sixty and aware that the days in which to make his mark and rebuild his fortune were dwindling, approached the fort's gates. There, no doubt cupping his hands over his mouth and yelling, he outlined a deal for his son, who would have been surprised to hear he had been made a baronet of Nova Scotia, just like his father. A princely endowment of land along the Atlantic coast was Charles's if he would surrender Acadia and transfer the fort "to the allegiance of the King of England." Charles would continue to be in command. The only difference was that his father and stepmother would also take up residence there "for his security," whatever that meant.

In his 1673 book *The Natural Description and Natural History of the Coasts of Nova Scotia*, Nicholas Denys, who watched events unfold firsthand, says nothing about the tone of the son's words as he thanked the king of England "for so much good-will towards him." Alas, he said, he already had a master and could "accept no rewards" but from the king of France. This answer obliged the father "to use the very finest language on earth to persuade him." Those rhetorical flourishes seemed to have rubbed the younger man wrongly. Charles told his father that neither he nor his wife would ever enter his fort. The elder La Tour retreated to his ship. The next day, Charles received a written ultimatum: surrender or the English would take the fort. Denys fails to record how long Charles La Tour, who had just thirty men behind the fort's walls, mulled the threat, just that he replied "that the commander and his father could do as they thought best, and that he and his garrison were entirely ready to receive them."

An English force laid siege to the fort. When that failed, every English soldier and sailor disembarked from their ships to begin an all-out assault. A day later the English gave up. This was a matter of some consternation to La Tour senior, who had told the English commanders that they would encounter little resistance from his son. Fearing for his safety if he returned to England, Claude begged his son to grant his parents sanctuary. Charles agreed under one condition: that he keep his previous vow. His father and stepmother would never enter the fort. Home would be a small dwelling just outside the walls, which must have been somewhere near where I stood.

History tells us that the dwelling was large enough to accommodate the parents' manservants and maids along with Claude's shame, which had to be immense. For a man with children it's a chilling thought: Did the son ever find it in his heart to forgive his father? Did Claude ever get to play with the grandkids? Or was it just he and his bride, long ago grown weary of each other and taking it out on the help as they faded quietly into history?

The most dramatic father–son confrontation this side of Darth Vader and Luke Skywalker was a mournful tale, although not nearly as mournful as the one that followed. The next year, as a reward for his stout defence of the fort, King Louis made La Tour his lieutenant-general in Acadia. It was no great prize. The French presence then was still just a handful of traders and missionaries scattered from Cape Breton to the mouth of the Saint John River, where La Tour built a trading post to control the largest river and richest source of furs in Acadia. By then, England's King Charles I, anxious not to jeopardize his French-born queen's dowry, had ordered William Alexander Jr. to abandon his settlement. The only remnant of the short-lived Scottish colony would be a name, Nova Scotia, along with a flag and coat of arms that remain to this day.

I've come across no explanation as to why Cardinal Richelieu, the craftiest of politicians, did what he did next. I mean to take nothing away from Isaac de Razilly, at eighteen a knight of the Order of Saint John of Jerusalem—the Crusader knights—and, during the Wars of Religion, the commander of a squadron of French ships in the successful siege of the port of Saint-Martin, who later lost an eye in an engagement with the Huguenots. Richelieu, that shrewd spotter of talent, sought Razilly's counsel on maritime and colonial matters and appears to have followed his lead when it came to New France, where he suggested blocking further English incursions north of the thirty-sixth parallel and also importing a few thousand French colonists to develop the colony's resources and to secure the crown's interests.

But nothing I've read explains precisely why Richelieu felt compelled to then appoint Razilly as the new lieutenant general of New France knowing that La Tour already held the post. Razilly, who had served as a ship's captain under the great Champlain, actually declined Richelieu's first offer of the job. Yet a man can only be asked so many times. In early 1632 Razilly signed an agreement to take possession of Port Royal and, under the terms of a newly signed treaty, to make Acadia a French colony. He made his headquarters in LaHave, on the southwest coast of Acadia, many miles south of La Tour's stronghold at the mouth of the Saint John River. For three years, from a distance, they ran things amicably together. Though neither of them quite understood who actually ruled what, they showed mutual restraint, steering clear of each other's affairs. Who knows for how many more years, even decades, the détente could have lasted? But Razilly died. Personalities changed. Events, as they so often do, acquired a momentum all their own.

———

We are fortunate that around this time Charles de Menou d'Aulnay sat down in an artist's studio. We can look directly upon the forthright eyes, aquiline nose and rosebud lips. Above the hint of a double chin the cheeks are full. The hair, which would soon begin to thin, is at that point luxuriant and backcombed into a Trumpian mound. He wears his moustache and narrow goatee as symmetrically as a cross. I look for the arrogance and status-consciousness that were said to ooze from this kinsman of Richelieu, this aristocrat whose people, as far back as the early twelfth century, were chevaliers, crusaders, a king's chamberlain, even a commander of lances who served with Jeanne d'Arc. I don't see it, even though d'Aulnay would have studied under the Jesuits with the nobility and gentry of France and later attended the leading martial arts academy of his day, studying, as one historian put it, "equation, fencing and tilting, and the polished arts of the courtier."

Everything I've read leads me to believe that from the moment he arrived as Razilly's lieutenant, d'Aulnay thought himself above the rough-hewn La Tour. The disdain was said to be as mutual as it was obvious. While alive Razilly managed to keep the rivalry in check. When he died Acadia began to resemble some big-city borough left with a power vacuum after a mafia don's demise. Let me provide one example: in 1636 d'Aulnay married and soon after sired the first of his eight children. At this point La Tour, the widowed father of three daughters, realized he needed a male heir. He sent a trusted friend to France, where his main duty was to find La Tour, who previously doesn't seem to have paid such matters much attention, a bride.

Around this time d'Aulnay relocated his headquarters from LaHave back to the Port Royal area, where the land was fertile and his colonists could begin draining and diking the flatlands using cultivation techniques that are still admired today. From there, on a clear day it must have seemed like d'Aulnay could almost see across the Bay of Fundy to La Tour's Saint John fort. From these two vantage points, no more than sixty nautical miles apart, their rivalry for control of Acadia played out. It began as small trade squabbles and evolved into legal claims and counterclaims. Open warfare, when it finally came, had an inevitability to it.

To add to the epic nature of the saga, a heroine had arrived, as the result of La Tour's hunt for a bride in France. Françoise-Marie Jacquelin was possibly a barber's daughter and maybe a Paris actress, but most certainly a member of some lower French line of nobility. In twentieth-century depictions she is either portrayed as a middle-aged coquette painted by Raphael, or a wrathful Valkyrie—tall, fierce-eyed, with a sword clutched heroically in her hand. We do know this much: when she arrived at La Tour's principal settlement at the mouth of the Saint John River, it was aboard a merchantman that also carried cannons, mortars, muskets, pikes and ammunition.

I want to leap ahead in time now because in the mid-1600s so little was really going on amongst the white folk in this all-but-empty place that any writer with an interest in pace and flow would feel justified in hitting the fast-forward button. So let me quickly tell you this: a few weeks after her arrival, Madame La Tour's husband and d'Aulnay had some sort of fracas at the latter's Port Royal fort. The La Tours ended up in D'Aulnay's hoosegow. When Charles La Tour returned to Saint John he learned that the king had revoked his commission as governor and ordered him to appear at court back in France to explain the dustup with d'Aulnay.

Those with his interests at heart told La Tour that he was doomed if he returned to France. They urged him, as a show of good faith, to surrender his old fortress on the south shore of Nova Scotia where the showdown with his father took place—the very fortress I went in search of—since the king had ordered d'Aulnay to appoint a disinterested third party to act as caretaker of the fort. Then and only then could La Tour's supporters possibly be of some help to him.

I am not naive. I know that facts, particularly long-ago ones when not much was written down, are works of imagination. A story emerges, which may or not hold much in the way of truth, but in time it hardens into something greater: myth. There may have been a very good reason for d'Aulnay's next course of action; that is just not how history views his decision. In the overall narrative of what has become known as the Acadian Civil War, the burning down of every last one of La Tour's buildings after he had, in good faith, vacated his Nova Scotia fortress simply seemed to confirm d'Aulnay's fondness for moustache-twirling villainy.

More than that, we somehow feel for La Tour, a classic under-dog. He could have been a twelfth-century Berber besieged by war-lords or the proprietor of a small, family-owned hardware store in the shadow of Walmart. By 1641 he had been on this earth for forty-eight years, but life in the wilds of the New World was not get-ting any easier. D'Aulnay had turned the French court against him. As he scrambled to regain the initiative, La Tour did himself no favours by reaching out to the booming New England colonies for supplies, as a market for furs and also for reinforcements against d'Aulnay. Meanwhile, his wife was burnishing her legend by avoid-ing d'Aulnay's ships on the way to and from France to lobby to have the charges of treason rescinded against her husband.

In the many words spilled by novelists, script writers and histori-ans on the tragedy that lay ahead, those of Denys were the closest to firsthand reportage: The next winter La Tour sailed for Boston, leav-ing his wife in charge of the fort's small Saint John garrison. D'Aulnay attacked but was repelled by Madame La Tour. Two months later, while her husband was still in Massachusetts, a larger force of ships again sailed across the bay. It was, memorably, Holy Week. For three days and nights Madame La Tour and her men rebuffed the attackers. On the fourth day a Swiss sentry took a bribe to let d'Aulnay's men inside the fortifications.

Even then there was no quit in Madame La Tour, who Denys wrote was "as noble a woman, as brave a fighter and as heroic a character as can be found in the history of the New World." She led the charge against the interlopers. For how long the resistance continued is unknown. Denys said that Madame La Tour surrendered "at the last extremity," and only then under the condition that d'Aulnay "give quarters to all," which I take to mean that their lives would be spared. History would learn how d'Aulnay reneged on his word. How he clapped Madame La Tour and her men in irons. How, right then and there, he ordered every man hanged except for one, who was allowed to live so that he could act as executioner.

D'Aulnay's wickedness was such that Madame La Tour was bound and a rope noose hung around her neck "as though she had been the greatest villain." From a vantage point a few feet away from the makeshift gallows, she was made to watch every agonized last breath. Legend adhered to her until the very end of her life, which occurred just three weeks later. She was said to have been physically ill, her spirit broken by the slaughter. The Acadians believed that d'Aulnay poisoned her. They believe so to this day.

You will perhaps be happy to hear that d'Aulnay did not die a peaceful death in old age, surrounded by family, content in all he had accomplished. There is a common pattern in the lives of many of the tragi-great figures who tried in succession to build this place in the early years of the seventeenth century: when I think of the dotted line in the history books that represents d'Aulnay's trek from the chateaus in France, through his fundamentally aimless acts of aggression that led to no gold and a premature demise when his canoe capsized in the icy Annapolis River, I see the same themes at work as I do in the lives of Poutrincourt, Biencourt, Alexander, La Tour and those whom followed: aspiration, hardship and mostly thwarted ambition. To a man, they had bad luck. The great forces of history and economics conspired against them. If character is truly fate, then some of them were doomed from the start.

Nova Scotia by then was still just land, from the white way of looking at things. It would be a century before it would start to fill up and become landscape, and another two hundred years before the landscape would start to look as we know it today. A reconstituted fortress called Fort Anne now stands at the the site from which d'Aulnay left to commit his atrocities. It is a place where, once you know a little about what happened, the past can spread out behind you, like a river in time that also carries you rushing forward into the future.

It can be a bit much, seeing things this way, in this place where so much of what is important has already happened. It can leave a person haunted by history that took place before they were born, and sometimes never even took place at all. If a physical object has no known narrative, I will just impose one, filling in the blanks as I go. Once, great wooden ships slid down that slip that is only driftwood on a beach now. That country store—its interior home to swifts, the exterior signage trumpeting the names of the proprietor and the kinds of wares he sold, faded to white—was the hub of a thriving town when the rail line passed by. Did an English ranger once stare down a musket barrel at a Mi'kmaq warrior standing where the plaque for some small-town worthy now hangs? Did a privateer once stride across the cobblestones visible through the broken concrete in the twenty-first-century village street? Did Joe Howe one day show up at that farmhouse, now collapsing into the ground, knock on the door and try to interest an owner in a subscription to a newspaper within which he couldn't read a single word?

Cross marking the point from which the Acadians
departed during the Expulsion.

———————

# THREE

# Scheen of Sorrow

*The Buried Past—Doctor Fitz—Broussard and Beyoncé—The Battle for a Continent
—The King of Ganajahhore—Annapolis Royal Falls—An Obstinate,
Intractable People—Louisbourg—Fanning the Flames of Bunker
Hill—Halifax—The Gore Did Flow—Winslow—Colville—
Toute Passe—Le Grand Dérangement*

One June afternoon, on the hunt for ruins once again, I watched a
man slowly amble across a patch of well-tended grass. Jonathan
Fowler walked at an even, stately pace. From his right hand dangled
something bright, ungainly, long and narrow: the EM38B geophysical
sensor, which measures how well soil, and whatever is in it, responds
to an electromagnetic field. In his left hand was a handheld computer, which provides readings that to my untutored eye look like a
straight line. Fowler tells me I'm wrong. When the meter image is
blown up, the straight unbroken line becomes a series of what he
calls little "warbles." By themselves, they may not look like much.
"But that little warble here may connect to the other warble over
there . . ." he says, letting the sentence trail off.

Tall and spare with brainy wire-rimmed glasses, Fowler wears
his ball cap backwards as if he's a grad student at Saint Mary's
University in Halifax rather than an associate professor of archaeology there. For the past fifteen years, he's been driving to the pretty

place where the Gaspereau River, named after the fish that swim and breed there, empties into the Minas Basin. Here, Fowler pushes a tent peg into the ground as a starting point. Then he walks ahead, carrying a converted garden hose reel from which a white line marked at five-foot intervals unravels. Using the homemade contraption, he lays out a grid of straight lines about a yard apart. When he's staked out the area of interest, he fires up the sensor. Straight-armed, he lifts it to shoulder height to get a bearing. Then, deliberately, he starts to walk.

What he seeks are things that shouldn't by rights be in this flat, fertile valley. During the last Ice Age, glaciers dragged basalt boulders from a volcanic lava sheet about ten miles away down to the marshlands that were emerging as the surrounding waters receded. When the Europeans arrived, the size, shape and hardness of the big rocks made them ideal building blocks. The Acadians, the French folk who settled the area, liked to gather the basalt rocks together and use them as footings for farmhouses and barns and retaining walls for their cellars. By themselves, basalt boulders exhibit only minute magnetic qualities. Bunched together, as a wall or foundation, they are highly magnetic. They show up as warbles on Fowler's meter. But so do other things. When something has been burned at a very high temperature it becomes highly magnetic as well. Once, the very land was aflame here, which shows up on Fowler's sensor, too.

When the data at the Grand-Pré National Historic Site looks promising, Fowler and his students pick a few square yards. With trowels and shovels they begin to dig. Using screens, they sift through the soil like gold prospectors. They measure. They take pictures. At some point they will stand back and try to figure out what they've got. By the summer of 2016 they had excavated more than twenty sections of land in the area where what was probably the largest Acadian settlement in the history of the world once stood. They've found big things like the footprint of a cellar some of those Acadians built with their own two hands and the outline of a house made by an English-speaking New England immigrant who was handed their land after the French were expelled. After all this time and effort, Fowler and his people have uncovered evidence of the New England military occupation, as well as a parish church and cemetery. Even the thrill of finding smaller things—a silver cross, coins from the early 1700s, shards of pottery and earthenware, a pipe that seems to have been the handiwork of Thomas Dormer, a pipemaker from 1750s London—never gets old for Fowler, a man of unfettered enthusiasm.

In his undergraduate days he studied history and archaeology at the same school where he now teaches. Then and there, Fowler got hooked on the story of the colonization of Nova Scotia. His honours thesis was on intermarriage between the Acadians and the Mi'kmaq, the First Peoples who had been here for millennia when the white people arrived. When he moved on to Acadia University, just a few miles from Grand-Pré, he happened to open the journals of John Winslow, the plump, complex figure who led the British effort to eradicate once and for all the French influence in Nova Scotia.

He's never been able to shake off what he read. While other Acadia students were watching the school's football team, the Axemen, do home-field battle, Fowler hiked and drove around the Annapolis Valley with a purpose in mind: to picture what Winslow saw when he arrived at the centre of the flourishing Acadian world in 1755. Like everyone with an interest in such things, Fowler knew that before the great purge thousands of people once lived around Grand-Pré. "What I wondered was where had it all gone," he said, standing in a place that, on a warm summer day with only a few people poking around, has the air of a spiritual site where some miracle or mystery has occurred.

The Grand-Pré National Historic Site is the construct of someone else's conception of what the capital of the Acadian world was once like: the pretty reproduction of the small Saint-Charles-des-Mines (Grand-Pré) church where they worshipped; the stately trees and sombre hedges through which they walked; the stone statue of Evangeline, the fictional heroine of American poet Henry Wadsworth Longfellow, who gave the world the Acadian story even though he never actually visited Nova Scotia. Instead he discovered the germ for his saga in the Harvard University library in a history by Thomas Chandler Haliburton, a Nova Scotian politician, judge and author who gained a measure of fame for his own literary creation, the Bluenose peddler Sam Slick.

Fowler, on the other hand, is a man of science. In his early days he worked on a Hungarian dig that had been around for a long time. Every so often Jenö Fitz, an archaeologist who had been working on the site since its discovery, would show up with his cronies. "Doctor Fitz," as he was known by one and all, was an old man by then, but still liked to make his way gingerly up and down creaky ladders to the various levels of the dig to see the progress. Sometimes Fowler, who has been digging in Grand-Pré since 2000, feels a bit like Doctor Fitz. "It is a bit humbling to look up one day and realize that you've been here sixteen years," he tells me.

Truth, in the archaeological sense, doesn't come easily. In my notebook I'm writing down his view that archaeology, by its nature, reveals the everyday, and that all people contribute to the archaeological record, not just the literate and the powerful. The archaeological record therefore holds enormous potential to expand our understanding and appreciation of those who came before us. Whole worlds, he means, wait underfoot to be discovered and explored. Gaining a better understanding of long-ago events and minds means tapping into a discipline known as "cognitive archaeology." For that to happen, a person needs to realize what is right before their eyes. They also need to be able to take the material and make what can only be described as a creative leap, to draw some conclusions about why and what the people of the past were thinking when they made or used the objects under consideration.

I underline those words, because writers are always looking for easy metaphors. I see some parallels between what Fowler is trying to do with his sensor and squiggles and what every writer about history, in ways not nearly so scientific, attempts with notepad and tape recorder: to pick through the present to look for clues of the past; to try to construct a big story from shards of glass, bits of pottery, old musket balls and other detritus of long ago. "He who seeks to approach his own buried past," the philosopher Walter Benjamin once wrote, "must conduct himself like a man digging." And, I suppose, there is truth to that.

Fowler, who has a knack for making the complex sound concrete, tells me about a simple iron pot, now on display at the site's museum, that a farmer in the area found when digging out his barn. It was a little like one of those Russian nesting dolls: inside the first pot was another pot, and inside *that* pot were some delicate glass cruets—small containers that might have contained oil and vinegar—carefully wrapped in moss and birchbark. Just by looking at them, he could tell that the pots and containers had been used by Acadians and were made some time in the early 1700s.

Then came the magical leap forward. History tells us that those were dangerous times. From there, if you're Fowler, it doesn't take much to envision a local farmer under armed guard waiting for the English ships to come, and his disconsolate wife, realizing that the time was short, trying to hide the possessions that they treasured. By then, some of her neighbours might have run for the woods or left to join their kin far away. She might have followed, had she known about the hardships that awaited her and her family. On the day of which we speak, all she would have understood is that whatever happened, somehow, sometime, they intended to return. And, so she bundled up her prized possessions—dishes, jewellery, even some glass cruets that had been in the family for generations. Then she buried them in the ground for better days, not knowing that the flames were coming.

So event-filled were those years after d'Aulnay's death that it is best to summarize them in the simplest form possible, like a plot outline for a movie on Netflix: his remaining backers fought over and over again with Charles La Tour and his people. Hapless Port Royal was pillaged. La Tour not only improbably emerged as the new governor general of Acadia but also, in perhaps the most head-spinning twist in this multigenerational drama, married his great rival's widow.

In the decades that followed, other than a brief period during which it was captured and held by the Dutch, the French and English passed Acadia back and forth. When it was France's turn, despite Louis XIV's imperial designs in North America, it ran Acadia more like some distant, forgotten business than a true colony, as was the way in those days. Between 1670 and 1710 Acadia—its boundaries, owing to the conflicting claims of England and France, as vague as they were ephemeral—had eleven different French commanders or governors. One year its administrative headquarters was in Port Royal, the next way up on the Saint John River Valley, and the following year, somewhere in between.

Acadia by then was the oldest continuously settled French colony in North America, but it was by no means the most important.

Canada, as the colony along the St. Lawrence River was known, figured bigger in Paris's plans because it gave the French an entrée into
the richer fur-trading territories and better missionary access to the
First Peoples. In theory, instructions from France guided the actions
of all officials in New France. But a return voyage from La Rochelle
to Quebec took a minimum of three months, and a journey on foot
and by canoe from Quebec to Port Royal would take weeks. So
neither Quebec nor Versailles did much to support Acadia, which
received few troops and a paucity of settlers during these years when
it was essentially on its own.

In a classroom in the centre of Halifax I learned that the great
battle for the continent was then underway. Like every Nova
Scotian kid, I heard the place names for the first time, repeated like
liturgy by a devoted, underpaid teacher: the Plains of Abraham,
Louisbourg, the dyke lands of Acadia. In a textbook I saw names
that still ring through history: Wolfe and Montcalm, Winslow and
Cornwallis. It would be decades before I understood that, during
these moments that defined us, they were at it again over in Europe,
where uncertainty over the line of succession to the Spanish throne
had ignited yet another power struggle between King What's-His-
Name and an alliance of countries and dynasties that still make my
eyes glaze over reading them. And that, by the last decade of the seventeenth century, North America remained a critical, distant theatre
in this old-fashioned, old-country war.

Like many people bad at math I am drawn to numbers, because
they are at least something concrete to hold on to. I find it helpful to
know that as the 1600s closed some 250,000 English settlers could
be found in all of North America, but just a handful of them in
modern-day Nova Scotia. The French on the continent numbered just
fourteen thousand. Of those, only a thousand or so made their homes

within this province's boundaries. A census taken in 1686 found ninety-five families with a total of 583 people at Port Royal, the settlement's trading centre. A few Acadians had migrated from Port Royal around the Minas Basin and also to the village of Beaubassin, located on the marshy isthmus joining peninsular Nova Scotia to what would become known as New Brunswick. Since the English tended to come and go—soldiers, some enterprising folk from New England looking for trading opportunities—most of the people here were still Mi'kmaq, who held the balance of power in these bloody, unsettled days.

At Sir Charles Tupper School, the girls in blue jumpers and the boys with crew cuts and corduroy pants that made a *zubba, zubba, zubba* sound when they ran learned a version of events governed by the aforementioned Walter Benjamin's view that "history is written by the victors." So we didn't hear much about the French "sea wolves" operating out of Acadia, who wandered the shipping lanes and fishing banks preying on New England vessels. To my knowledge there was never a mention of larger-than-life men like Pierre Maisonnat, usually known as Baptiste, who captured nine vessels in six months in 1692 and had already taken several wives in France and Holland before marrying an Acadian woman in Port Royal. Nor did we hear a peep about Joseph Broussard, who went by Beausoleil, the Acadian Che Guevara who led the Acadian militia and the Mi'kmaq in armed resistance against the English and whose bloodline can be traced today to the pop star Beyoncé and her sister, Solange.

In a classroom where we pledged allegiance to Queen Elizabeth and sang, each morning, of "Wolfe the dauntless hero" who "planted firm Britannia's flag on Canada's fair domain" we didn't hear a damn thing about the Wabanaki Confederacy, the alliance between the Mi'kmaq and the other First Nations from the Maritime provinces, formed to repel the English. In fairness, they might have been too much for a child's sensibilities. In the worst bloodbath, the Deerfield Massacre in Massachusetts, forty-eight New England settlers were slaughtered and scores of captives taken north to Montreal for ransom or enslavement by Mohawk and French, although at least one prisoner chose to live the rest of her life among the Mohawk. The Mi'kmaq and Maliseet carnage along the Acadia–New England border understandably earned the enmity of the New England Puritan colonists, who felt that all "savages" were equally loathsome and blamed the Mi'kmaq every time an Algonquian war party snuck over the border from Canada to raid one of their settlements.

The English, with retribution in their hearts, just kept coming. Historian Naomi Griffiths has calculated that between 1690 and 1695 every single Acadian village endured at least two raids by the expansionist English. Some fared worse than most. In 1707 two New England expeditions unsuccessfully laid siege to Port Royal. Three years later a Yorkshireman led the final English assault on the fort. When Francis Nicholson was a boy he somehow became a page in the household of a marquis, which gave him lifelong connections to people in power. It was such a connection that led Nicholson to join in an unsuccessful overland assault on Montreal and another by sea, equally fruitless, against Quebec. It would have stuck with me, I think, if I had learned as a young man that this small string of failures led Nicholson and some Mohawk and Iroquois chiefs to travel to London to try to stir up interest in the North American war.

The ranking Indian personage in their group was a young man whom the English called King Hendrick, even though his native name was Tee Yee Neen Ho Ga Prow, often shortened to *Tiyanoga*. Also in attendance was Oh Nee Yeath Ton No Prow, called by his hosts the

"King of Ganajahhore"; Sa Ga Yean Qua Prah Ton, whose Christian name was Brant; and Elow Oh Kaom, who for no known reason was called "King of the River Nation" during the visit. Usurpers from Europe have been parading the First Peoples of North America through their streets since Christopher Columbus, with six captives in tow, marched triumphantly down the roomy avenues of Barcelona and Seville in the fifteenth century. This time, touring London in carriages and being introduced to Queen Anne as American kings, they seemed more magnificent than miserable.

Their role in our story ends there. But in 1710, leading a fleet of five warships and thirty transports, Nicholson left Boston bound for Port Royal. The British and New England troops drove the outnumbered French behind the walls of the fort. Weeks later a few hundred Frenchmen—proud but starving, their clothes in rags and tatters, many of them no more than adolescents—marched out of the fort with drums flying and flags waving. But it would be three years later, with the Treaty of Utrecht ending hostilities in Europe and America, before things were clarified: France ceded all of Newfoundland, mainland Nova Scotia and Hudson Bay to England. All France held on to was tiny Île Saint-Jean, later to become Prince Edward Island, and Île Royale, known nowadays as Cape Breton.

The treaty decreed that any Acadians who wanted to leave with all of their effects could, provided they did so within a year. Every modern-day Nova Scotia schoolkid knows that if the Acadians had wanted to stay, they could have done that as well. All they had to do was swear allegiance to Queen Anne, the last of the Stuarts.

I've spent lots of time around Acadian folks, at political rallies, in nightclubs, in churches, in fiddle bars on the western coast of Cape

Breton, in old-folks' homes along the Bay of Fundy—Acadians, through some lucky fluke of nature and geography, enjoy one of the longest lifespans anywhere in the world—and even over a glass of moonshine that made steam come out of my ears in the garage of a complete stranger in southwestern Nova Scotia.

The biggest collection of Acadians I've been around at a single time was in Moncton, New Brunswick, just the other side of the Nova Scotia border. The occasion was the inaugural World Acadian Congress, finally held more than 280 years after Acadia passed for the final time into English hands. The setting was soullessly generic, the University of Moncton being a new school in a city trying to forget its railroad-town roots. The blandness isn't what sticks with me. What lingers after all those years was the palpable sense of joy. They were there, I recall, from the United States, Europe and all over Canada. How great it felt, people told me in different ways over and over again, to be back in the land of their ancestors amongst people who understood the things that didn't need to be said. I witnessed tears and lots of backslapping and new friendships-for-life being forged. One old fellow with the bright eyes of an optimist and the smoky accent of the bayou said, "It's a miracle," and then repeated himself not once but twice.

There was a lot of talk about the Acadian identity that day. But my memory is that, in the emotion of the moment, words mostly failed people. So the best explanation I've heard about what sets Acadians apart, and why, despite everything they've gone through, they are still who they are, comes from a source closer to home. Alan Melanson's people witnessed the way-back-when historical events you just heard about at firsthand from an ideal vantage point: the area around Annapolis Royal that would become known as Melanson Settlement because that is where his people settled.

In all that time, they've stayed close to home. From the balcony of his house, the tenth-generation Acadian can see the five miles to where archaeologists just like Jonathan Fowler have found Melanson homesteads. Two afternoons a week during the summer months, Melanson dons circa-1700 Acadian duds and leads historic tours through nearby Annapolis Royal. Most nights, during the good weather, you can find him in a local cemetery, wearing Victorian mourning clothes, conducting graveyard tours. "I'm either five foot eight or five foot eight and a half, depending upon whether I'm wearing wooden shoes or shoes with heels," he likes to say.

If you wander over to Fort Anne—once the site of Alexander the Elder's fort, later home to a succession of fortresses built by d'Aulnay and others—you'll see someone who looks an awful lot like Alan. His twin brother, Wayne, still works at the fort, where Alan himself toiled as an employee of Parks Canada. Besides the same build and facial-bone structure, they share a buoyant personality that Alan declares is characteristic of his people. "We love music and food and dancing and getting together," he says. "We say, 'Don't take life too seriously. Enjoy what you have today. Be happy with what you have, because nothing is forever.'"

When he's on the job Alan tries to give his Acadian everyman a little personality, a little *savoir faire*. Technically, what he does is play-acting. But he likes to think that somewhere in his stories about what life was like for his people, some essential truth emerges. "The story of the Acadians," he says, "is a story of self-sufficiency, of independence and resurgence. A lot of people would have been destroyed by what happened to us. We endured. We have always tried to do the best we can with the situation we are presented."

Like most things I know about them, this makes my admiration for the Acadians grow. The seigneurial system, based on the old

European feudal system, ensured a subservient tenant–lord relationship in New France—the area that would become known as Quebec,
where most of the French had settled. Since the land grant system
was looser in Acadia, there wasn't really an elite there. Acadians,
consequently, weren't always good at paying taxes or listening to
their priests. Since they so seldom were under any direct control, they
decided where they would settle and what they would do once
they got there. When there were disputes, they worked them out
themselves, often with the clergy serving as unofficial judges.
When the British took over the colony, Acadians showed their reluc-
tance to be governed by anyone by migrating away from the area
around Port Royal and Annapolis Royal to places where they were
even less likely to be under English sway.

For all that streak of independence, they could get along. Before
the English captured Port Royal, farmers, fishermen and merchants
lived side by side in a by-and-large happy state, and soldiers and missionaries arrived regularly from Europe and elsewhere in the French
empire. Their relationships with the First Peoples were particularly
praiseworthy. Scholars think that the old story I recounted in the
prologue about the Mi'kmaq girl and the strange men on the small
floating island may mean that the Mi'kmaq were the first native people in North America to make contact with Europeans. Familiarity
alone could explain why the Mi'kmaq leaders welcomed the arriving
French colonists, while every other French attempt to establish colonies in North America was met with armed resistance. But the truth
is that First Nations people would seldom have as good a relationship with whites in this land as the Mi'kmaq had with the Acadians:
they did business together, sent their children to the same schools and
intermarried often enough that Jonathan Fowler wrote his whole
undergraduate honours thesis in anthropology on the subject.

Mi'kmaq historian Danny Paul says the Acadian culture even seems to share values that the Mi'kmaq hold near and dear: "mutual respect for neighbours, democratic practices, welfare of the community before oneself, and a desire to be left in peace, to name a few." Like the Mi'kmaq, they believed that "maintaining the integrity of one's personal honour was the guiding principle upon which relationships with others were built," Paul has written. The Acadians borrowed some Mi'kmaq words and customs and vice-versa.

Most Acadians, though, could not write or read. Putting a youngster to work in the fields was viewed as more important than time spent in school. Acadians put much stock in tales, legends, laments and folk songs that kept their history alive. Because immigration from France had dramatically slowed in the early years of the eighteenth century, the rate of consanguinity, inbreeding, was eyebrow-raisingly high. Nonetheless, as a group the Acadians were healthy: children, of whom they tended to have lots, reached adulthood at a higher rate than they did in Europe; because they grew their own food—and perhaps because they didn't live in close, big-city proximity—they were free of famine and epidemic. Consequently, the population tended to be young and growing, a factor that would not have endeared them to their English overlords.

Like all people everywhere, they fought and fornicated. They got smashed on beer brewed from the branches of spruce trees and on cider made from the abundant apples. The filled their stomachs after those long days in the fields with recipes that hadn't change much since their ancestors came from France, like fricot, a stew that could include clams, chicken, rabbit or whatever else was on hand. Acadians, both men and women, liked to puff away on clay pipes that for some reason came mostly from England.

Limited in-migration meant that after three or four generations everyone in the various settlements was related to one another. The census of 1671 contains forty-seven Acadian surnames. In the next forty years, dozens more would materialize as a person took on another name, based on where they were from or their job. Since kinship was the main criteria for social organization, families tended to mass in certain places, which explains why even today there's a Comeauville, where most of the residents are Comeaus, and nearby a Saulnierville, home mainly to *les Saulniers*.

In settlements like those, Acadians worked every day of the week, although their beliefs prescribed some forty religious "idle" holidays. They worked well in groups, sometimes resorting to festive working bees for everything from processing wool to pulling fabric. A priest in Port Royal once said of them, perhaps hopefully, "One sees no drunkenness, nor loose living and hears no swearing or blasphemy. Even though they spread out four or five leagues along the shores of the river, they come to church in large numbers every Sunday and on Holy Days." The English weren't so appreciative of their virtues. One English governor of Acadia called them "perfidious, headstrong, obstinate, and as conceited a crew as any in the world." Another thought the Acadians "a proud, lazy, obstinate and intractable people, unskilled in the methods of Agriculture, not [willing to be] led . . . into a better way of thinking."

The latter is just plain wrong, since the Acadians bent geography to their will. Instead of clearing forests, they settled in the coastal low-lands, which became salt marshes when the tides came in. There they built earthen, sod-covered dykes just tall enough to keep out the water when the tides peaked. To drain the dyked marsh, they employed a technology that they had imported from France—the *aboiteau*, a log sluice with a hinged gate that would let the freshwater out when the tide was low, but shut when the tide came in. Someone with a sharp pencil once figured out that in the century between the colonization of Acadia and permanent British rule, Acadians cleared just five hundred acres of forested upland. On the other hand, they desalinated more than thirteen thousand acres of tidal wetlands, which explains how they came to be known as "*défricheurs d'eau,*" meaning "those who reclaim land from the sea."


Whenever possible I walk through those lands, the mere sight of which, Howe gushed, is enough to "make you sigh for the possession of the little Paradise, and almost foreswear mingling in the city again." I do so because they are beautiful and also because when I am there, in air sheltered by mountain ridges and warmed by rivers and the waters of the Minas Basin, standing in glacial soil fertile enough to grow corn, apples and grapes of wine-making quality, it helps to remember that we are all everywhere the product of our geography.

Equally true is that we are always, if we are to survive, who we need to be. The Acadians lived in a world without true geographic borders, without discernable wealth or military might, balanced between giants. Naomi Griffiths, the historian, has written that the signature feature of the Acadian identity was their stubborn belief that, despite being a border people between two superpowers, they had a right not just to live on their lands and to be consulted on things that affected them, but also to have a say in the important decisions and matters in their lives. This, a reviewer of one of her books noted, gave the Acadian saga the tension of a Shakespearean tragedy as the reader watched events inevitably approach, driven by the very factors that helped make these people who they are.

I think some other qualities also help to give the story of the

Acadians its narrative flow. If it hadn't all sounded so grand, the events to come wouldn't have resonated as they have through time. If their dream hadn't been so innocent, their tragedy followed by their almost-biblical resurrection wouldn't have become what I think of as the defining yarn in this province. What I mean is this: in 2016, when I was writing this book, the thirty-four thousand Acadians and francophones in Nova Scotia made up less than 4 percent of the population. Their story is more than dusty old history in a place where struggle remains the byword and in a province where reminders of life's ephemeral nature come daily. We have seldom seen shining moments of triumph, at least never for long, in Nova Scotia. Pluck and fortitude, the ability to put your head down and just trudge forward while lashed by rain, snow and wind, I have long thought should be emblazoned on the provincial crest. I've been drawn back to this story, as a schoolboy in a classroom, as a journalist and as someone trying to take the long view of history, over and over again because it seems like an ancient fable that tells us something fundamental about ourselves. Forward, the old story says, have courage, endure.

Events by now were overtaking the Acadians. To the northeast, on Île Royal—still, because of the Treaty of Utrecht, part of France—a fortress rose into the sky. Named after Louis XIV, the Sun King, Louisbourg would in the 1720s become many things to France: the natural epicentre of its lucrative Grand Banks fishery; a trade hub linking it to North America and the West Indies; and most important, a sentinel guarding the entrance to the Gulf of St. Lawrence and Quebec, France's most important continental holdings. "If France were to lose this island . . . it would be necessary to abandon the rest of North America," Louisbourg's governor wrote, prophetically, to Versailles around this time.

To protect this small town at the end of the continent, Louis erected the largest, most sophisticated fortifications North America had ever seen. Through a trick of time I saw it half-built, when a massive restoration was underway, and I had a day off from my first newspapering job in Sydney, the industrial epicentre of Cape Breton. It would have looked nothing like the Dunkirk of America that it would become, the fortress and walled city that at one time housed the third-busiest seaport on the continent. With Europe again a battlefield, the war between France and England had once more spread to North America. Louisbourg, home to Swiss mercenaries and elite artillerymen, was the base of a band of privateers tenacious enough to capture three dozen New England merchant ships and fishing vessels during the first year of the conflict. Within weeks of a 1744 declaration of war between France and England, forces from Louisbourg raided the mainland English fishing centre of Canso and tried and failed to retake Annapolis Royal. Britain retaliated, tying up shipping to and from Louisbourg.

Things stood in a stalemate. And there they might have stayed had Massachusetts governor William Shirley not been under immense pressure from his colonists to do something permanent about mighty Louisbourg. In May of 1745 four British ships and some four thousand New Englanders descended upon the fortress. Six weeks later, news that the greatest citadel on the continent had fallen triggered wild enthusiasm throughout New England, where fireworks were set off and the liquor flowed. So important was the victory to the New England psyche that even now the worrisome-sounding Order of the Founders and Patriots of America claims on its website that the confidence from that unexpected victory "bred and nurtured the independent spirit that carried over to 1775 and fed the flames of resistance at Lexington, Concord and Bunker Hill."

At the time, the victory seemed mostly symbolic. The Treaty of Aix-la-Chapelle returned Cape Breton and Louisbourg to France just three years later. The French, in expansion mode all across the continent, rebuilt Louisbourg and forged a trio of new fortresses to protect the vital trade and travel route up the Saint John River Valley to Quebec City. With the help of their Mi'kmaq allies, the French began reasserting themselves in the region in any way they could.

So the gore it did flow: in the outlying Acadian settlements, where marauding New Englanders torched farms and seized women and children as hostages, and in the English-controlled strongholds of Canso and Annapolis Royal, where Mi'kmaq warriors killed and scalped soldiers, took prisoners and put homes to the flame. At one point, New Englanders chased down some Mi'kmaq warriors sailing in captured English ships. The Yankees shot two dozen of them as they swam for shore. As a warning, the corpses were decapitated and the severed heads impaled on pikes surrounding Canso's fort.

Nobody, it seemed, was completely safe in those bloody days, not even around the great harbour known by the Mi'kmaq as Chebucto, where a humble English stockade with some gun batteries rose. The settlement had been born out of American outrage after Louisbourg was returned to France. Shirley, the Massachusetts governor, wanted a greater guarantee of protection from the marauders of Louisbourg.

For a settlement with the grand ambition of providing an English checkmate to France's massing power, Halifax had a woeful start. Ordinary settlers were promised fifty acres of land apiece, while every army officer above captain was entitled to six hundred acres. Each and every one of them was told that they could expect "a civil government . . . whereby they will enjoy all the liberties, privileges and immunities enjoyed by his majesties subjects in all other of the Colonies and Plantations in America under his Majesty's Government."

Yet the yield from the recruitment campaign was meagre. The novelist and historian Thomas Raddall called most of the 2,500 newcomers staring out from the decks of the ships that entered Halifax harbour in the spring of 1749 "the poor of London, a rabble of cockneys wholly unfit for a life in the American wilderness, attracted simply by the promise of free victuals." The colony's governor, Edward Cornwallis—fresh from hunting down the survivors of the Battle of Culloden in the Scottish Highlands—bitched and moaned about the quality of the settlers, some of whom only wanted partial passage to New England, others who were so poor that they didn't have shoes, socks or shirts. Desertions were frequent. Those who stayed were often dead drunk since, in addition to the liberal daily grog ration, thirsty settlers consumed ten thousand gallons of rum during the first six months there.

By then, many of the settlers were still living aboard the transport ships in the harbour. Cornwallis had about three hundred houses roughed in and erected a barricade of felled trees around the perimeter of the town, along with a couple of log blockhouses. That first winter, typhus tore through the weakened population. It is said that one in three settlers died. Many of them were buried in a small cemetery just outside the southernmost defences. The scene of Halifax that Raddall sketches at this point in time—"rumpled rum-primed grave diggers, the shivering guard of redcoats, watching the forest, the perfunctory parsons, the unwilling mourners, the pine coffins with their carved initials, and the air of gloom over all"—is enough to make you turn your own collar up against the cold and reach for the rum bottle.

For those who survived, it must have seemed like death lurked everywhere beyond the palisades. The Mi'kmaq saw the founding of Halifax, without negotiation, as a violation of earlier treaties with the British. Four times, the Mi'kmaq raided Halifax during the seven-year conflict known as Father Le Loutre's war. Even more harried were the settlers of Dartmouth, on the eastern side of Halifax Harbour, who endured eight raids during the early years of war.

During the first fracas, two settlers were scalped and two others decapitated. When a detachment of English rangers was sent after the raiding party, they returned with the heads of two Mi'kmaq men and a scalp of their own. Afterwards, in a decision that would damn his memory nearly three centuries later, Cornwallis offered a bounty of ten pounds sterling for every Mi'kmaq scalp—a proclamation to this day akin to genocide in the view of the Mi'kmaq nation—and raised two companies of rangers to scour the land around Halifax, looking for Indians. The body count continued to mount. In the summer of 1750, Mi'kmaq and a few Acadians, lead by the troublesome Beausoleil, attacked Dartmouth. Some twenty people died during what would be known as the "Dartmouth Massacre." The British gave chase, returning with a single Mi'kmaq scalp. In further retaliation they sent several armed companies to Chignecto, where the Acadians lived. There, the dykes were breached. Hundreds of acres of crops were ruined when the salt water poured in.

One day, after spending too much time staring at a computer screen, I got in a car and drove northwest from Halifax at a good clip. The sky was cornflower blue with just a fleck of cloud, the temperature in the double digits with enough humidity to hint that rains were coming somewhere down the line. I needed to know what the men of Acadia saw and felt when they were led blinking into the daylight

260 years ago. Could they too hear crows caw and some other unidentified birds sing? Did a nice breeze stir the trees and the tall grass then as it did today? Did the sun warm their skin as it did mine?

No one knows the exact location of the church at Grand-Pré, the spiritual centre of the Acadian nation. What is known is that more than a century ago a poet, historian and optometrist named John Frederic Herbin, bless his heart, bought the land where it was thought to have stood. Later he sold the property to a local railway, which in turn ceded a parcel to la Société l'Assomption, a mutual insurance company owned and managed by Acadians, who have long, long memories. The structure they built here is as much reminder as reconstruction.

By the middle of the eighteenth century, how confused the Acadians must have been. By then, they thrived as they had never thrived before: reclaiming new land from the sea, putting additional acreage under cultivation, expanding their trading markets to include Louisbourg and Boston. Their population had swelled to just under fifteen thousand, compared to a paltry five hundred British in Annapolis Royal and Canso to go with the few thousand who had settled Halifax. Yet there had been no clear winner in the French–English conflict: Louisbourg had been lost and then returned to the French. The British, after founding Halifax, struggled to expand British settlement any further. Both sides, for very sensible reasons, wanted the allegiance of the Acadians.

By then, most every adult Acadian male had taken an oath of fidelity to the British monarch, but most of them made their oaths conditional on an exemption from compulsory military service. Claiming to take no side in the French–English conflict, they declared themselves content to clear their lands and live their lives. As the English demands drew more incessant, Acadians, in protest and fear, departed the Nova Scotian mainland for French-controlled areas—Île Royal, Île Saint-Jean and the disputed area of modern-day New Brunswick. By the thousands they left Grand-Pré, Pisquit, Rivière-aux-Canards, Cobequid and Port Royal. But thousands more stayed. They were known as the "neutral French." That is how they saw themselves; that is how they wished to be seen.

I will spare you the lengths to which the neutral French went to avoid being dragged into the incessant warring between the British on one side and the French, the Catholic clergy and the Mi'kmaq on the other. Yet the beginning of the Seven Years' War, which would once and for all decide the victor in the Anglo-French imperial conflict for the continent, meant their fate was sealed. Britain's colonial officials were already contemplating the removal of the Acadians in 1755, when a combined force of New England and regular British soldiers drove the French military from Fort Beauséjour, just inside the present-day New Brunswick border, cutting the Acadians off from the French in Quebec. Afterwards, deputies from several Acadian communities once again refused to pledge unconditional allegiance to the British crown. When the British found evidence that Acadians had helped defend Beauséjour, Charles Lawrence—flaccid of face and body, a company commander before he became governor of Nova Scotia, where he would be judged cruelly by history for his inhumane treatment of the Acadians—had the justification he needed.

Whenever I've visited the church at Grand-Pré I've always been alone and there's only ever been silence. This, to me, is the proper state of affairs in a place of such solemnity, where the spirit just naturally tries to connect with something bigger than yourself. I imagine the Acadian men praying in silence as they waited. On September 5, 1755, John Winslow, a member of one of New England's most prominent families, summoned 418 men from the surrounding Acadian settlements to assemble in the church at Grand-Pré. They must have been wary of such an order: when Winslow arrived weeks earlier, he had ordered his soldiers to build a stockade around the churchyard. Not long after that, three British ships arrived in the basin, claiming they were there to transport troops. When the Acadian men approached the church, they filed past long lines of armed soldiers.

Based on Winslow's journals, he just got right down to it, telling the assembled group that he had received the king's "final resolution to the French Inhabitants of this his Province of Nova Scotia, who for almost half a Centry have had more Indulgence Granted them, then any of his Subjects in any part of his Dominions. What use you have made of them, you your Self best know." For all we know, a collective cry filled the room as Winslow started in on the specifics: all of their land and buildings, cattle and livestock were to be seized by the crown. Every last French inhabitant was to be removed and transported by ship elsewhere. Winslow said that he would do his best to ensure they weren't "molested" and were able to take all their money and household goods with them. A few were released to spread the word. The rest were the king's prisoners, the fenced-in churchyard their prison yard, and the chapel where they slept, under guard, their jailhouse.

For five days they waited. Then a local English-speaking priest arrived and told them that the moment for departure had come. The young men were supposed to go first, but refused without their fathers. "I Told them that Was a word I did not understand," Winslow wrote in his journal, "for that the Kings Command was to me absolute & Should be absolutely obeyed & That I Did not Love to use Harsh Means but that the time Did not admit of Parlies or Delays." He ordered his troops to fix bayonets and advance towards the Acadians. Finally, in one of the most dramatic moments in his mostly orderly diary, Winslow "took hold" of one of the dissenters and ordered him to march, which he did with the others following.

I'm walking now where they would have, east from the church, past the site where graves of their people had been excavated by Fowler and his team. Nowadays, anyone moving in that direction does so between a neat row of hedges, across a seldom-travelled road and then through an empty parking lot with grass emerging through the cracks in the pavement. Eventually you come to a blue sign announcing that you are entering the Grand-Pré Dyke.

I know that while he was alive, Alex Colville, the realist painter who lived nearby, could often be glimpsed at funny times of the day or night sitting here at his easel. He was working on the disquieting images upon which his fame rests: a horse galloping at breakneck speed down a track towards a train, a cow lying on a marshland under a full moon. That makes perfect sense; the Grand-Pré marshland may have reminded him of the Lowlands of Europe through which he tromped as an official war artist in World War II. I've spent some time staring at Colville's paintings, which always seem to have something unsettling just below the surface, like a big fish lurking in a beautiful lake. A serious man, he once told me that in his work he hoped to capture a moment in time that was "enhanced by knowing how bad things can be and that this moment is okay." For that reason too, the dyke lands—in some places broken chunks of hardened mud, in others fallowed field with hardwoods with a farm silo or two off in the distance—was a good place for Colville to work.

In his journals, Winslow said that the first batch of Acadian men advanced slowly. At one point they must have stopped altogether, because they had to be prodded on by the British bayonets. As they walked their wives, children and parents tried to break through the red line to touch their menfolk one last time. The men wept as they walked. Being good Catholics, they prayed and sang hymns as they stumbled forward. One of those hymns was called *"Faux plaisirs, vains honneurs"* (false pleasures, vain honours), and another *"Vive Jésus"* (long live Jesus).

They might have also sung a lament called *"Tout Passe,"* which you can hear on a recording of the same name by an Acadian singer with a gorgeous voice named Suzie LeBlanc. It's a haunting thing, even in English:

Beneath the sky
All is in flux
Everything passes on

And no matter what you do
Our days flow faster than a torrent
Everything passes on

A great truth
Other than eternity itself
Everything passes on

Let us put mercy first
Time is precious
While, before our eyes
Everything passes on

Young and old
Bosses and workers
Everything passes on

We will take our place
And disappear one day
During our mortal sojourn
Everything passes on

Like the ship
That sails in the distance
Everything passes on

Without a trace
So go the honours, the chattels and the glories
Everything passes on

It would, in my opinion, be a mistake to interpret those as the acquiescent words of a docile people. Beausoleil was still out there in the forest, stirring things up. A thousand Acadians, according to the records of the day, lit out for other French territories rather than be deported. Scores more headed for the woods and hid along the seashore nearby, hunting and fishing for sustenance and living the outlaw's hard life. All told, ten thousand would be forcibly evacuated and made refugees by the time the Great Expulsion, *le Grand Dérangement*, was complete.

On the day I'm trying to picture, they trudged across terrain as flat as prairie, past rows of corn as high as a man. They walked through farmland that they had reclaimed from the waters of the Minas Basin, beyond homes and barns they had crafted with their own two hands. If a place where something awful happened can have a memory, right here would be the spot: a trail, now pitted with the wheels of tractors and other big machinery, that skirts the tops of the dyke lands from which the men of Grand-Pré would have been able to see the first of the anchored British ships.

Fenced-off cow pasture stands there now. Where the trail ends, next to a stunted apple tree at the water's edge, a friendly Lab-mix from an adjoining farm walks up, wagging his tail. Ahead are a couple of benches, a stone cairn and some all-weather displays that tell the Acadian story. Mostly the eye is drawn to a cross. It is iron, about fifteen feet high, with discreet ornamentation. It stood near an old creek on some other farmer's land until someone figured out that this was the point of departure for the Acadians. The first time I saw the cross was in a Colville painting in which a young woman twists on the saddle of her horse, looking back at it while her mount plods on.

Here, in real life, some of the Acadians also must have turned and looked back towards woods and farmland and the great headland of Cape Split, which in the lore of the Mi'kmaq marked the gateway between the land of the living and the land of the dead. How deep was the despair of Jean Apigne, Antoine Celestin and Feler Babin, of Blesse Leblanc, Francis Rous and Aman Gotro as they prepared to board the British ships? Did Norez Daigre, Oliver Hebert, Anselmer ales Mangean or Fabien Dupuis fall to their knees? Or did Marcel Sonner, Jean Doulet, Delene Leuron and Augustin Hebert merely hang their heads in resignation?

When I look at Winslow's list and read the names of Rener Babin, George Cloatre, Tunuislaps Forest, Norez Commo, Dominque Pitre, Renez Sosonier and all of the Landrys—Michelle, Auguste, Charles, Former, Etair, Alexandre, Etim, Rener, and so many others—my heart sinks because I know what happened next: the cruelly overcrowded belowdecks where they waited for weeks before departure; the hard voyages that amounted to death sentences for so many aboard the innocently named vessels, *Hannah*, *Swan* and *Sally & Molly*, that carried them to New York and Massachussetts, Pennsylvania, South Carolina, Georgia and Virginia.

On that mournful day it was just as well that Jacques Celeve, Feler Babin, Lewis Pierre Cloatre and Paul Boudro (the spellings were Winslow's) had no inkling of the poverty, starvation and slavery that waited in their new homes in the American states, or in France and the French colonies in the Caribbean and off of Newfoundland. Just as it is best that they had no idea what would happen to their land when they left. Winslow's orders were clear: burn the villages and homes so that none of the French would return. By the time his men were done, 255 Acadian homes from the Grand-Pré area had been put to the torch along with 276 barns, another 155 outhouses and a single church.

We don't know whether the British let them linger for a minute on the crest of that small rise of land, or just kept them moving that day, at the end of which Winslow sat down at his desk, dipped pen ink and wrote, "Thus Ended this Troblesome Jobb, which was Scheen of Sorrow." I just hope that they memorized what they saw there. I hope they kept it in their hearts like those small treasures buried in the ground in l'Acadie, waiting for centuries for the arrival of a man besotted by the ache of their story, with his archaeologist's shovel.

Yearly, descendants of Scottish Highlanders gather in Nova
Scotia at the only cairn outside Scotland commemorating the
Battle of Culloden.

# Someplace, Somewhere

Where I live, in Halifax, the capital of Nova Scotia, it is perfectly acceptable within seconds of meeting a complete stranger to ask them where they are "from." If, in 2017, they happen to say "away," chances are good that they mean a village in Guangdong Province, some teeming Mumbai suburb, a cypress-ringed Lebanese town or maybe, just maybe, a condominium complex in Calgary from which they vamoosed once the price of oil crashed. Time was when this simply wasn't so around here. Back when the privies of Halifax were emptied into wheelbarrows that trundled through muddy streets teeming with grog shops, if you asked a person where they were from, they might have said Boston, where things had gone bad, or the slums of London, which they hoped to never see again. Through an undecipherable brogue, they might have answered Waterford, Ireland, via the Grand Banks fishery off of Newfoundland, which they knew as *Talamh an Éisc* (the land of the fish). If you asked a butcher named Johann Horn, he would have said Strasburg; a candle maker named Andreas Priebtz would have replied Dresden; a gunsmith who went by the name of Johann Krahl would simply answer Weimar.

Record keeping wasn't always the best in those days. But everything I've read leads me to believe that if Franz Joseph Timming, whose arrival at age thirty-one marks the point at which my personal story joins the larger story of Nova Scotia, had been asked such a question on the streets of Halifax, he would have said Vaud (pronounced VOH) in a French accent because this is how they spoke in the canton in western Switzerland from which he came. The question, to me, is always: Why? I've been to Vaud, long before I knew it was where my great-great-great-great-great-grandfather was born. It does not look like the kind of place somebody voluntarily leaves, so I can only assume that things were not going well in the old country when he and the others decided to board a leaky scow bound for British North America, as Canada was then known.

In Nova Scotia, where Governor Cornwallis sought suitable settlers to compensate for Halifax's cockney rabble, land and victuals were free. The handbills and posters that appeared in in the northern part of Germany and the smaller states of the southwest, in the Montbéliard region in the foothills of the French Alps and the cantons of Switzerland—where people's minds were unbiased by any firsthand knowledge of Canada, let alone a tiny corner of it protruding into the Atlantic Ocean—made Nova Scotia sound like a land of dreams for good labouring men. In Rotterdam, my forefather and the others were assailed by competing agents from other colonies who told woeful tales about Nova Scotia's climate, its lack of decent farmland and the ferociousness of the Indian attacks. Some, heeding those words, left for other places. Even so, when the *Gale* departed from Rotterdam for Halifax on June 12, 1751, there were 214 men and women aboard.

They represented the usual range of people necessary for settling new lands: saddlers, weavers, butchers, carpenters, farmers, furriers and shoemakers. There were bookbinders, bakers, stonecutters, glovers, joiners and tanners. There were lots and lots of farmers. According to the passenger list there was just one stocking weaver, my ancestor, who also happened to be one of three Swiss who made the crossing aboard that ship. I don't envy him one bit: the over-crowded tween decks where a moderate-sized man had to stoop to walk; the shared berths; the food that turned rancid and wormy; the drinking water swimming with long, green, slimy growths that tasted so foul that it had to be laced with gin, brandy and sometimes vinegar so it could be choked down.

Timming's was not the worst crossing among the immigrant ships carrying "Foreign Protestants" to Nova Scotia: the *Sally* would lose forty passengers en route, as would the *Pearl*. Aboard the *Gale*, on a later voyage, twenty-nine men, women and children died during a long and stormy passage with violent westerly winds. On August 8, 1751, when that same ship, carrying my grandfather five times removed, docked in Halifax, there were nine fewer names on its pas-senger list than when the voyage began seventy days before.

This was no triumphant arrival, signalling the start of something great. Some of the immigrants didn't make it beyond that hard first winter, which they spent quarantined on a frozen island in the middle of the harbour. Those who survived found themselves in drafty bar-racks far from the main colony or in a slummy lane in the interior. The soil was poor. Disease swept through the newcomers. As the months turned into a year, Timming and the others put in hard labour helping to build the new garrison. It had to be a relief when the colony's governor finally announced that 1,400 of them were being moved to a place on the southern shore of Nova Scotia, which was blessed with a decent harbour, better soil, and land that was said to have been cleared some time ago by the Acadians.

The place had a Mi'kmaq name, which the English naturally changed to honour their royalty—in this case the ruling monarch, George II, whose ancestral title was Duke of Brunswick-Lüneburg. There, because of a steep hill rising from the harbour, the main streets were laid out in an east-west fashion parallel to the shore. The north-south cross streets rose sharply from the water's edge. For organizational reasons, Lunenburg was sectioned off into divisions, each named for the British officer in charge. Each division had seven sections, and each section was subdivided into fourteen lots, each in turn forty feet by sixty. Timming, who is variously known in the records of the time as Timmon, Timon or Dimon—but whose name within twenty years had taken on the more permanent form of Demone—drew lot B-9 in Strasburger's Division. It turned out to be partway along Lincoln Street, the third street up from the harbour, which, like the settlement's other principal east-west streets, was forty feet wide.

Lincoln Street looks somehow narrower when you walk it now, even in the shoulder season when the summer tourists and their cars are gone. Kinley the druggist, the gallery once inhabited by the photographer John Knickle, Stan's Dad and Lad Shop. The hardware store, which has been variously a meat market, tailor shop, dry-goods store and, furthest back of all, a house owned by Henry Neil, the mariner. The office space once inhabited by a tinsmith named Lemuel Wambolt. Fussy places where you can buy quilts and eat curried mussels, get your back adjusted by a chiropractor named Flavin and learn to tap dance like Bojangles Robinson.

Heading east, it is a couple of blocks before you reach houses. Since Lunenburg's old town is one of only two urban places in

North America to be designated a UNESCO World Heritage Site, the wooden homes are real beauts—stately, radiantly coloured, with lots of elaborate mouldings and many good examples of the fabled local dormer known as the "Lunenburg bump." The metal plaques from the town's heritage society explain that they are old, but still generations younger than the ones erected by my ancestor and his neighbours the Gerlings, the Bertlings, the Gauers, the Langilles and the Meyers. The old Timming lot is on the harbour side of Lincoln Street, two doors from where it intersects a street called Hopson. A Temperance Hall used to be on the street corner, back in the days when such places could be found in most every town in Nova Scotia. It's long gone now. So is my people's first residence on this continent. In its stead is a two-storey residence the colour of fresh grass. The four-bedroom house has a front veranda on Lincoln and a back deck on Pelham Street offering an unobstructed view of the harbour. The house, at 324 Lincoln, seems to have had an addition off to the right. Along with its dormer windows, the most eye-catching architectural feature is a trio of roofs, each resembling a cresting wave. It was for sale the day I visited, with an asking price of $699,000, which is nothing grand by the standards of Lunenburg— which, in 2016, were grand indeed.

Until I discovered Timming, I was mighty confused about where we came from and who we were. Then a whole bunch of things began to make sense. These Foreign Protestants, who were mostly German Lutherans, with their love of order and efficiency, their proclivity for hard work and discipline, had nowhere to go but forward. Upon their arrival they were granted woodlots that had to be cleared within two years or forfeited, along with garden lots and grants of livestock. (As an adult male, Franz Timming received five sheep, a sow and a goat.) Ahead were harsh winters and summer droughts.

The settlers didn't always get along with each other, or with the British administrators who, characteristically, decried the slow pace of development.

There were worse tribulations. As the Mi'kmaq and French fought on to resist colonization by Britain, the Foreign Protestants paid the price. Six people from one family were killed and a woman and her four children were carried off during one raid, five people from two families in another. In one early year there were four raids on the Lunenburg Peninsula: families attacked in their homes, soldiers in the blockhouses, two men and some boys who had the misfortune of being caught swimming with their family out in the hinterland. It got so that most people abandoned their farm lots—including, I'm assuming, my predecessor, who had been granted thirty acres a few miles northwest of the settlement, and retreated behind the walls of the fortifications. Winthrop Pickard Bell, the chronicler of the Foreign Protestants and the settling of Nova Scotia, has recounted with presumed restraint that, for those who did not leave farm for town, the number of raids and their intensity increased.

My knowledge of science is not only scant, but also based almost entirely on theories that square with my world view. I do, however, tend to side with the relatively new study of behavioral epigenetics, which has essentially concluded that traumatic experiences in someone's past leave molecular scars adhering to your genes. What I conclude from this is that if you've fled some far-off land where life was so grim that you were willing to endure hardship and death to leave it, and if you then find yourself in a place where the impenetrable woods are said to teem with people who, with justification, want to take your scalp, it can put a scare into you that can last for generations to come. It goes with all the other things an ancestor bequeaths you: in my case, the Lutheran belief that no priest is needed to seek God's grace, along with the resolve that allows you to bury two children before they reach the age of three and still do your duty—becoming an ensign in the militia, donating money for the building of a church that, in a later incarnation, still stands today. As well, there's the Get 'er Done attitude that compels you to continue to pick up new land as it becomes available, because onward and upward has always been the point of this new life in this new world.

When we think about the founding DNA of this place, we all think first about the Mi'kmaq and the achingly sad way that they were engulfed by those who followed, and later the French, forlornly clinging to their small foothold here. Then I think about the period during which the province was by and large peopled, which is where we are in our narrative. It's a curious amalgam of cultures and histories, of disparate strands that have woven together over time to give this place its distinctive warp and woof, the singular way its people look upon the world and express themselves in a poem, a prayer, a song or an inventive layering of cuss words.

Technically, the newcomers who arrived in Nova Scotia during this period had a choice. Canada wasn't a penal colony like Australia, then being built by indentured slave labour. But it wouldn't be quite true to say that everyone arrived of their own volition, either. They were all fleeing something, whether misfortune, war, calamity or economic collapse. It was wilderness then, as it is still mainly wilderness today. Yet this, for a whole variety of reasons, is where they chose to make their stand. They arrived with unquiet hearts. They came with dreams that they followed, twisting and turning, sometimes losing the trail altogether, sometimes forgetting what they came in search of in the first place, sometimes never rediscovering their way again. Their stories, old as time, are being repeated as you read this. Maybe that is why they tend to stick with a person. At least, they do with me.


The New England Planters—after the founding of Halifax and the appearance of the Foreign Protestants, the third major influx of population in Nova Scotia in barely a decade—dreamed of land. Sam Slick, the Yankee trader created by Nova Scotian humourist Thomas Chandler Haliburton, called them a breed "tolerable pure yet, near about one-half apple sarce and t'other half molasses, except to the eastern where there is a cross of the Scotch." They came because New England even then was filling up. In the early 1600s Connecticut had only eight hundred people. A century later the number had grown to thirty-eight thousand. In the next ten years the population doubled. Thirty years later, which is about where our story now finds us, 141,000 lived there. Almost exclusively tillers of the soil, they were running out of room. Families were large, with fifteen children not uncommon. Speculators got involved, gobbling up vast tracts. Soon the best land in the lower Connecticut Valley was occupied. What remained was full of swamps, hills and rocks. The land-hungry farmers left, searching for new frontiers in Upper New York and Pennsylvania and as far south as Georgia, before turning north.

Through western Massachusetts into the wooded valleys of New Hampshire and Vermont they trekked, swelling the population in those places too. In Nova Scotia, now under the same flag as New England, the French threat was gone now that the Acadians had been removed and Louisbourg, as of 1758, was once and for all captured and its fortifications demolished. One day the governor of Nova

Scotia published a proclamation in the *Boston Globe*: since the enemy could no longer disturb and harass here, the time had come to people and cultivate the lands vacated by the Acadians. The Planters—so named because their predecessors arrived to plant a new England on the Atlantic coast of North America—heeded the call. To the north, the head of a family was promised not just one hundred acres of wild land and another fifty for each member of the household, but also an elected assembly similar to the ones back in the Thirteen Colonies. In Nova Scotia, they understood, existed freedom of religion, a necessity for the New England Congregationalists, with their abiding belief that each church congregation be allowed to run its affairs autonomously. In return for this, all they had to do was plant, cultivate and improve one-third of their holdings each decade, until all was under cultivation.

In 1760, as Franz Timming was baptizing the fourth of his ten children, working his fields and acquiring new land to cultivate— thirty acres here, another thirty there—the Planter ships began to arrive. First from Massachusetts, then a flotilla from Connecticut, and finally four ships carrying Rhode Islanders. In time, Massachusetts fisherman also arrived, mainly settling farther down the coast. "By the end of the year 1760," historian R.S. Longley told the Nova Scotia Historical Society two centuries later, "Annapolis County had a new Massachusetts, Kings County a new Connecticut, and the present Hants County a new Rhode Island." He called the whole of the Annapolis Valley, with a Planter population of nearly two thousand, "a new New England." Joseph Howe, visiting the Planter village of Bridgetown in 1838, found the people devoid of "stateliness and humbug," instead bursting with "energy of character" and "the germs of future prosperity and advancement." They brought new institutions, like the town council. They restored the old Acadian farmlands to their former glory. They built towns and homes that to this day thrive amidst the province's struggling rural economy.

Henry Alline grew up in one of these places: Falmouth, on the banks of the Avon River. There he indulged in the usual youthful recreations, which he described as "frolicking and carnal mirth." Yet he was a conflicted young man. Even before his family had relocated there from Newport, Rhode Island, he had been touched by the spirit of God. For many years, Alline later recounted, he wrestled constantly with his soul, "groaning under a load of guilt and darkness, praying and crying continually for mercy." Then one Sunday after wandering in some fields near the family farm, he returned home, picked up a Bible and turned to the Thirty-Eighth Psalm, whereupon "redeeming love broke into my soul with repeated scriptures with such power, that my whole soul seemed to be melted down with love."

Not long after, Alline, who has fascinated me from the moment I learned of him, felt the call to "labour in the ministry" and "preach the gospel." This he proceeded to do on horseback, canoe, snowshoe and on foot throughout the Nova Scotia wilderness and the settled parts of New Brunswick, turning up in bigger settlements and villages and hamlets where a few Planter families huddled. What a sight he must have been, materializing from the woods. "His form was slender, frail and even ghostly," according to one contemporary, while another described his "light complexion, light curly hair, and dreamy blue eyes."

In later years Alline was increasingly affected by consumption, tuberculosis, which ultimately killed him. Historians said that he showed the usual signs of the affliction, his gaunt, pale, sickly appearance contrasting sharply with his hyperactive, sometimes feverish mental state, all adding to the perception of Alline as some sort of backwoods John the Baptist, eyes ablaze, preaching the Word in tents or the open air, where he met people as he found them.

The end was nigh, this uneducated man from this simple farming family told these poor, untutored souls who might not see another stranger until the next time this saddlebag preacher returned. The devil, he ranted and railed, waited to carry them to an apocalyptic hell. His message that divine rapture was there for all who embraced his "New Light" theology caught fire in the wilderness. In sermons delivered as he crisscrossed the entirety of Nova Scotia, Alline told the Planters that they had a special, predestined role to play in God's plan for the world. Their very backwardness and isolation removed them from the corrupting influences of not just Britain but also New England, then in the midst of chaotic revolution. Nova Scotia, he thundered as his revival spread, would lead the world back to God. The newcomers weren't just some outpost of New England on the remote fringes of the empire. They were special, he told them over and over again. They were distinct, "a people highly favoured of God," he intoned, as his words by their power turned them from Yankees into Nova Scotians.

In those days, if you had a sturdy horse and a strong spirit like Alline, you would have seen the strange blend forming—the Mi'kmaq but also, not far from the Minas Basin, a scattering of Irish described as "indigent" when they arrived from Ulster in this place, which for obvious reasons they renamed Londonderry. The end of the Seven Years' War meant the Acadians were, by and large, free to go where they wanted. Many of those who survived the deportation preferred to settle in Quebec, in France, or in some French territory, such as the islands of Saint-Pierre-et-Miquelon near Newfoundland, present-day

Haiti, French Guiana in South America or the American territory of Louisiana, where, as modern-day Cajuns, they now hoot and dance and make spicier versions of some of the dishes they grew up on back in Nova Scotia. Amazingly, some came back to Nova Scotia, in leaky, decrepit boats or just on foot. This time they agreed to take the British oath of allegiance, allowing them to stay, but only in small groups, in designated areas, always far from their original lush lands, which had been given away to the English, fostering an aggrieved sense of resentment that simmers to this day.

Mostly, if you encountered a human being in the late eighteenth century in Nova Scotia and they did not speak Mi'kmaq, they spoke English, and chances were that they had not been here long. When the musket balls flew in the Thirteen Colonies, not everybody was a hotheaded Son of Liberty determined to throw off the British yoke.

Some—the best estimate is 19 per cent of the soon-to-become United States' population of two and a half million—counted themselves still loyal to the king for a wide variety of reasons: it was in their best interests or because they thought the revolt would fizzle. Maybe they feared the chaos that revolution could bring, for it was already bad enough for them in a place where unruly patriot mobs were within their rights to take the land and property of those unwilling to sign an oath of allegiance to the United States and even to tar and feather them, leaving the victims blind, scarred and frequently dead. Some were not born loyal but became so by circumstance or geography. Some were traitors. Some were just opportunists who wanted free land in the Canadian territories of Quebec and Nova Scotia. Some were just born loyalists, their belief in the mother country, historian Walter Stewart wrote, "as unshakable [if sometimes as uncomfortable] as belief in God itself."

In any case, they came. By the tens of thousands they poured across the border by foot, cart, horse, carriage and ship. By sheer force of numbers the British loyalists—English and Europeans, but also former black slaves who had been granted their freedom—overwhelmed their sparsely populated new home. Stewart calls the arrival of the loyalists "the pivotal event in Canadian history—the end of our childhood, the commencement of our formation as a country." Nowhere was this truer than in modern-day Nova Scotia, where the twelve thousand people then living there were engulfed by twenty thousand United Empire Loyalists.

Some of them had done okay in the colonies, but few were moneyed elite possessing fine educations and purses heavy with gold. Many of them were soldiers, their units disbanded, their lands gone. Others, said the provincial surveyor William Morris, were "Gentlemen, Bargers, Taylors, Shoemakers, Tankers . . . who have neither the fear of God nor man before them." Aboard the *Apollo*, which in 1783 departed New York for Nova Scotia, were eight mariners, eight carpenters and five labourers. There was a single cooper, carpenter, cord weaver, stonecutter, navy pilot and hairdresser. The only passengers aboard the ship who did what today would be considered white-collar work were a pair of merchants: Robert Wilkins, formerly a captain in the King's Loyal Company in Massachusetts, who arrived with his wife, three children and three servants, and a New Yorker named John McIntire, who came with his spouse, children and seven black slaves in tow.

We—or at least I—don't know if Wilkins and McIntire were present at the gatherings at Charles Roubalet's smoky tavern near the Paulus Hook ferry, the favoured New York watering hole of loyalists during the last years of the Revolutionary War. As Stephen Kimber recounts in his book *Loyalists and Layabouts: The Rapid Rise and Faster Fall of Shelburne, Nova Scotia, 1783–1792*, those get-togethers were raucous-sounding affairs featuring entertainment by magicians and musicians and even some foot-stomping dancing. Sooner or later, after quaffing a few pints and smoking a few pipes, they would get down to the real business at hand. One thing united the loyalists meeting in taverns and pubs all over New York in those nervous days: a deep-seated hate of the Americans that glowed hot as they pondered where to go next. Britain, by then, was too foreign a place for which to decamp. Canada was too cold and too French for the loyalists. The West Indies too far away, fever-ridden and foreign. By process of elimination Nova Scotia, the closest British territory to New York, became the natural location for their new loyalist mecca.

They chose a place that had been showing up on European cartographers' maps as far back as the 1500s. Champlain sailed past Sawgumgeegum, which was later rechristened Port Razoir and would one day become Port Roseway. The early Acadian settlers were repeatedly burned out by pirates and New England privateers. Settlers kept being drawn there anyway: New England Planters after the expulsion of the Acadians, and later some Irish immigrants accompanying the land speculator and adventurer Alexander McNutt, who named the townsite, optimistically, New Jerusalem, though it was no such thing. In the final years of the American Revolution McNutt's land was rescinded and laid aside for the United Empire Loyalists, who knew of its deep, expansive harbour and the surrounding acres of timberland that promised settlers a start in the lucrative lumber trade with England and the new United States.

When they landed in Nova Scotia the loyalists fanned out across the province, to Halifax, the Annapolis Valley, Cape Breton and even modern-day Prince Edward Island. Mostly they headed to Port Roseway, about eighty miles from Halifax, which from a standing start within eight months had more than double the population of the provincial capital. With twelve thousand inhabitants, Shelburne, as Port Roseway had been renamed, suddenly possessed more people than Trois-Rivières and Montreal combined. At that moment, in all of North America only Boston, Philadelphia and New York were larger than this town, which Governor John Parr grandly described as "the most considerable, most flourishing and most expeditious [city] ever . . . built in so short a time . . . ," as well as "an ornament to the British Empire." Yet a scant thirty-three years after its founding, only 374 people remained among the town's decaying wharves, unoccupied buildings and grass-covered streets. If its rise was glorious, its fall was downright breathtaking. There's no other way to put it: whatever could have gone wrong in the settlement once known as Port Roseway did.


One day on some hardscrabble ground down Nova Scotia's south shore, I met a man named Richard Gallion. For thirty years he had packed a pistol and patrolled the highways and byways of Ontario as a member of its provincial police. By then he was retired, back in the village of Shelburne, where he had been born. He got out of his vehicle and we shook hands. My memory is that he was tall enough to look down upon me and had a solid build, made even squarer—it being February—by a puffy winter coat. I know this much: he was a black man, late fifties, with grey in his thinning hair and moustache, a broad nose and seen-it-all eyes. He had history in this place where, though no formal record of it existed, his people were known to be buried.

During the American Revolutionary War, as I just mentioned, you had to choose sides. Gallion's ancestors, slaves in the colonies, decided to fight with those loyal to Britain in return for land, rations and, most of all, freedom. Landing in New York in the final days of the revolution, some of the black loyalists were met in some cases by their old masters from the south, who seized them in the streets and even hunted them down and dragged them out of their beds. George Washington insisted that all the ex-slaves be returned to their owners, but Guy Carleton, the British governor-in-chief of North America, refused. And so, when the ships finally left New York Harbour in 1783, nearly three thousand free black loyalists headed for Nova Scotia, many of them to Port Roseway, where the white loyalists had already settled. "Hard to imagine what was going through their minds," Gallion told me as we walked, feet crunching the snow. "How excited they were."

As we trudged on he told me some things that I knew and other things I hadn't heard before. It's common knowledge, for example, that the black loyalists never did get the land they were promised. Instead they ended up in a place where the ground was rocky and barren, which someone called Birchtown after the British officer who helped evacuate them from New York. The wind was punishing as we walked, which made the place seem even bleaker, understanding as I did that so many black loyalists spent their first winters there, in pits hacked into the frozen ground. Once, a person walking where Gallion and I did would have seen the ragged black settlers climb out of their huts and begin walking to Shelburne, which Port Roseway had by then been rechristened, where the only work available would have been as servants to the white settlers for wages as low as fifty dollars a year.

For some, the period of indenture went on so long that they might as well have remained slaves. Lydia Jackson was pressured into signing what she thought was a one-year term of indenture that turned out to be for thirty-nine years. She was then sold to a man who beat her mercilessly even when she was eight months pregnant.

In his autobiography, black loyalist leader Boston King wrote about people having to sell their clothes and blankets and eat dogs and cats to avoid starvation. In Shelburne, where negro "frolicking" or dances were banned, they were conned out of their rations and whipped for the most piddling crimes. It is hard to know whether they were better off than the blacks who arrived here as slaves to their white owners, even though the preferred phrase was "servant." (A story is told that when one such "servant" repeatedly ran away and was recaptured, his master cut a hole in his ear, passed a rope through it, and dragged him on the ground behind his horse.)

Despite all of their misery, a group of disbanded soldiers one day got it into their heads that the blacks of Birchtown were stealing their jobs and were responsible in other ways for the white men's own sad lives. With clubs, they chased them back to their shantytown, where they then put many houses to the torch. When the man who would later become England's King William IV arrived for a visit in the late 1780s, he wrote home that he had never seen "wretchedness and poverty so strongly perceptible in the garb and the countenance of the human species as in these miserable outcasts."

There seemed to be no shortage of unhappiness in this place whose shining moment would be so woefully short. The white loyalists, as Kimber has written, left the chaos of New York with a wide range of emotions: bitterness over Britain's decision to give up the fight, despair over their futures, anger towards the American victors. For most there was "anxious anticipation of what the future would bring." We know that the hopes of some came crashing down when the first boatload of newcomers arrived at Port Roseway in May of 1783 after a hard nine-day voyage. The harbour lived up to expectations. But instead of neatly laid-out streets and town lots, there was only forest as far as the eye could see. At that point, many of the women just sat down on the rocks on the impenetrable shoreline, lowered their gazes and wept.

When I walk the streets of Shelburne, I never feel despair. You can, even after all this time, understand the newcomers' stubborn belief that this could become something more than a dumping ground for the remnants of New York's loyalist population. Framed Georgian houses went up alongside the log homes. Businesses too: stores, saw-mills, blacksmith shops and fishmongers along the waterfront, its growing number of wharves fingering out into the harbour.

The hope was that Shelburne would be a "new and improved New York City"—a city that in Stephen Kimber's words would be "cosmopolitan, but more refined, more royal, more loyal and cer-tainly more exclusive than the place they were leaving forever." Consequently there were fancy-dress balls and parties with lots of toasting of the king. There were newspapers—the *Royal American Gazette*, launched by some brothers from New York and, soon after, the *Nova Scotia Packet and General Advertiser*—and other signs of civilization like coffee houses, churches with sermons about eternal damnation, justices of the peace who could marry, and in time, a court where all manner of sins would be accounted for. The latter was needed because, beneath the veneer of civility, Shelburne was a frontier town. Riots erupted over land allocations. Well-off new-comers treated their slaves harshly. The raucous behaviour was exacerbated by something else: the astounding number of taverns and "dram shops" in Shelburne where rum was available for three or four shillings per gallon during the early days of the settlement.

Nowadays when I visit Shelburne, which lives on as a small fish-ing port and regional service centre, I like to walk up to some old house with no car in the driveway and peer in. I get weird looks from passersby and even the occasional "Can I help you?" which is to be expected. If someone looked back out at me from inside all that, I could have said it was Lorenzo Sabine who sent me, which wouldn't have made any sense, but would at least have provided a distraction while I made my escape. Sabine was a Whig, an American who supported independence from Britain during the American Revolution, who later became a member of the U.S. House of Representatives from Massachusetts. He was mostly known during the American Revolution for his outlandish view that perhaps not every loyalist needed to be tarred and feathered. He had his defenders, for which I am thankful because they enabled him to publish several volumes of his major opus, *The American Loyalists, or, Biographical Sketches of Adherents to the British Crown in the War of the Revolution, Alphabetically Arranged.*

I found those sketches so interesting that once, after opening a volume, I looked up from my desk and discovered that it was dark out and I hadn't moved in so long that my legs had gone to sleep. In there, skimming some pages while digging deeply into others, I found the folks who ended up in Shelburne, even if just for a short time:

Joshua Gidney, from a place near Poughkeepskie, New York, had been imprisoned during the war "for his agency in spiking a cannon of the vicinity of King's Bridge."

Francis Coyle, a New Yorker, got caught up "in the excitement of the time [and] paid a guinea a foot for a house lot." A few years later, wrote Sabine, "he could hardly have sold his property for one-tenth of its cost."

Benedict Byrne of Maryland or Virginia entered a loyalist corps during the Revolutionary War, was taken prisoner, but escaped in New York, where he was employed as a harbour pilot. Byrne later went to England to obtain compensation for the money his loyalties had cost him as well as for his services in the United States, but returned empty-handed.

Mederich Cameron owned three houses in the city of New York and had two of them demolished so that he could transport the bricks to Shelburne to build a new house there.

Joshua Hill, formerly of Delaware, was convicted of treason and had his estate confiscated in the United States, with his personal losses estimated at ten thousand pounds.

John Fountain grew a fine vegetable and flower garden in Shelburne, where he apparently "let the boys eat currants at a penny each."

John Cowling, a Virginian, was impoverished by the war and opened a school in Shelburne, where he was assisted by his wife, Phoebe. After he died she opened a shop and carried on.

Archibald Cunningham was a merchant from Boston, where he had been a high-ranking Freemason. In Shelburne he became a clerk of the peace and registrar of probate, as well as "a man of reading and observation [who] left valuable papers."

Abraham Dove of New York kept a hotel in Shelburne, where he died.

James Dove (relation to Abraham unknown) was a magistrate and a merchant.

Robert Barry, an eminent merchant, was "distinguished for qualities that adorn the Christian character and throughout his life was highly esteemed."

James Frank, who died in Shelburne in 1809, was a pilot to the royal fleet in New York Harbour. "In March 1776 Lord Sterling sent a secret mission to take or destroy him," Sabine wrote enigmatically of Frank.

Robert Huston, an Irishman who fought with the British heavy dragoons in the revolution, worked in navigation and trade when he got to Nova Scotia.

Adam Hubbard spent lots of time around the water at Sandy Hook, New York, where he was for a time a lighthouse keeper. He waited until he had moved to Shelburne to drown.

Tunis Blanvelt, an active "bush-ranger" in the war, kept a boardinghouse in Tusket, Nova Scotia, where he moved and spent the rest of his days.

William Hill brought his family of eighteen and their eight servants here from Boston.

Nathaniel Gardiner commanded an armed schooner called the *Golden Pippin*, was captured by the Americans, and then escaped from jail to New York, from where he made his way to Shelburne.

James Humphreys Jr. started out studying medicine, but disliked the profession so much that he turned to printing, publishing a paper called the *Pennsylvania Ledger,* "which it was said was under the influence of the friends of the British Government."

Peter Anderson, a New Yorker, moved from Shelburne to Saint John and died in Fredericton, New Brunswick, at age ninety-five.

Joseph Bell, born in England, who emigrated to New York just before the revolution, "suffered much for his loyalties" and went to Shelburne in command of a company of exiled loyalists.

From the start, Shelburne was a here today, gone tomorrow place. Before the last refugees turned up, some of the early arrivals had already left for other parts. Some of them were speculators who tried to turn a quick profit by selling the land they'd been granted in Shelburne, and then taking their money and heading elsewhere. Most of the white loyalists who planned to stay were the wrong type of settlers—tradesmen and ex-soldiers who knew nothing about coaxing a living from the area's mean soil. They made lousy decisions. They didn't plan ahead. When the British government stopped provisioning the settlement, they started departing too, leaving more of the barely used homesteads to moulder in the damp and snow. Many headed back to the United States, where opportunities were opening up left and right. Some eventually lit out for the tubercular poverty that awaited them in Halifax, where, one of the loyalist leaders, wrote, "it is not possible for any pen or tongue to describe the variety of wretchedness that is at this time exhibited."

When the black loyalists from Birchtown got their chance they took it too, decamping in the last years of the eighteenth century for

Sierra Leone, the world's first free colony of African blacks. Life there was so tumultuous that a visitor would later christen it "a pestiferous charnel house." Yet they hung in: two centuries later their influence was still strong enough that Valentine Strasser, a twenty-five-year-old descendant from the Nova Scotia émigrés, seized power to become Sierra Leone's president and the youngest head of state in the world. Not for long, mind you. Four years later he was deposed by military coup, which was the same way he came to power. When a British newspaper caught up with him in 2012, he lived with his mom and spent his days drinking gin by the Sierra Leone roadside.

By then, back in Nova Scotia, a few members of the original black loyalist families still lived in the Birchtown area, although most of them had migrated down the road. The old settlement had new life, thanks in large part to a novel by Lawrence Hill called *The Book of Negroes*, which brought the story of the loyalist blacks of Nova Scotia into the light in somewhat the same way that the story of Evangeline had brought the saga of the Acadians to the world. Thanks to this book, I found myself one day in a big Halifax hotel ballroom, eating canapés and rubbing shoulders with the participants in the inaugural summit of black Canadian political leaders. They were there because the Black Loyalist Centre, the longtime dream of Richard Gallion and so many others, had just opened in Birchtown, making Nova Scotia the natural site for such a gathering. Once, black people couldn't wait to leave Birchtown, but now the traffic was headed in the other direction, I learned. Folks came from all over, from thousands of miles west in Canada and down in the states from whence Gallion's ancestors originated, to see the museum. It may be apocryphal, but I'm told that one of the first people at the site got out of their car, knelt down and kissed the ground, just like they were at least coming home.

———

The notion of home is an intriguing subject. To some people, being anchored to a place means more than others. For them it's hard, nigh impossible, to forget the old country no matter how long they call somewhere else home. Sometimes, during this period of arrival in Nova Scotia to which we've now turned our attention, people came in such numbers that their descendants felt compelled to erect some marker in their honour, something that spoke of all they had left behind. Way up on the northeast shore of Nova Scotia, halfway between the isthmus connecting it to the rest of the continent and the causeway linking the mainland to the island of Cape Breton, is a clearing in the woods that eventually opens up into a lane bisecting some low-level vegetation. The first, and so far only, time I was there it was late July, 28 degrees Celsius and calm. Not at all, then, like it normally is on the Saturday nearest April 16, when the old men don their kilts with their clan tartans, their tasselled sporrans, their little tams and long woollen socks and join the kids studying Gaelic at the local high school, the bishop of the Archdiocese, the local politicians and the plain, ordinary folks making their way down the lane.

A piper leads them. On white bandy legs the oldtimers head into the open. They stop, ramrod straight, their features broad and Hebridean, in front of a stone cairn. Then, though they've done it so many times before, they read the inscription:

TO THE MEMORY OF ANGUS MACDONALD, HUGH MACDON-ALD, JOHN MACPHERSON, SOLDIERS OF PRINCE CHARLIE. THEY FOUGHT FOR SCOTLAND IN THE CLANRANALD REGI-MENT AT THE BATTLE OF CULLODEN IN 1746. BORN IN MOID-ART, SCOTLAND 1712 AND 1716. CAME TO MOIDART, NOVA SCOTIA 1790–1791. BURIED HERE 1802–1810.

Then, the lines below:

LET THEM TEAR OUR BLEEDING BOSOMS, LET THEM DRAIN
OUR DEAREST VEINS, IN OUR HEARTS IS CHARLIE, CHARLIE
WHILE A DROP OF BLOOD REMAINS.

Since such things matter in these parts, it is noteworthy that the aforementioned Angus MacDonald had a son named John "Ban" MacDonald, who himself had a son named Donald MacDonald, who in turn sired a boy named John Alexander MacDonald. Among "Johnny Joe" MacDonald's offspring was a girl named Ella. She consequently married a McVicar. Every April 16 the result of that union is present at a spot where his great-great-great-great-grandfather was laid to rest a couple of centuries earlier. After all this time Bill McVicar, who spent 42 years working at the 5 cents to $1 store in nearby Antigonish, has been able to put together a few facts about old Angus and John MacPherson, both of whom came from Kinlochmoidart, a hamlet in the district of Moidart in Inverness, Scotland: that they had the good and bad fortune of being born in one of the most picturesque and rugged areas of the Scottish Highlands; that when they came to the town of Pictou in 1791 aboard a ship called the *Dunkeld*, they were already old, old men.

Except the stack of rocks isn't known as the Settlers' Cairn or the Cairn of the Old Fellas. Such is the nature of the offspring of those early settlers that, instead, it commemorates one of the defining events in Scottish history: their bloody defeat by the British near Culloden Moor, marking not only the vanquishing of the Jacobean military but also the end of the Scottish rebellion and therefore the Highlands of the clans. Bill McVicar, in his 70s himself, tells me how his forebear, along with John MacPherson and Hugh MacDonald, was already with Prince Charles Edward Stewart—"Bonnie Prince Charlie" to his supporters and "the Young Pretender" to his opponents—as he rode to meet the redcoats at Inverness. The way he talks, I can almost see the battlefield: a cold, stormy morning, the snow and rain blowing through the flat and featureless plain, the skirl of the pipes as the Jacobeans marched, then the thunder of death as the cannonballs started to rain down before, in the words of one narrator, the "cutting and slicing" began.

It was all over in less than twenty minutes. A thousand Jacobite soldiers died that day on the moor and later in the mountain villages where the English dragoons—some under the direction of Edward Cornwallis, the founder of Halifax, others taking their orders from James Wolfe, who would defeat Montcalm on the Plains of Abraham—hunted down fleeing Highlanders. That's what they recall at the only cairn to the Battle of Culloden found anywhere in the world, other than in Scotland, where on April 16 some mighty strange things have happened over the years: Scotch whisky has been ceremonially poured on the hard soil; bracing themselves in the wind, oldtimers, with exaggerated gestures, have recounted the Scottish version of the battle; toasts have been made and respects in English and Gaelic paid. When it is all over the crowd relocates to a parish hall to hear music that hasn't varied a note since the *Dunkeld* anchored nearby.

Somehow the MacPhersons and Angus MacDonald avoided the butchery. Instead they were imprisoned in Kelso and Edinburgh before being released under the general pardon of 1747. The old men's joints would have creaked and their old hearts ached when they boarded their ship. The kelp had failed. Their clan system had been destroyed, the kilt and the tartan banned for everyone other than Highland regiments serving in the British army. It was the peak of the Highland clearances, terrible days in which tens of thousands of men, women and children were evicted from their homes to make room for large-scale sheep farming.

The great migration was underway. Prince Edward Island, one of the first places encountered on this side of the Atlantic, was a natural landing place. So was Nova Scotia, where in 1773 a ship named the *Hector* carried 190 settlers, mostly from the Loch Broom area of Scotland, into Pictou Harbour. The arrival of the *Dunkeld* and other ships filled to the gunnels with Highlanders virtually doubled Pictou's population. The newcomers were so miserably poor that John Parr, the lieutenant governor, dug into his own pocket, sending them meat and salt herring to see them through the winter. That spring, many of the Highlanders began to move east, often by canoe, in search of more hospitable climes. Angus and Hugh MacDonald and John MacPherson stopped in Antigonish. Some kept moving right through to Cape Breton, where there was plenty of room.

It can be a confusing thing to travel in the same direction as those old-time Highlanders nowadays, crossing a causeway by car and chugging up the west side of Cape Breton, where so many of them ceased their wandering. Past settlements named in their honour— Campbell, MacKay, Beaton, MacKeen—and the places from which they came (Inverness, Dunvegan, Strathlorne and Glencoe). The last census I looked at showed that 1,275 Nova Scotians, a fraction of the twenty-four thousand identified in 1931, still think of themselves as Gaelic speakers. The bulk of them I know to be in Cape Breton, where the up-and-down lilt of the language never fails to thrill me, both because it is pleasing to the ear and because it is just great to know that it can still be heard.

In the village of Mabou, where the undecipherable Gaelic street names might as well be written in ancient Phoenician, I like to stop by a pub named after an old fiddle tune by Dan R. MacDonald, the most prolific of all traditional Cape Breton composers. Inside the Red Shoe as the old music filled the air and some little kid step danced in the Scottish style—stiff in the upper body, anything going from the knees down—I once eavesdropped as a couple of old fellows, faces creased from time and weather, spoke "the Gaelic" to each other as naturally as pensioners passing the time at a Tim Hortons in Parry Sound.

One night on one of my many visits, I talked one of the staffers at the Shoe into leading me outside to a small building that is today a store room for the pub's perishables, but way back when was the residence where the aforementioned Dan R. MacDonald lived for a while. Dan R. would hitchhike to dances or ceilidhs (Celtic hootenannies) all around the island. Since Scottish tradition says that if a fiddler shows up at your door, you must take him in, this shy, corpulent man with his Coke-bottle specs and his funny patois that mixed Gaelic with quotes from classical literature, could end up staying at some friend or relative's home for weeks on end. When it was finally time to leave, he would pay for his lodging the only way he knew how: with a new fiddle tune or two that added to the hundreds and hundreds he wrote during his life.

I love that story. I love too that the last time I was at the Red Shoe, son in tow, we stood by the bar next to the former premier of the province, himself a renowned fiddler and step dancer. A few feet away a piper's cheeks inflated like a bellows. The fiddler slurred her notes like a drunk, then made raw, otherworldly sounds as, one by one, the dancers made for the floor.

It seemed like the happiest place in the world even though I knew it wasn't always so around here. At the start of the nineteenth century most of Cape Breton's 2,500 inhabitants were fishermen who lived along the coast. The arable land in the interior was pristine, almost untouched when, in 1802, the first shipload of ragged settlers from the western Highlands and islands of Scotland landed here. They were a sad lot, many so destitute that their Scottish landlords cancelled their rents and debts and even paid their way, just to get them off the land where they had lived as subsistence farmers. The exodus from the outer islands was staggering. At the peak of the migration in the late 1820s, more Highland Scots were moving to Cape Breton than anywhere else in North America. Fifty years later, nearly two-thirds of Cape Breton's seventy-five thousand people were of Scottish origin. "In large part," wrote historian Stephen Hornsby of this period, "Cape Breton had become a Scottish island."

There would have been no certainty in those days. No more confidence that what lay ahead would be better for the Scots than it was for the Germans, the Swiss and French seeking something superior to what they left behind, the English fleeing revolution, the Acadians returning like spawning salmon to their homes. If some common identity was starting to be forged by these peoples who found themselves by coincidence and grand design in this formless, improbable place, it must have been undetectable to them, lost in their own long journey. The MacNeils of the Isle of Barra, led there by Donald "Og" MacNeil, who returned from the seige of Louisbourg in 1756 to sing the island's praises before being killed in the siege of Quebec three years later. But also the people of John MacCodrum, Iain Mac Fhearchair—one of the classical Gaelic bards in Uist—and those of Angus "An Saor Mor" MacDonald, the big carpenter from Carinish, who settled along the Mira River.

Yes, destinies were being forged there by the MacLeans, MacKinnons, MacLellans, Beatons and MacIsaacs, all from South

Uist, who flocked to the west side of Cape Breton. The same could be said for the other Scots who came pouring out of places like North Uist, among them people named McKeigan, all descended from Donald MacKeigan (known as "Domhull Og" or "Young Donald"), who decided to make their stand at a spot somewhere between the Mira River and Glace Bay. That, in retrospect, may have been a mistake: they arrived poor and the land there was unyielding. But I'm overjoyed that they did.

My grandmother was a McKeigan. I imagine her own father, Angus, being small in stature since he was born only a decade or so after the deprivations of the Nova Scotia potato famine of 1845, which, in the words of an emergency legislative body struck to deal with the crisis, reduced entire settlements throughout Cape Breton to "poverty, wretchedness and misery." He would have grown up hearing all about it. By firelight in the Cape Breton night he would have heard other things too: the smell of heather on the Highlands and, sooner or later, the sound of death on the moor in a place called Culloden.

Statue of Joseph Howe at the Nova Scotia legislature,
where he fought for the freedom of the press.

# FIVE

# Ace, Joe and Me

*Laying-On of Hands—The Nature of Greatness—The Rambles—In Another Skin
—Liverpool Badass—The Packet and the Privateers—Enos Collins—
The Hill—Bodies Twitching—The Group of Twelve—Let the
Vivisection Begin—The Press Is (Sort of) Free—Spent
Force—Walking the Joe Howe Line*

The most pleasant thing I could think of to do while working at the first job that mattered to me was to sit in the quiet newsroom on a Saturday at the *Chronicle Herald* building in downtown Halifax. Since there was no Sunday newspaper in those days, the pressure was off; if the city was rocked, as it was in 1917, by the largest manmade blast before the bombing of Hiroshima, if the naval convoys were massing out in the basin as they did to cross the North Atlantic to take on the Axis powers, I like to think that I would have headed outside on my own volition to see what was going on. Otherwise the Saturday reporter was just an insurance policy. Mostly you just sat there nursing a hangover as the police scanner squawked somewhere off in the distance.

Often the only other human you saw on those days was the sports columnist W.J. "Ace" Foley, who had started his newspapering career for the same paper back when Jack Dempsey was the heavyweight champion of the world and Newsy Lalonde was setting the NHL ablaze with a thirty-three-goal season. Small and pink as a bunny, Ace would toss a fedora right out of *The Front Page* onto his desk. I know he loved cigars—his memoir *The First Fifty Years* shows him chewing on one that's as thick as a blackjack—although oddly I can't recall him ever firing one up during those smoke-filled days. I remember that he would sit down, his hair slicked back, his nose straightforward, and two-finger his column, "An Even Break," on an Underwood typewriter now sitting in the Nova Scotia Sports Hall of Fame. Then he would walk over to where you were, pull up a chair and start to talk.

He would tell you about ancient prizefighters from Cape Breton you had never heard of and hard-hitting catchers in the old colliery baseball league, about some guy who had made it in the NHL long enough to have a cup of coffee and some ball game that started on a Wednesday and ran right on until the following Saturday before somebody broke the tie. The last thing I may be imagining; after all this time I really don't know. Details weren't important. The tales, every one of them, were wondrous. I felt blessed to hear them.

When I first started working on the paper it was fashionable in Halifax to call it the "*Chronically Horrid,*" but we all learned plenty in that building, which was full of the usual collection of dipsomaniacs, problem gamblers and folks who had found the Lord not a moment too soon, people who would go on to great things and those who would fizzle out in a blaze of glory. Newsrooms then were what we as a society used to have instead of asylums.

I was lucky enough to make my appearance before the Internet, when dailies like the morning *Chronicle Herald* and the afternoon *Mail Star* were licences to print money. We did extravagant things like cover the OPEC meetings in Venezuela and, because of the imperial connection, maintained a bureau in London to go with a person or two in Ottawa. Every now and then the publisher, Graham Dennis, who had his suits made in London, would show up in the newsroom and hand everyone a big fat bonus cheque. I loved writing in the same pages that brought the people of Halifax the news that the Wright brothers had gotten a plane off the ground in Kitty Hawk. This, in my overly romantic way, I loved too: that when I heard one of Ace's stories I was connecting to the historic past, through the laying-on of hands.

I don't mean in the obvious way, that the first paper ever published in Canada—a single, half-sheet of foolscap printed on both sides called the *Halifax Gazette*—was published weekly here when Halifax was a newly founded city and that by working for the latest of its successor papers I was part of that long and storied lineage. What I mean is this: it's entirely possible that when Ace Foley worked his first shift in 1920, someone yelled, "Copy!" On elfin legs he would have hustled over to where the ink-stained wretch sat. Then, perhaps not even looking up, this fellow—for they were most always fellows in those days—would have held his story out for the new kid to grab and leg up to the composing room.

You will have to indulge me for a second, because if that seasoned reporter was as old then as Ace was when he gave me those Saturday tutorials in Nova Scotia sporting history, he could have been a working hack himself in 1874 when the first edition of the *Morning Herald*, another predecessor to the paper where I now worked, hit the streets of Halifax. Back then, when press wars were everywhere in this country, all Canada cities of note had competing papers supporting each of the two main political parties. Halifax had an even dozen papers in those days. But it was a smaller place then. So, it's entirely possible that our nameless journalist—the one thing we know about him is that, besides being male he would have been sallow, since news people until recently rarely saw sunlight and survived on a diet of coffee, cigarettes, hooch and bile—at some point toiled across town for the main competition.

Now I can finally get to the point of all this conjecture. I'm bending forwards and backwards because at one point there was a paper in Halifax called the *Novascotian*. It is said that there's never been a paper like it in this province, which is saying something in a town with the kind of newspapering history that Halifax has. The man who ran it was one of a kind too. Which is why it makes me so happy, however contrived this exercise is, to think that when Ace handed me one of his wife Dorothy's cookies it was with the same small hands that would have accepted copy from the hands of our anonymous scribe, whose own hands, a score of years before, could have accepted the barely dry pages of the *Novascotian* from someone whose fame has hardly dimmed after all this time.

It is a thrill to feel that this succession of exchanges is all that separates me from Joseph Howe, that I am joined to him the way a dog on the end of a chain is linked to its master. When I started writing this book I did extensive polling—well, I asked a few people—about who they thought was the greatest Nova Scotian of all time. A number of them said Angus L. Macdonald, the premier who helped bring the province out of the dark ages, and Sir Charles Tupper, who snuck Nova Scotia into Confederation. The brewer Alexander Keith and the Nobel Prize winner Willard Boyle each garnered a couple of votes, so did the prizefighter George Dixon and the father of the cooperative movement, Moses Coady. Eventually someone answered Joseph Howe, for which I let out a long sigh of relief, since I had long ago made up my mind.

People have strong opinions about the nature of greatness. A few years ago, when the CBC asked Canadians to choose the most storied

Canadian to ever walk this land they picked Tommy Douglas, the father of medicare, and who can argue with that? The scales are less heavily weighted in Howe's favour, for a whole bunch of reasons: he was as human as human could be. His ego was profound. He was, in one huge way, on the wrong side of history. When his main work was done, wrote one of his biographers, "dullness succeeded enthusiasm, cynicism faith," and from that point on his story became "one of fading day and falling light." All of which may be true, but Howe had heroism in him.

Never once did he occupy himself with small matters. His sparking resumé—crusading publisher, defender of the freedom of the press, father of responsible government in Canada, premier, opponent of Confederation, then nation builder—ensured that he was here, there and everywhere like no other person I can think of in those days. In his time he spoke better than any politician, or man, in the country. Off the cuff he uttered words that would stand as the newsman's credo: "When I sit down in solitude to the labours of my profession, the only questions I ask myself are: What is right? What is just? What is for the public good?" I don't know if Joe Howe was truly great. Maybe the most I can say is that I think he was the greatest man to come out of Nova Scotia during his time, for which he himself will be our guide.

One day in the early years of the twenty-first century an Australian-born, Oxford University–educated man named Michael Bawtree was walking with a friend down Hollis Street in downtown Halifax. When they passed the provincial legislature, with its statue of Joseph Howe in full rhetorical flight on the lawn, his friend looked at the likeness, and then at Bawtree, and finally back at the statue again.

"You should do a play about him," he told the actor and writer, who by then had spent more than forty years in Canadian theatre and television. "You look like him."

Bawtree at that point was semi-retired and white-haired.

"I said to myself, 'That's not a bad idea,'" Bawtree told me one morning, many years later.

I was there to see him not just because that short exchange spawned an initiative to celebrate the bicentenary of Howe's birth, but because Bawtree, who has played Howe on television, radio and stage in three countries, and has written books and plays about him, has spent more time thinking about and inhabiting the man than anyone on Earth. If anyone knew Howe, Bawtree did.

"He always had that restless desire to do something important," he said in his actor's voice, when I asked what made Howe tick. "He just felt that he was destined for something big, and that never disappeared. It continued with him for his entire life."

Bawtree aged 78 at the time, was seated at the dining room table in his rambling old house, just down the street from the site of the theatre festival he founded in the college town of Wolfville. He chuckled in a "can you believe it" way at the image of Howe—"who said that sometimes it seemed like his readers' idea of a free press was that that they should get his paper for free"—scouring the countryside for subscribers and money to keep his publishing enterprise going. Bawtree doubts that hitting the road in that manner was an unpleasant experience for Howe, "who just had this wonderful, absolutely genuine capacity to be with people."

As premier, to the chagrin of Halifax's upper crust, Howe still loved to dine at the homes of marginalized black folks living near Halifax. Empowered to write a special report on the impoverished Mi'kmaq, Howe one day visited a First Nations community and discovered that the chief was out. Waiting for his return, Howe and the chief's two young daughters passed a couple of hours in pleasant conversation, even though they spoke no English and he didn't know a single word of Mi'kmaq. Once, at a big outdoors political gathering in Windsor, Howe, who was giving the keynote speech, couldn't be located. One of the organizers happened to take a stroll and found the guest of honour lying on the grass, sharing a picnic with a family Howe knew and had not seen in a while.

His humanity shone through in the series of sketches that started appearing in the *Novascotian* in July of 1828, theoretically based on his intermittent stagecoach "rambles" through the province, but really just a distillation of his incessant travels across Nova Scotia. Howe, alas, was a man of his time. "Gentlemen of colour," he opined, were imbued with "ignorance and idleness." Acadians he thought "a simple and affectionate people." "Paddies," on the other hand, "go laughing and fighting, with their hats on the sides of their heads or their hands in the apertures of their breeches, into any country where the soil is favorable for the growth of Potatoes." Though no admirer of their "ribbons and flounces," he had an eye for the ladies, whether "sable beauties" with their "wooly heads" or the women of the Annapolis Valley, where "not an ugly female have I seen."

Like many self-educated men he wanted to show the world that he was no bumpkin, a desire that could manifest itself in quotes from his voluminous reading and pithy zingers about peoples and places that he had never met or seen. But the man who speaks from the pages of these rambles is a fine fellow who, thanks the owners of the Western Stage Coach Company for supplying the means "by which a man may get a look at the country, without having to hire a sorry gelding at the rate of a shilling a day for every ounce of flesh upon his ribs," who prays from the bottom of his soul for the health of one of his fellow passengers, a girl with "consumption's touch . . . upon her," who, passing through the Annapolis Valley, finds his eyes start to water, dashes a clenched fist into the roof of the coach and exclaims to the alarm of his fellow passengers, "This is my own, my native land."

Through Howe we see the province of 143,000 as it was in those days. Heading north from Halifax, he liked Windsor. But he loved Kentville, then home to just thirty houses, yet raucous enough that a person "may run about, like Blair's soul, knocking at every outlet, but in vain—Port stands sentry in one place—Madeira in another, while Claret at the head of Bacchus' light infantry, fairly cuts you off from every retreat." Howe thought the folks of Cornwallis lazy and indolent. Annapolis, old Port Royal, he found past its prime, its buildings old and showing signs of decay, the village characterized by a "lack of enterprise and spirit," and he had little better to say about the loyalist settlement of Digby, a shadow of its former self, where the good folks "made sad complaints of the dullness of the times."

Yet there were hints of progress too. "From Blomidon to Digby gut, there is an almost unbroken line of cultivation," he wrote. The township of Granville, to his eye, contained "a succession of fine farms." There were three hundred residents in the Acadian hamlet of Claire and another two hundred in nearby Tusket, and he saw encouraging enough signs to predict that the nearby settlement of Sissiboo would one day grow into a town—which, in time, was true. To the east, New Glasgow, "a thriving little village" with buildings "of very recent erection" caught him by surprise. He seemed to have had low expectations for Pictou, a place of "miry" streets and "barbarous politics" which he understood to be home to "dirty-phiz'd radicals and red-headed Highlanders." Instead, from a standing start forty years earlier it was now home to 1,500 and had "progressed in a manner very creditable to the zeal and perseverance of the original settlers and their descendants."

At a pace of six and a half miles an hour he travelled, crossing rotting wooden bridges and lumpy, barely passable corduroy roads. The stages—the sections of road covered by one team of horses before another was substituted—were about fifteen miles apart. At each stopping place, there would be a stable with attendants and, usually a place to dine, at Mrs. Wilcox's in Windsor and Mrs. Fuller's at Kentville. The inns—Fultz's, Blanchard's, Hiltz's—were of variable comfort.

He went where his subscribers lived, not necessarily where the stories lay. Not everything he saw made it into print. Even so, I'd have loved to hear what he made of a town like Liverpool, where in the early 1800s things were as good as they would ever be. It was still a young town then, a fishing port founded by New England Planters who came in such numbers that the *Dictionary of Canadian Biography* declared it, in its early days, "essentially a New England community in Nova Scotia." As such it had been mostly sympathetic to the sentiments that led to the American Revolution—until, that is, it was not.

It is said that residences retain some stamp, however faint, of their previous inhabitants. The imprint of Simeon Perkins's presence on an old house on a leafy Liverpool street is deep. The day I arrived, much of the furniture was covered by drop cloths. Some of the ancient brown floorboards had been lifted. Jack posts seemed to be everywhere in an effort keep the walls, floors and ceilings stable. There was mist in the air, as if bad weather was coming, as I walked beneath dormers and past gabled windows, through a green wooden door and into eighteenth-century gloom. The day was mild, but since there was no insulation and the peeling plaster walls were thin, I could feel the damp in there as I nosed around.

I had the impression of walking in another's footsteps as I moved. I've seen a picture of Perkins, a profile of his right side, the nose and chin curving towards each other in an arch, soulful eyes, a spectacular comb-over that seems to run from ear to ear. I already knew his voice from his voluminous diaries, which are seldom demonstrative— "I hear my little son is sick there. My sister, wife to Burnham, is low. Benjamin Adgate's mother is dead"—but possess a simple poetry through which you sense the difficulties of everyday life. ("Nothing remarkable for some time. The people are in poor circumstances. Everything needed is very high, their pay uncertain, the land hard and rocky, very few cattle of any kind.")

Perkins was a man of enterprise, opening a store, trying his hand at fishing and lumbering and trading with everyone: the Mi'kmaq, the British colony of Newfoundland, Europe, the West Indies and particularly the Thirteen Colonies, where he was born and still had friends and relatives. Later a judge and politician, he was a force in the affairs of Liverpool throughout his long life. I would have loved to have had a word, because Perkins, despite his strong Congregationalist beliefs, his whoop-dee-do hairstyle and pillar of the community stature, was also a badass.

On September 13, 1780, a pair of Yankee privateer ships surprised and captured Liverpool. The townspeople, Perkins noted in his diary, were "Disheartened & did not Incline to make any resistance as they Looked upon our Situation Desperate." Their spines stiffened after Perkins engineered the capture of one of the American captains and then, by means of prudence and diplomacy, arranged for the recovery of the fort and the mutual release of prisoners. Within a few hours the "Dubious and Difficult affair" was over, he wrote, and "every thing [was] restored to its former Situation without any Blood Shed."

He sounds like a law-abiding citizen, like a simple man who just wanted to get along. Yet these were unruly days around here. Out of the fog a Yankee ship would appear, sails trimmed, cannons blazing, in the harbour in Pictou or Yarmouth, Cornwallis or Digby to pillage and plunder. The Yankee raids—conducted with powers conferred by the governors of the Thirteen Colonies—became so frequent that at the end of 1775, Nova Scotia's lieutenant governor declared martial law throughout the colony. In time, the residents and ship owners petitioned the government in Halifax for the means to protect themselves "from further insults and depredations." That meant ammunition for the onshore militia. It also meant letters of marque that gave Nova Scotia ships the right to "surprise, attack, vanquish, and apprehend" any vessel armed by and belonging to the rebellious Colonies and then to bring those ships and their plunder into any port within the province.

The men aboard those Nova Scotian ships weren't eighteenth-century navy men fighting, when the motivation was purest, to protect what was near and dear. The impulse was commercial. The American Revolutionary War had disrupted Liverpool's trade. Divvying up the proceeds of the captured ships fed families. During the peak years of privateering, it also turned Liverpool into the kind of rowdy, rambunctious port that makes you wonder if you're in the right place as you enter the quiet twenty-first century village that it is today: cattle drives crossed the province just to bring beef there; bakeries from as far away as New York and Quebec made bread to feed the men arriving. Countless barrels of gunpowder, cannons, muskets and cutlasses poured into the town, recounted marine historian

Dan Conlin. "Privateers and their prizes crowded the harbour, requiring new wharves and warehouses. Auctions of captured ships attracted schooner loads of Halifax's wealthiest merchants along with crowds of seamen bidding on some of the more affordable luxuries. Privateer parades, funerals and noisy celebrations added new rituals, mixing patriotism and economic optimism."

All this began with a few ships. In my reading I've found two vessels that hold the honour of being declared the first of Liverpool's legendary privateers. One was a schooner named *Lucy*, of which I could find little information other than that she was owned by a group of Liverpool merchants that included Simeon Perkins. The other was a schooner named *Enterprise*. Her commander was Captain Joseph Barss, the most fabled and feared of Nova Scotia privateers. *Enterprise* was also partly owned by Perkins, who would be financially involved in five of the six privateer ships that sailed from Liverpool at the turn of the eighteenth century. Perkins threw his weight behind the *Enterprise* because he wanted revenge after his own ship, the *Bouncing Polly*, was taken by an American privateer. On her first cruise, the *Enterprise* took twelve prizes. Yet she wasn't the most famous Liverpool privateer ship. Nor, for that matter, was the brig *Rover*, also part-owned by Perkins, which would return from its first voyage from the Caribbean during the Napoleonic Wars escorting captured prizes whose holds were full of Madeira wine and sperm oil. Her later voyages were even more memorable.

*Rover*'s captain was described as a man "considerably beyond the ordinary size, of an exceedingly quiet demeanour and retiring disposition." On deck though, Alex Godfrey was all resolve and derring-do. What he did off the coast of Venezuela in September of 1800 is still a maritime legend. There the *Rover* had been such a nuisance to Spanish shipping that a trap was set, using a small schooner as bait. When it was sprung, Godfrey manoeuvred his lighter vessel between the trio of Spanish ships, swinging his guns back and forth, firing first to one side then the other like Al Pacino in *Scarface*. He then made for open water, seeing the fore-topmast of the biggest enemy schooner crack and fall, turned back and led a boarding party onto her deck, despite being outnumbered five-to-one by the Spanish. When the musket balls stopped flying and the bloody cutlasses were lowered, fifty-four Spaniards lay dead and dying on deck that day, while not a single Nova Scotian life was lost.

When the subject of Liverpool privateers comes up the *Rover* is mentioned in the same breath as the *Charles Mary Wentworth* and the *Duke of Kent*, two other vessels owned in part by Perkins that also live on for their deeds in the Napoleonic Wars. Yet there's a higher pedestal still. Only one ship from this province—or this entire country—did what a former slave carrier-turned-mail carrier managed to do during these warring years. I bring up the name of the *Liverpool Packet* because when North America was ablaze during the War of 1812, this two-masted topsail schooner of Baltimore Clipper design prowled the Atlantic. She was only fifty-three feet long, just under nineteen feet in the beam, and had a hold just six and a half feet deep. But this small ship carried five cannons and forty-five men armed with muskets and cutlasses. From Liverpool, with the aforementioned Joseph Barrs at the wheel, the *Packet* left over and over again, capturing fifty American vessels during just ten months. No ship was more feared than the *Liverpool Packet*, no privateer more reviled by the Yankees than Barss, who would be twice captured and would be dead at forty-eight, his health broken by the American prisons.

I bring up the *Packet* because her combination of nerve and enterprise, the way she bedevilled the Americans and showed open contempt for the British government in Halifax, was emblematic of the best we had to offer in this time and place. But I also mention her because she was owned by a man named Enos Collins, whose path had long been intertwined with Perkins's. The second son of Hallet Collins's twenty-six children earned his keep by going to sea on one of his father's Liverpool ships. But Collins was also eventually the first mate on the *Rover* and served as first lieutenant on the Perkins-owned *Charles Mary Wentworth*. By the time the last shot had been fired in the War of 1812, three of Collins's ships, laden with supplies for the beleaguered British Army, would successfully break through a naval blockade off the coast of Cádiz, Spain. By then he had already begun using the profits from his privateer ships to lay the groundwork for a personal fortune that in time was said to be the largest in the British Empire. Which is interesting, even it's not really why I'm telling you about him. I bring up Collins now because he takes our story in a roundabout way right back to where it needs to be: to Halifax and to Joe Howe.

Among the daunting challenges facing Nova Scotia when I sat down to write this book—the hollowing out of the countryside, the last-century skill sets and industries, the aging population—is the simple fact that for a whole variety of reasons, few people want to move here. The numbers over and over again show that those hard-driving immigrants who are willing to do three jobs today so that their kids can own a block of apartment buildings tomorrow are loath to call Nova Scotia home.

This is less apparent in Halifax, where the hustle of Tripoli and the bustle of Taipei can sometimes be glimpsed, particularly in the new suburban areas, but also in the old city in which I like to poke around. Students stream by on the way to class. Hijab-wearing mothers push strollers. Oldtimers, perhaps dreaming of some village in the old country, amble by, hands clasped contemplatively behind their backs. In these streets, not far from where big political decisions are made, banks, hospitals and universities hum and cruise ships and shipping lines unload, there are moments when I feel I have never experienced such a profound silence as the one around me. When those moments arrive, whether day or night, I can shut my eyes and visualize in a swarm of detail what this place would have been like.

Halifax, by the time of Waterloo, had experienced a succession of booms and busts during the incessant fighting that began almost from the moment Edward Cornwallis founded the new garrison town. The end of the War of 1812 brought more trying times: economic depression as the garrison was disbanded and the naval fleet reduced and the rich West Indies trade collapsed, along with a series of epidemics. All the while, boatload after boatload of Scots, English and Irish, almost every one of them poor, arrived. With peace, respectable streets began to appear and some first-rate commercial buildings—some made of brick, others of stone—materialized, making the town seem solid, as if it were here to stay. Some of its defining features had begun to appear: a star-shaped series of walls and trenches atop Citadel Hill for the next time the Americans threatened; the town clock that rang out the time nearby. One writer of the moment declared of Halifax that "its streets are laid out with regularity, its spires have a picturesque and even magnificent effect," while a visiting Scot spoke in approving fashion about the upper levels of Halifax society, who showed "more refinement, more elegance and fashion, than is to be met with probably in any town in America."

Great fortunes were beginning: Samuel Cunard, the industrious son of British loyalists, was breaking into the shipping business.

Alexander Keith, a Scottish immigrant who had arrived at the end of the War of 1812, had begun brewing his India pale ale, which became a staple for those working on the town's fortifications. Arriving at the rather mature age of thirty-seven, Enos Collins had acquired some premises on Water Street, signalling that there was hope for this place beyond being a military base in time of war. Back then, a man in search of elevated thoughts could find them in Halifax, which had all manner of churches, including one started by black refugees from the southern United States after the War of 1812. It had a university. It had libraries. In keeping with the enlightened spirit then sweeping the province, it even had a lecture hall, the Halifax Mechanics' Institute, in which the inaugural talk was delivered by Joseph Howe himself. Howe, seemingly at the centre of everything in those days, was also a member of the town's foremost, and probably only, literary society. During meetings, the society members would work on satires about the follies and affectations of the day, which sometimes appeared in Howe's *Novascotian*. His was the best-read paper in a town where the journalistic instinct was so keen that the founding editor of the competing *Acadian Recorder* would jump in a boat and row out into the harbour to meet vessels as they arrived in port just to could get the scoop before his competitors.

I don't want to give you the wrong impression. Halifax was a tiny, congested place where few of the town's fourteen thousand residents lived more than a half-hour walk from one another. Too many people to count were near destitute. Riots, as a result, were frequent as the town's two-thousand-or-so soldiers clashed with the slum dwellers in the miserable huts and shanties of Water Street and the area between the garrison and the harbour known as "The Hill," where could be found more sin and misery than in the rest of the province combined. History, we all know, is imposed after the fact. If I had been a scribbler working for one of Halifax's bevy of newspapers as the Georgian era gave way to the Victorian age I'm not so sure I would have realized I was alive in great times. There was no decent water supply in Halifax. A few sewers by then had been built, but most waste was just dumped into cesspools. Once the sun went down it was mostly dark—the town being lit at night only by the meagre glow of seal- and whale-oil lamps on the central streets—and dangerous, since it would be years before the town's ragged group of police constables dared embark on regular night patrols.

By then Collins, Cunard and the other members of the town's wealthy merchant class, enriched by the wars, had begun to move from their mansions in the shadow of Citadel Hill to the suburbs to the south of Spring Garden Road. Even that beautifully named street must have seemed like an elemental place to someone strolling east towards the harbour, past the corrections house, the jail and the poorhouse. Cemeteries seemed to be everywhere—for the Anglicans, Methodists, and even the paupers who died in the poorhouse. Lots of graveyards were needed because anything could take you in those unsanitary days when death came by typhus, dysentery, diphtheria, yellow fever, malignant measles or scarlet fever. Smallpox swept through the town in 1827 and again a year later. Six years after that, whether through tainted water or from Irish immigrants discharged from their vessels and lodged in the poorhouse, cholera ran rampant through Halifax. By early September it resembled one of those European plague cities, complete with bonfires lit to drive off "noxious vapours" and death carts rumbling through the streets to collect the mounting corpses. The wagons made the rounds early each morning, eventually conveying the dead to the cemetery adjacent to

Fort Massey, Halifax's richest and most prestigious Presbyterian church, where the crude coffins were dropped into long trenches and hastily covered with earth.

On top of everything else, Halifax was a violent town, particularly if a man happened to venture down to the groggeries and brothels on Barracks Street, today the site of trendy brew pubs and the arena where the local junior hockey heroes play, but back then a rookery of cold tenements that smelled of filth, disease and danger. Destitute Irish and blacks lived seven to a room there and the streets crawled with soldiers and sailors, drifters and transient workers ranging from circus performers to deserters who had jumped ship from some far-off port of call. Gone by then, I believe, was the old-time practice of branding criminals in some visible spot on their faces or bodies in lieu of formal criminal records. But the denizens of Barracks Street still looked malnourished, diseased, "squalid and poverty struck" according to one correspondent.

The profusion of saloons was so great that little seemed to have changed in Halifax since the late days of the eighteenth century, when a visiting clergyman observed that the business of one half of the town of Halifax was to sell rum and the other half to drink it. When R.H. Dana, the author of *Two Years Before the Mast*, "investigated" Barracks Street around the time of which we speak he declared it a "nest of brothels and dance-houses" in which the prostitutes "looked broken down by disease and strong drink" and were so syphilitic that he put the odds of catching it or any number of other venereal diseases at ten to one.

I routinely walk by the site of one of the worst dram shops and brothels from yesterday, the Waterloo Tavern, the site of an almost constant stream of brawls, assaults and even murders. Much of the mayhem was thought to be the work of the proprietor himself, a man named James Bossom who was fond of using his shillelagh, the heavy end of which had been hollowed out and filled with cement, to calm excitable customers. The Bossoms were a bad crew who tended to come to a bad end. As proof I offer the tale of James's son, James Jr., who by his early teens had already grown into a cruel thug with his own motley collection of followers. One day after a night's carousing, young Bossom showed up at a nearby saloon demanding that the proprietor come out to fight. Instead, Smith D. Clarke shot Bossom in the eye. Clarke would have hung for it had the young Queen Victoria, in a magnanimous mood over her impending marriage to Prince Albert, not issued a string of pardons to various felons across the empire around that time, including the Halifax tavern owner.

Punishment for lawbreakers like Clarke was less harsh than it was years earlier, during the anarchic days on the high seas. Back then the laws required that, after execution, the tar-covered bodies of pirates be displayed in public, hanging from chains in an iron cage called a gibbet, as a warning to other sailors. In the early 1800s it is entirely possible that a ship entering Halifax's harbour had to pass between a hanging corpse on McNabs or Georges Island in the middle of the harbour and another one suspended and rotting at Point Pleasant Park, where I now walk my golden doodle. Decades later, people were still sometimes hanged right in the centre of town, on the common, where on a summer's night you now might see Frisbees flying through the air and little kids taking their first freestanding steps.

The last hanging there took place back in 1844, which is the same year that a barque named *Saladin* sailed from Chile, bound for England with a cargo of valuable fertilizer, silver dollars and copper. The ship was found stranded near the northeastern end of the province. Boarding the *Saladin*, the captain of a passing vessel found six inebriated men "acting suspiciously." Four of them were found guilty of murder and sentenced to death by hanging. A gallows was erected on the South Common, now the site of a hospital. Hundreds turned out, children in tow, to see the condemned men arrive in a prison wagon surrounded by the red-coated members of the 52nd Regiment and then to watch the necks snap and the bodies twitch.

Through this town, one step ahead of his creditors, steady on the ground as the press on which he printed his *Novascotian*, strode Joe Howe. For all the duelling and rioting, this was no wide-open frontier settlement. Nor did it much resemble one of those New England towns, with their democratic tendencies, from whence many of the residents had arrived. In Nova Scotia, political, economic and judicial power was the exclusive possession of a cabal of Halifax businessmen, high colonial officials and learned folk. It may be illuminating to know that by then Nova Scotia's elected House of Assembly could only pass laws if the governor, appointed by the British Colonial Office, and the Council of Twelve, who were appointed by the governor, approved. In the early, precarious days of the colony the Council of Twelve was dominated by military officers, but in time Halifax's growing merchant elite took control, ensuring the town's dominance over the colony.

Inevitably Collins, who in photographs always had the harrowing look of someone who had endured youthful hardship, joined the council. At that point his privateering days were behind him. Like many a self-made mercantilist of yore, Collins did the best with what he had, using the profits from the booty captured by his privateer boats to purchase an impressive array of wooden docks and ironstone warehouses on the Halifax waterfront. He bought and sold, moving into new businesses when he saw opportunity. In 1825, along with the shipping magnate Samuel Cunard and some associates, Collins formed the Halifax Banking Company, commonly referred to as Collins Bank since it was headquartered in one of his ironstone waterfront warehouses. It is noteworthy that five partners in the venture, including Cunard, were members of the Council of Twelve, while the other seven were their friends or relatives.

There are lots of examples of how the business elite's unhealthy dominance of Halifax's affairs played out. I think one, in particular, is illustrative: a group of businessmen wanted to set up a bank in direct competition with the Halifax Banking Company. They rounded up 184 supporting signatures, including Howe's, on the necessary petition for incorporation, which was subsequently approved by the provincial assembly. But when the all-powerful Council of Twelve got hold of the document, they went into a room, closed the door and returned with a series of amendments sharply watering down the powers of the competing lending house. Collins's bank, which in time became the Bank of Commerce, one of Canada's largest financial institutions, did okay. So did the other concern, in time known as the Bank of Nova Scotia, by the twentieth century also one of Canada's Big Five banks.

I raise this affair because it was a galvanizing moment of sorts. Political reform was then being called for in Nova Scotia in the same way it was being called for throughout England and most of its overseas colonies. All causes need a champion. By then Howe, a married father, a bon vivant with a knack for getting himself into financial difficulties, had moved the *Novascotian* into bigger, swankier quarters opposite Province House. He was as reverential towards Britain as his father had ever been, but his belief that great things lay ahead for this province was equally unshakable. Howe, who thought that it was personal duty to promote the rise of provincial literature, published multivolume histories of Nova Scotia's laws, money-losing epic poems by an author known as "the Bard of Elenvale," and even something called *Letter on the Doctrine of Personal Assurance*, the only work by his father ever to see publication. In the *Novascotian* Howe wrote tirelessly, promoting the province's progress to the point of cringeworthy boosterism. The prospectus inserted in the first issue of the paper summed up his political creed as simply "the Constitution, the *whole* Constitution, and *nothing but* the Constitution," which meant that he generally supported things as they were.

Yet, he had eyes; Howe could see what was going on. A few years earlier the provincial assembly had imposed a tax on foreign brandy. This being Nova Scotia, the customs collector had arbitrarily decreed that a lower duty was sufficient, even though he failed to inform the assembly about his decision. The assemblymen might never have known that provincial coffers were being shortchanged had Collins not had the temerity to petition for a refund on the brandy duty that he did pay. When the assembly tried to enshrine the neglected levy in law, the council, controlled by Collins and his cronies, fought that too. As the story played out, Howe sat in the provincial legislature, dutifully recording the debates for five and six hours a day. When he put down his pen he had 480 pages of notes. Like all great newspapermen, when he found a story—whether the existing checks and balances of the political system were enough to safeguard the interests of Nova Scotians—Howe rode it hard and long. In time his questioning in the *Novascotian* grew not just louder but more pointed. His focus moved from the provincial level to Halifax's local government, which made things complicated since both his father and half-brother were members of the elite coterie that ran the town and province as its own.

It wasn't something that Howe wrote that brought everything to a head. The letter that appeared at the bottom of the second column of page two of the January 1, 1835, edition of the *Novascotian* was signed "The People," and a friend of Howe's named George Thompson wrote it. In old-timey language it made serious allegations: that the affairs of Nova Scotia "have been for years conducted in a slovenly, extravagant and unpopular manner" and that the hard earnings of the people were being lavished on an aristocracy "who repay their ill-timed generosity with contempt and insult." Most serious was an accusation that the police and the magistrates appointed by the Council of Twelve to run Halifax had pocketed at least thirty thousand pounds meant to go to the province's poor, distressed and destitute.

You can almost see the potentates' bow ties spinning like Catherine wheels as they read those words. Was there much debate before the magistrates officially complained to the governor, who then passed the whole thing on to his attorney general, the province's highest legal official? How many people had to sign off before he, in turn, charged Howe with "seditiously contriving, devising and intending to stir up and incite discontent and sedition among His Majesty's subjects"? Libel chill isn't some twenty-first-century notion. Being charged with criminal libel was a constant fear of newspaper editors in British North America in the mid-1800s, when those with money threatened expensive legal suits against anyone who dared to criticize them. By taking him to court, the pashas of Halifax intended to ruin Howe professionally and financially. That this time might be different must have become apparent a day later when they picked up the *Novascotian*, in which Howe warned matter-of-factly that even if he lost in court his accusers would not "bear their banners unsullied from the field."

———

Any private citizen can go and visit the legislative library at Nova Scotia's Province House, across the street from the old offices of the *Novascotian*. The last time I entered the squash court–sized room with its claret-red carpet and three-sided balcony, its hanging staircase, its mammoth portraits of long-ago citizens of note, its eight alcoves adorned with wrought-iron mayflowers—Nova Scotia's provincial flower—only one other person was there: the library's manager of information services. Anne Van Iderstine, who speaks quietly, perhaps from a lifetime of shushing folks, sat at a desk at the front of the room, about where the judge would have been seated. "The defendant's dock would have been about there," she said, waving a hand off to my right. The building across the street from the legislature wouldn't have existed in 1835. So it is possible that when Howe took his seat, scanned the jury and visitor's gallery and then looked out the ten-foot window he could have seen clear down to Halifax harbour.

Inside the room, which served as the Supreme Court of Nova Scotia until 1862, the air conditioners hummed and moaned the last day I visited, keeping the temperature to a tolerable level. Howe, on the other hand, said it was "hot as a furnace" and "crammed to overflowing" when his trial began. It could have just seemed that way. The Halifax establishment was out in force, including some of the very magistrates who were the targets of his withering attack. Howe said that when he looked back at the gallery he saw more of the "middling" members of the society—the folks who "had suffered some exaction, had some complaint to expose, or had had justice denied or delayed" and had put their grievances in letters that arrived in such volume that they filled the entrance to his *Novascotian* offices. He was, in a legal sense, completely alone. Every lawyer he had contacted said that he had no case since, as the law then stood,

it was libellous to publish anything calculated to degrade a person or
to disturb the public peace. Famously, he borrowed a law book. For
a week this man who hadn't been inside a classroom since age twelve
pored over the volume. When he finally stepped away from his desk
he told his wife that if he "had the nerve and power to put the whole
case before a jury, as it rested in [his] own mind, and they were fair
and rational men, they must acquit [him]."

Nonetheless, Howe was nervous when he stepped into the court-
house. He only had time to memorize the first two paragraphs of his
address, which, after the prosecution laid out its case, began this way:

My Lords and Gentlemen of the Jury,
I entreat you to believe that no ostentatious desire for display has
induced me to undertake the labour and responsibility of this
defence. Unaccustomed as I am to the forms of courts and to the
rules of law, I would gladly have availed myself of professional aid;
but I have felt that this cause ought to turn on no mere technicality
or nice doctrine of law, but on those broad and simple principles of
truth and justice to which an unpractised speaker may readily
appeal, and which an impartial jury can as clearly comprehend. I
have felt, besides, that if the press is to be subjected to a series of
persecutions such as this, it is indispensable to the safety of those
who conduct it that they should learn to defend themselves.

Believe me, also, that the notoriety and excitement of this
proceeding are foreign to my taste. Men of my profession, whose
duty it is to mingle in public contests, and while watching over the
general interest, to wrestle with those who menace or invade, are
too often reproached with the invidious tasks they perform, and
suspected of a morbid fondness for contests into which they are

impelled by a sense of the obligations that public faith and common honesty call on them to discharge. Those who know me best well know that I would rather give the little leisure that a laborious life affords to my books and my fireside to the literature that ennobles, and the social intercourse that renders society dear, rather than to those bickerings and disputes by which it is divided, and by which man is too often, without sufficient cause, set in array against his fellow-man.

Howe had no choice in the matter, he argued. He printed the offending letter for the same reason that he would later fight to keep Nova Scotia out of Confederation: because it was his nature, because he could not help himself.

He knew the magistrates well. Some of them were family, others he deeply admired in their private lives. If the question to be decided by the jury was whether he had some wicked or malicious motive in printing the letter, he said rest easy, for he had none. The problem, he explained, was that he also knew these men as magistrates whose job included "the guardianship of morals and the public peace," who made legislation, who collected and dispensed revenues, acted as trustees of property and auditors of the town's accounts. The problem, he said, was that that he knew them as the jury knew them, "as almost every man in the community knows them, to be the most negligent and imbecile, if not the most reprehensible body, that ever mismanaged a people's affairs."

For the jury's sake he pointed out that he hadn't written a single line of the letter mentioned in the indictment, that he gave no advice in its preparation and that he hadn't added or taken out one word once it came into his possession. The moment it landed on his desk he had no choice. As startling as the charges the letter contained were, Howe believed them to be true. "And strong in that belief, I published the letter," he said almost with a sigh, "and should have betrayed the trust I hold, had I caused it to be suppressed."


Michael Bawtree, who has recreated Howe's courtroom star turn too many times to count, doesn't just get up and wing it. "I am an actor who starts with a text," he likes to say. So he took Howe's whole six-hour libel defence and tightened and shortened, summarized and paraphrased. He distilled it until he had eighty polished minutes for his performance. "If you make sense of a text—its emotional range as well as its logic and intellect—you will come close to the person," he says. No recordings exist of the man. But so much has been written about his gifts of oratory that Bawtree felt that he had much to go on as he crafted his performance.

Howe's father came from Boston, so it's possible that he had a New England cadence, though not the "Pahk my cah in Hahvad Yahd" dropped "r" we, in the twenty-first-century, hear in movies. Everything Bawtree knows about Howe makes him think he would have eschewed any showy hand gestures—"He was just natural, and if you are a natural speaker you driven not by technique but to communicate your voice"—as befitting an orator who once wandered into a London debating club and left twenty minutes later to cries of "Why isn't this man our prime minister?" from the assembled crowd. Sometimes, when Howe was getting down to the business of speaking, he would pull his coat off of his shoulders and allow it to dangle loosely from his arms, which Bawtree would do too. Though these were the days before microphones, Howe sometimes spoke to crowds of five thousand in a farmer's field, so Bawtree figures he had a rounded voice that was good at projecting. "He was a man who loved words," he says. "If you love words you want them to be heard."

As Howe's words rang throughout the small room, the magistrates must have known their day would be long. The sinking feeling had to strike them the moment the defendant took the routine language of a libel indictment—that he was "wickedly, maliciously, and seditiously contriving, devising, and intending to stir up and excite discontent and sedition among His Majesty's subjects"—and turned it into a stirring profession of loyalty for the British crown as well as a blanket condemnation of the magistrates themselves. If the king were in the courtroom, Howe went on, "these prosecutors would shrink before the indignant glance of the Sovereign, whose trust they had abused. His Majesty would tell them that he who robs the subject makes war upon the King, that he who delays or withholds justice excites discontent and sedition . . . that they were the rebels, and that against them and not against me, this bill of indictment should have been filed."

I imagine Howe at times thundering from the heavens like Henry Drummond and at others murmuring as reasonably as Atticus Finch. "His sense of humour was my sense of humour," Bawtree says. So it was easy for him to do justice to the accounts of the trial, which frequently mention the laughter of the audience and, for all we know, the jury members themselves as Howe gathered steam and confidence. At the same time, reading Howe's words after all these years, you can still feel an anger that was deeply personal. These men had dragged him from his home and had him "arraigned before you as a criminal"; they hoped to destroy his reputation, his livelihood and the financial future of his family. In the apologetic manner of a colonial Tom Hagen, Howe said that they had "placed me in a position where the performance of a disagreeable duty is essential to my own safety . . . and to the public safety also." They should remember that, he said with a verbal shrug, as the vivisection continued.

Purely by coincidence, precisely 181 years after Howe's trial I found myself walking up and down a busy arterial street named in his honour. Joseph Howe Avenue, by then, was the home of the newspaper where I worked, the slimmed-down, Internet-challenged *Chronicle Herald*, which had decamped from Halifax's historic core. The sky was flint grey, the temperature raw, the wind moving hard, mostly from south to east on day 39 of a work stoppage with no end in sight. By then the adrenaline buzz of the first few weeks on the picket line had given way to the numbing reality that we could be doing this for a very long time. Patterns had begun to emerge: a group milled about the entrance to the paper's parking lot; some of us tried to pass the tedious hours doing laps up and down the street like religious penitents. Sometimes we did so together. Sometimes we just trudged back and forth in single file.

On those days, this project well underway and my MP3 player on the blink, my thoughts sometimes turned to Howe. I didn't think a great deal about the trial itself: the deft manner in which he demonstrated how the town's worthies had fleeced the citizenry; his epic takedown of the commissioner of the Bridewell, the reform school of the day, and the regulator of the Poor Asylum, for appropriating funds that were supposed to go to the down-on-their-luck. Like everybody familiar with his story I knew about his acquittal, which took the jury just ten minutes, and his subsequent proclamation in the *Novascotian* that "the press of Nova Scotia is free." After all of this time Howe, who was carried through the streets of Halifax after his acquittal, gets credit for bringing freedom of the press to

Canada, but that's not really true. Nine years later his successor as proprietor of the *Novascotian* was forced to give up his paper and was marched to the hoosegow because he couldn't pay the libel damages awarded to the government of the day. What Howe's court victory did do was to make a shambles out of Halifax's old-boy government. A slew of resignations followed. New appointments were ridiculed. Rancour ruled.

According to Howe's biographer Murray Beck it was months before things had quieted enough for him to hop on a horse and take a head-clearing ramble in the countryside. For three weeks Howe zigzagged around, in the midst of another provincewide recession, covering a distance of two to three hundred miles. All the fresh air gave him time to think, and what he thought about was that if he wanted change—if he really wanted the people of Nova Scotia to possess the same rights as their equivalents in England—scribbling away in a newspaper wouldn't do. Beck figures that on this road trip Howe first started thinking about running for public office, which he did, successfully, a year later.

He was a reformer, seeking a government responsible to the people rather than some far-off monarch. Howe had company at a time of widespread discontent towards the small, powerful local elites that had sprung up to control the governments in Britain's colonies. This discontent boiled over into armed insurrections in Upper Canada (now Ontario) and Lower Canada (soon to become Quebec). Howe chose finesse and patience over gunpowder. It took eleven years, during which coalition governments failed and Howe was in and out of the legislature. Here's how contentious the whole thing was: Howe's electoral success so outraged his opponents that he was forced to fight a duel with John Haliburton, the son of the chief justice. When Haliburton missed, Howe fired his pistol into the air, further adding to his legend. But when Nova Scotia ushered in British North America's first responsible government—James Uniacke was premier, but everyone knew it was Howe's victory—he could rightfully claim that it had been achieved "without a blow struck or a pane of glass broken."

Once in power, he had no great knack for governing, whether as provincial secretary or later as premier of a precarious majority or in his failed bid to build a railway from Halifax to Quebec. He lost a provincial election, then bounced back, securing an appointment as colonial fisheries commissioner. When Sir Charles Tupper, his main political rival, invited him to be one of the Nova Scotian delegates to the Charlottetown Conference in September 1864 he declined, leading to one of the great "what ifs" in Nova Scotia history.

In Charlottetown, the governments of Nova Scotia, New Brunswick and Prince Edward Island planned to discuss political union as a way to gain clout in dealing with the Province of Canada. We all know that things got away from the easterners: the representatives from Canada's Great Coalition cabinet, who showed up as uninvited guests, wanted to create a federal union, mainly out of fear of being annexed by the Americans. When the meetings broke up, that is conditionally what they had.

Howe thought from the start that Nova Scotia would become a second-class partner in the larger union. He feared that the higher Canadian tariffs would handicap the Maritime colonies when it came to exports and domestic consumption. He thought the voters should be consulted before such a major step was taken. (Tupper, using his power as premier, just pushed a resolution favouring Confederation through the legislature before he had an election to face in 1867.) Yet instead of cutting and running to accept the editorship of a paper in New York, Howe decided to stay and fight, telling anyone who would listen that the deal was a bad one for Nova Scotia. He led a delegation to London, not once but twice, to oppose the passage of an act of union and later to repeal it. He wrote and spoke, cajoled and wheedled. Nothing worked. Much of what Howe feared would happen to Nova Scotia after Confederation simply did. Yet once he realized that the tectonic plates of nationhood were fusing together he negotiated an agreement that provided better terms for Nova Scotia, then entered John A. Macdonald's cabinet, where he did his part for the new dominion, acting as an intermediary in the first Riel rebellion and helping to bring Manitoba into Canada.

Yet his role as a nation builder wasn't really what I thought about while I trudged back and forth on the avenue named in his honour. As the days turned into weeks and the weeks into months, I thought more often about the manner in which Howe was remembered in a newspaper reminiscence published a day after he died, worn out, at sixty-nine: "The news of his death will be known in the country towns and will spread to the scattered villages . . . The farmers driving along the country roads will stop to talk over his life and tell anecdotes of his conflicts." From time to time, as the days mounted and my mood darkened, I thought naturally about his trio of journalistic questions—"What is right? What is just? What is for the public good?"—which used to stand high and proud on a billboard advertising the paper where I once worked and someday hoped to work again. It was a different time, I knew that. When Howe gave voice to his newspapering creed, this area where we walked with cardboard signs around our necks was virgin country. Deer and rabbits ran wild around here. Cattle chewed grass in the pasturelands. Treetops, when the weather warmed, threatened to shut out the sun.

The Yarmouth waterfront during the great days of sail.

# SIX

# Making It Pay

*Tough as Wrought Iron—Brier Island—The Usual Pioneer Beginning—Seaborne*
*Units of Production—Miles of Canvas—Merchant Capitalists—The Deep—*
*The Graveyard of the Atlantic—The Wandering Years—St. Elmo's*
*Fire and the Belaying Pin—The Seafaring Maiden—Conjuring*
*the Old Ghosts—The Spray—Casting Off*

The essential book written by a Nova Scotian—not the best or most skilfully rendered one, or the most informative or insightful book, or even the one that has touched me the most deeply, but the one that, in my opinion, gets most directly to the essence of this place and its people—is one that has been printed and reprinted dozens and dozens of times. At least one edition, the 1949 one with the Arthur Ransome introduction, has a navy-blue cloth cover with gold foil lettering and pictures clear and maps precise enough to give a reader a true understanding of the size and scope of the enterprise. I borrowed a copy of that edition, three by six inches, faded and dog-eared, possibly salt-water-stained, the dustjacket long gone. Since I have never given it back to the person who owns it, in the eyes of the law I am a felon. All I can say in my defence, Your Honour, is that I am drawn to Joshua Slocum's story like a big man is to beignets, and throw myself on the mercy of the court.

The photograph in the front of my stolen edition of *Sailing Alone Around the World* shows the mariner at about the age when a newspaper reporter caught up with him on the Boston waterfront, after he had completed the great adventure. The newspaperman declared Slocum "as tough as wrought iron and as lively on his feet as a chicken." The captain had "hard horny fists," like those of heavyweight boxing champion Gentleman Jim Corbett. The newshound observed that the mariner still sported a vivid scar over his left eye from being blown out of an upper topsail yard during rough seas. Slocum, going by this photograph, had a face for the wall of some forgotten museum: a biblical prophet's stern and sober mien; the cheeks sunken; the eyes, everyone who met him noted, unwavering and devoid of warmth, as if they had seen terrible things. But his family talked of him as a loving if undemonstrative husband and a tender father. Slocum had cracked the Greek classics, and any careful reader of his prose knew that a poet's heart beat beneath the breast of a man who wrote, "I was born in the breezes, and I had studied the sea as perhaps few men have studied it, neglecting all else," a line that I long ago committed to memory.

Yet I have to wonder about him sitting there, answering a reporter's questions. I wonder if he might have said to himself, in that uncanny way Slocum had of looking at something, stripping it of emotion and seeing it clearly for what it was: here you are, a man in your fifties. Three of your children and your one true love have died aboard ships far from a home. You have shipwrecked and lost two clippers, shot one crewman and been charged with the murder of another. America's newspaper of record has pilloried you on its editorial pages. You are barely on speaking terms with your current wife, who spent her honeymoon delivering a case of oil from Boston to Montevideo and, during the marriage to come, would endure shipboard mutiny and pestilence as well as being wrecked and stranded in the jungles of Brazil and then having to make a five-thousand-mile journey back to America in a homemade thirty-five-foot canoe.

Slocum was never one for self-delusion. After once commanding and owning part of one of the greatest ships afloat, he had been reduced to living by his wits: scrounging for work along the Boston waterfront, a crazy scheme to deliver an iron-clad warship into the midst of a Brazilian civil war and trying to fish for cod, at which he was an abject failure. He was broke and old and must have understood in his heart that his way of life was over. Everywhere he looked, he must have been reminded that he was a man out of time and place. Every time he peered into his wife's eyes, he must have seen disappointment and reproach, whether it was there or not. And yet here is the greatest thing among the many great things about Joshua Slocum: he had another act still in him. Whether to forget about the squalid state of his life, because he had nothing better to do—or perhaps because he knew all along that men for centuries were destined to speak his name—he spent more than a year rebuilding, plank by plank, a sloop that had had been sitting derelict in a Massachusetts field. He did so, he wrote, because he "had resolved on a voyage around the world."

I read those matter-of-fact words a long, long time ago in the book that he wrote about the great adventure. I've been in the grip of Slocum—his skill and courage, his life of lonely adventure, his Emersonian self-reliance and his enigmatic end—ever since. Like all true obsessives, I've tried to walk where the source of my fixation has walked. Where he was born, "in a cold spot, on coldest North Mountain, on a cold February 20," but also the place where he had spent the first eight years of his life, Westport, which is the sole town on Brier Island, a place that can only be reached by car and ferry, but which, I assure you, is worth the trip. The main street in Westport is narrow and the little houses along it close together, particularly the oldest ones near the centre of the harbour where their foundations, the last time I was there, were dug into the side of the hill. Today, it's a smaller place than when Slocum made land here in 1895, his step light, "a thrilling pulse" beating high. Some one thousand souls called Westport home in the last years of the nineteenth century, including Captain George Clements Sr., who thought he could rid the island's gardens of insects by importing toads and snakes from the mainland and shipping over a pair of young alligators he found on a Florida hunting trip but which did not survive the Bay of Fundy winter.

There, Slocum's upbringing had been harsh: a brutal, embittered father beat him and forced him at age ten to put in ten-hour days tanning hides. Nonetheless, he waxed nostalgic about the little shop around the corner that he hadn't seen for thirty-five years, the roof where he and the other boys searched "for the skin of a black cat, to be taken on a dark night, to make a plaster for a poor lame man," and Lowry, the local tailor who carried his gunpowder loose in his coat pocket and would sometimes, in a moment of distraction, put his lighted pipe right in there with it.

Slocum made a short excursion to see friends at St. Mary's Bay, an old cruising ground. Fog and headwinds forced him into Yarmouth, where he "spent some days pleasantly enough." There, as he would meticulously account, he brought some butter and a barrel of potatoes on board and filled six barrels with water, which he stowed under the deck. In a Yarmouth shop Slocum saw a tin clock selling for a dollar and a half, but because the face was smashed the merchant let him have it for a dollar. The bad weather gave him time to stow everything securely and to take the topmast down. Slocum pulled on the lanyards and checked the gammon connecting the bowsprit to the stem of the boat. Then he did what sailors do: he waited.

One day, I stood roughly where Slocum would have moored the *Spray*, his sturdy little boat. It was long-sleeve weather, the sky cloud-dappled. An onshore breeze blew spume into Yarmouth Harbour and carried a chip bag down the wharf and onto the deck of a herring seiner. I was in a ruminative mood. I wanted to see the place from which Slocum left port in his tubby, homemade craft to plow through three oceans and complete the first single-handed circumnavigation of the globe. That was reason enough to be in Yarmouth. It just wasn't the only reason.

By the turn of the twentieth century, no one was fresh off the boat anymore. A century and a half after the arrival of the first generation of immigrants to this province, some of their innocent optimism remained. When most people to this day think of Nova Scotia, the image they have in their heads—great wooden ships with miles of canvas and a province inextricably bound up in a global system of ocean-bound commerce and warfare—is rooted in the mid-1800s. In the dying embers of the province's great days, Slocum found himself in the town that, more than any other, was emblematic of the age.

New Englanders joined the Mi'kmaq here first—Seven Years' War refugees from Yarmouth, Massachusetts, who may have named it after their old home. Later planters from Sandwich, Massachusetts, arrived to take up the Acadian lands cleared out by Lawrence. It was the usual pioneer beginning: the supplies failed to arrive and there was four feet of snow. Twenty-seven of the cattle they brought died; the rest had to be slaughtered for food. In 1762 Yarmouth had its first birth, first death and first marriage. Sixty years later the town consisted of only eighty buildings and 550 people. And yet all was not hopeless: there were those links with New England. It was near rich fishing grounds. On the other side of the Bay of Fundy, Saint John, New Brunswick, was already growing in prominence as a port as well as a timber hub and, in that symbiotic arrangement with which Yarmouth would soon become acquainted, blossoming into a shipbuilding centre of note.

When you think about wooden ships, you're probably like me: caught up in the romance of all that wood and canvas, the stirring notion of these free spirits, unfettered by the constraints of civilization and even the very land, chasing some star on the horizon. That, of course, is a bunch of hooey. As two historians named Eric Sager and Lewis Fischer have pointed out, the true way to understand ships and what they meant to the development of this province is to view them as units of production in a transportation industry. Ships were and are places where men and women worked, no different from fish plants and steel mills. By the turn of the eighteenth century nothing had changed much around here since the arrival of de Monts and Champlain. This economy was still based on things caught, grown, dug or somehow captured from the land and sea and sold elsewhere. For a long time, this "elsewhere" was Europe, and the only way to get these staples there was on sailing ships, most of which were still built and owned in Europe. What shipbuilding there was in Atlantic Canada, particularly outside of naval dockyards, was on a minuscule scale.

We do know that in 1761, the year of its founding, Yarmouth's shipping list included one ship, a little schooner of twenty-five tons, the *Pompey*. A nineteenth-century historian named John Roy Campbell tells us that a year later the registry's numbers had trebled. In 1764, according to Campbell, Walter Sollows built the first vessel that was launched in Yarmouth County, on Fish Point in Cape Forchu Harbour. Thirteen years later the *Sally*, owned and commanded by Captain John Barnard, sank with all hands aboard, the first ship from Yarmouth to do so, though she would hardly be the last. Thirty years after Yarmouth was settled, twenty-six vessels, a total of 554 tons between them, belonged to the township of Yarmouth. By 1815 the local fleet had doubled. Two decades later, with world trade growing at a high and steady rate, it had more than doubled again.

Later the same day, I stood inside the Yarmouth County Museum and Archives, where the pictures of many of the men who built those boats stare unsmiling and solemn from the old-timey photographs hanging from the walls. A former Congregationalist church, it is a stunning building with forty-foot ceilings, a ton of dark wood and glass and the kind of pulpit where Father Mapple could have delivered his Jonah-swallowed-by-the-whale sermon in *Moby Dick*. It is loaded with wonders: the old Cape Forchu light, the wings of a flying fish, a carved emu egg, the wooden horse-drawn carriage that used to run between Yarmouth and the village of Tusket. Mostly it holds nautical stuff. One of the first things you notice are the flags hanging from the ceiling, from each of Yarmouth's twenty-three shipbuilders. There are also a bunch of ship portraits painted on glass by artists in Antwerp, Liverpool, near Hamburg, San Francisco, Hong Kong and Sri Lanka. The museum has, in fact, the third-largest collection of glass ship portraits in Canada. The man standing there beside me, Eric Ruff, has been working on a history of the collection for the past eight years. "I'm about halfway through," he tells me, raising his eyebrows sheepishly.

Ruff is England-born, a cheery man with a shaggy white sailor's beard, as befits a mariner who served on Canadian frigates until he and his wife moved to Yarmouth, where he became the museum's director and curator. Technically he's retired now. The converted garage in back of his house, an office that contains what I would estimate to be a thousand nautical books, says differently. Such is his commitment to Yarmouth's seagoing and shipbuilding history that he was up until 2 a.m. the previous night, whooping it up with the other members of the Yarmouth Shantymen as they entertained a collection of fellow sea shanty singers visiting from Toronto.

Ruff is enough of a scholar that even after a night of high spirits he can cogently explain that by the end of the American War of Independence, only a few hundred vessels were owned in all of the Maritime provinces. A bunch of things helped change that. Immigration, new markets for the fish found in the waters off of Nova Scotia, and a series of treaties and trade policies that increased English demand for colonial timber. At first, he tells me, most of the capital for shipbuilding around here, along with the men who did the exacting work, came from Britain. But enterprise will find a way, and gradually shipbuilding became a local industry in these parts, usually in places that boasted plenty of timber and the first rudimentary yards. By far the biggest shipbuilding centre in the Maritimes was Saint John, at the mouth of the Saint John River, from which came so much of New Brunswick's timber. Increasingly the ring of the broadaxe, the clang of the hammer, the *clip-clop* of the work horses could be heard throughout Nova Scotia, along the South Shore and any number of places along the Bay of Fundy, but more than anywhere in Yarmouth County.

The way Ruff explains it, Yarmouth's shipbuilders were really just merchant capitalists. Fish, timber or some other staple enterprises attracted their money. They built ships to keep transportation costs low and because, when wood prices were high, they could sell the ship as well as the timber. In time the biggest profits came to be found in carrying goods that belonged not to the ships' owners but to merchants in other distant places: a vessel carrying oil from, say, New York to London might earn eight shillings a barrel. A bale of cotton from New Orleans to Boston could fetch a pretty penny too.

"They liked to spread the risk," says Ruff. "Each ship had sixty-four shares. Sometimes, but only rarely, was it one person who owned all sixty-four. But that meant investing a lot of money. Most of the time there were multiple shareholders. Frequently the major shareholder sold four shares to the captain so that he had skin in the game. Usually one person became a manager-owner and received a fee for looking after all of the ships owned by the various partnerships."

In time, an elite formed. In a startling bit of research, historians David Alexander and Gerry Panting determined that about 2,200 individuals were investors in the four hundred or so vessels built in Yarmouth County during the shipbuilding heyday between 1840 and 1860. They also calculated that just 110 investors put up the money for two-thirds of the tonnage and that just twelve individuals funded about a quarter of the shipping capacity built there. All these years later, this group sounds remarkably homogeneous: nine of them traced their origins to the migrations from Massachusetts. Only one, an Ulsterman, was a bona fide outsider.

When they could, they liked to stick together. My bags, while Ruff and I putted around Yarmouth's lovely, restful streets, sat in a bed and breakfast of unaccustomed splendour. It had been built in the "romantic Italianate style," but with a few other distinctive touches—ropelike mouldings, portholes in the frieze band—that underscore its origins as a wedding gift from a shipbuilder to his daughter. John W.

Lovitt, who came from Massachusetts, bought and built ships with his father and two brothers. He went into business with his sons, who did the same thing with their offspring. Lovitt bought ships with his cousins and probably also with a son-in law. On the other hand, some of his contemporaries'—who must have had their reasons—steered clear of family. Loran E. Baker, who began his ship-buying career in 1854, had not a single relative among his eighteen shipping partners. Aaron Goudey had forty-six partners, none of them relatives. The same, it is my understanding, can be said of William Law, the proprietor of William Law and Company who, over the years, had seventy-eight different partners.

As Ruff rattled off the names from the glory days of Yarmouth, I wrote them down in my notebook. I had never heard of Law before, or Baker, Goudy or Lovitt. I was, on the other hand, familiar with the name of Killam, which he also mentioned. A big picture of Izaak Walton Killam stares down from a wall inside the library at Dalhousie University, where some of the research for this book was done and part of it written. *The Canadian Encyclopedia* called him "the epitome of the financial power of Montréal's St. James Street, secretive and austere" and "the richest Canadian of his day," which was the early decades of the twentieth century. For a magazine story, I once spent a few days sniffing around a mansion in St. Andrews, New Brunswick, owned by his widow, also for a time married to Killam's former business partner, a New Brunswick boy who became the British newspaper baron Lord Beaverbrook. But I didn't know until much later that for Killam it all started in Yarmouth, with a string of buildings that were standing along the waterfront when Slocum waited for the weather to clear.

———

Not much has been said yet in this book in a straightforward fashion about the ocean and Nova Scotia's connection to it. It can, weirdly, slip your mind. Or maybe a better way to put it is that the sea is so vast and difficult to apprehend, and works so deeply on your imagination, that it gives a person a sense of vertigo just to think about it. My people are landlubbers who made their lives in cities, the woods and the subterranean depths. If any of us ever thumped across the waves in a dory, if any of us stood heroically, harpoon in hand, eyes scanning the horizon for the waterspout from a whale's blowhole, somehow the news failed to reach me.

Yet everything in Nova Scotia is touched by the sea, which finds its way into our food and drink, the way our skin feels, how we talk and smell, the roll of our gait and even how we look at the world. Humans are mostly water, and that fact alone is often used to explain our affinity for the substance that covers more than 70 per cent of the earth. Yet what I feel when I'm floating on my back, suspended by the magic of chemistry off of some beach, isn't the universal impulse to connect with my watery self, or the place from which we humans emerged onto the land. It is giddy awe, mixed with a bit of old-time existential dread. It's the same feeling I get looking at the ruins around this province, walking alongside ancient rocks that tell the story of the past or looking up at a star in the night sky and knowing that by the time it reaches us, the image is so old that it probably doesn't even exist anymore. It's liberating, after a day in which your hard drive fried itself, to lie in the North Atlantic Ocean and know that you're nothing compared to the body of water spreading infinitely around you. It's just mighty humbling too.

In his grand, gloomy book *The Great Deep: The Sea and its Thresholds*, James Hamilton-Paterson points out that oceanographer Robert Ballard played classical music during his descent to take the first photographs of the *Titanic* on the ocean bottom west of Nova Scotia and rock music on the way back up because it would have been unthinkable the other way around. "Heaven," Hamilton-Paterson wrote, "is deep and thin, even faintly unserious." The Deep, on the other hand, "is utterly solemn." The words Hamilton-Paterson uses to evoke the abyss beneath the water's surface—"stately, funereal, mysterious . . . time's liquid correlative which gulps down objects, lives, all that was and will be . . . its amalgamation of height and depth, of gulfs of space and time"—come the closest to what the mere notion of the Deep evokes in me. I haven't been more than a few yards underwater. But I've stared over the sides of big ships and small sailboats waiting for something the size of Moby Dick to break the surface, as huge as the sum total of every one of my deep-seated childhood fears.

Not everything about the ocean makes me shiver. Islands have always provided more pleasant metaphors. A preserve where man can't ravage nature. A paradise where the mores of society don't apply. A sanctuary where humans can control what goes in and what, if anything, comes out. When writers from Thomas More to William Golding wanted to portray an alternative society, they set it upon an island. We care so much about them because, on some level, we understand how important islands are to the world, keeping threatened plants, people and animals alive and ensuring our collective sanity. So much literature has been spawned by stories like this that there's actually a name for the desert island genre: Robinsonade, from Daniel Defoe's novel *Robinson Crusoe*. Being crazed about islands is common enough that there's a word for it too—nesomania—and a reasonable explanation for the obsession: perhaps, on some deep level, we just understand how important islands are to the rest of the world.

But the significance of islands is dwarfed by the importance of the sea, which demands so much in return. The cenotaphs and memorials found in every Nova Scotia fishing community show that the relationship between people and the ocean has so often been a fatal one, particularly in the late 1800s when ships plied the waters around Nova Scotia as they never had before and never would again. The Maritime Museum of the Atlantic's database, which stops in 1999, contains almost five thousand shipwrecks. Unofficial sources put the real number at about five times that. Whatever the number, a good deal of them occurred during the so-called Golden Age of Sail.

Nova Scotia has its own "Graveyard of the Atlantic," which is how Sable Island, where at least 350 wrecks have been recorded since the early seventeenth century, is known. There have been 350 recorded shipwrecks around the "Graveyard of the Gulf"—St. Paul Island, off of the northern tip of Cape Breton, where nineteenth-century fishermen from the mainland each spring used to find the frozen bodies of shipwrecked seamen huddled in crude shelters, waiting for help that never came. For some reason the numbers are less precise in the waters around Brier Island, but there have still been enough shipwrecks there to earn it the undisputed title as the "Fundy Graveyard." Seal Island, not far from Yarmouth, earned no ominous nickname. Even so, when spring came residents from the closest mainland villages would climb into their boats and row to the island to find and bury the winter's dead.

What does it say about me that I'm drawn to stories like that one? Just as I'm drawn to the saga of Howard Blackburn, who was born not far from where that ghoulish ritual occurred and who somehow, on a trip out on the Newfoundland Grand Banks, got separated, along with a dory mate, from their fishing schooner.

Blackburn, who was eighteen, began to row for shore even though he had lost his mittens. When his hands began to freeze, he formed them into claws so that he could continue to grip the oars. Then he rowed some more. He rowed for five days and nights without food, water or sleep. His shipmate was dead by the time Blackburn made shore in Newfoundland. By then he had lost all of his fingers and many of his toes, as well as both thumbs up to the first joint. Back in Gloucester the townspeople passed the hat around. Blackburn used the five hundred dollars to buy a cigar store and then a tavern. In time he headed west to try his hand at the Klondike Gold Rush. When that didn't work he returned to Massachusetts. There, when Blackburn wasn't busy crossing the Atlantic solo in small boats, he made a small fortune as a sometime bootlegger during Prohibition.

The time just seemed ripe for legends. A great mariner needed the basic ability to read the navigational charts as well as knowledge of sextants, chronometers and other aids of celestial navigation and the evolving tools of dead reckoning, which revealed a ship's position without the help of the stars. Also necessary was the combination of experience and judgment to take a square-rigged Nova Scotia windjammer through hurricanes and rogue waves, to avoid the profit-shrinking equatorial doldrums and the icebergs that sometimes made their way into merchant shipping lanes off of Newfoundland. They had to be rational men, unperturbed when the glow of St. Elmo's fire appeared on their mast. They had to possess the ability to command seamen of varying intelligence, work habits and character, and, if need to be, the willingness to use the belaying pin or brass knuckles in the interests of getting a cargo from A to B. It's not something you learn in any classroom. George Spicer of Spencer's Island, at the other end of the Bay of Fundy from Yarmouth, went to sea at twelve, hardly uncommon for that time in that place, and had only limited training in navigation. He still crossed the Atlantic Ocean 107 times at the command of five different windjammers, ensuring his share of scrapes and close calls.

One day on a road overlooking the Annapolis River I walked up to a two-and-a-half-storey wooden house with a steep gabled roof. The Sea-Faring Maiden bed and breakfast was once the home of Captain Joseph Hall, a sea captain, shipbuilder and merchant who traced his lineage back to the New England Planters. Hall was a figure of note in his day. His daughter, who stares out with a puzzled expression from a photograph on an inside wall, is who lives on through the ages. In 1870 Bessie Hall, who was twenty, arrived with her father in New Orleans aboard a ship called the *Rothesay* to pick up a cargo of cotton. The voyage was delayed, causing a number of the crew to desert. When they finally left for Liverpool, the ship was shorthanded, with a crew of just six sailors, a first mate and an elderly carpenter along with Miss Hall and her captain father. Four days into the voyage, smallpox hit. Rounding the tip of Florida, the *Rothesay* was battered by mounting squalls. Before her father collapsed into a smallpox-induced delirium he told Bessie to take command of the fever-ridden ship. Using dead reckoning, she sailed through a series of gales. Finally, she reached the Irish Sea. When she made dock in Liverpool—making her reputedly the first female to take a ship across the Atlantic Ocean—she had been at sea for forty-eight days.

Women were prohibited from holding mate's or captain's papers in the nineteenth century. So Bessie sailed with her father for another year, married and settled across the basin from Annapolis Royal. From that vantage point she watched the ships come and go and raised her four children. I love the thought of her there, living her routine, landlocked life. She would hear a knock at the door. There would stand some grizzled salt from God knows where, whose ship had tied up nearby. Cap in hand he would introduce himself. Humbly, he would beg her indulgence. He hoped he was not interrupting her. He just had to meet the "girl" of legend.

I know from many fine books about Slocum that his early life was typical of that rollicking time. He was just sixteen when he shipped out from Saint John, New Brunswick, bound for Dublin, as an ordinary seaman. A year later he was a second mate, and at nineteen he had risen to first mate, which entitled him to be called "sir" by the crew and to eat his meals aft. Two years later Slocum had twice doubled Cape Horn and sailed around the world. As his hailing port he chose San Francisco, on the edge of the Wild West, which fit his enterprising nature. "At various times," his biographer Geoffrey Wolfe wrote, Slocum "sold fish, seashells, self-published books and pamphlets, autographed photos, lecture performances, pieces of coral, ships and furs. He was at one time or another a trader, gill-net fisherman, shipwright, carpenter, lumberman, charter captain and trapper."

While in Sydney, Australia, he met and married a lively, adventurous twenty-year-old woman from New York named Virginia Walker. From the time they married until her death thirteen years later, she sailed wherever Slocum sailed, learning the marine life, educating their children—all seven of whom were born aboard ships, several while at sea—and sharing in his adventures and disappointments, of which there were many of both. Their honeymoon was a voyage to Cook Inlet, to see if there was money to be made from the Chinook salmon runs. In Alaska, their ship was wrecked, but Slocum built a thirty-five-foot whaleboat from the bits and pieces of the wrecked vessel and sailed her back to civilization.

They took a packet, a fast-sailing carrier of passengers, packages and mail, as far east as Japan and Australia and then found themselves marooned on a beach in the Philippines after the owner was brought low by the stock market panic of 1873. There, a British entrepreneur and architect hired Slocum to supervise construction of a steamer. When it came time for payment, the architect instead offered him the ownership of a forty-five-ton schooner named *Pato*, Spanish for "duck." That he didn't bat an eye—Slocum busied the ship in salvage work before embarking on a voyage from Manila to the cod-fishing grounds of the Sea of Okhotsk off the coast of Russia—was as indicative of the rambunctious era as the nature of the man.

Head crowded with info, my notebook closed in surrender, I had a pint with Ruff and his wife in a packed Yarmouth waterfront pub which features a beer named in his honour. Afterwards, I took a stroll to stretch my legs, but also because Yarmouth is the kind of place where it is still possible to see how things were, mostly because the buildings are still here, looked after by the town's diligent heritage preservation folks, spruced up by some well-heeled transplants or lovingly restored by some local returned after making good far, far away.

The first time I was here, some forty years ago, I stayed in one of those houses, originally built by a ship's chandler but by then owned by a former senior official in the Nixon White House, there to finish his working years as a newspaperman for the town's weekly. He had a glamorous wife who looked like she would have had drinks with Henry Kissinger and a son who, I think, was a member of the CIA. I arrived by train at night and left before daybreak the next morning, so it was years before I saw the town in the light: the big, weighty houses of the merchants and shipbuilders with their wraparound verandas and curved balconies all done up in fancy eighteenth-century styles; but also the captain's homes with their stained-glass windows, their hedges and their widow's walks angled harbourside so that anxious wives could stare out to sea; the salt boxes on the unfashionable side of town where the men who built Yarmouth's great ships—in many cases seasonal, transient workers who went from shipyard to shipyard—and those who sailed on them lived.

The air was soft as I walked along Water Street past a lobster pound, a herring processor and a former cotton mill. Here was a terminal where the on-again, off-again ferry that ran between Yarmouth and Maine docked. There was a memorial to the 2,500 residents of Yarmouth known to have died at sea. Things grew quieter the farther along Water Street I went. A couple of cars coasted by. Someone approaching me crossed over to the other side of the street. Otherwise I seemed to be alone, which made it easier to picture the waterfront when five shipyards were going full tilt nearby and the port's registered shipping tonnage was equal to the whole of British shipping in the time of Henry VII and equivalent to the port of London's in the reign of Charles II, according to Campbell, the historian.

By the time Slocum took the wheel of the *Pato*, Yarmouth and the surrounding villages and hamlets had swelled to seven thousand people. The breakwater to protect the harbour and the lighthouse, which guided ships in and out of port with its brilliant light and later its foghorn, were still years off. But the town had a series of wharves up and down the waterfront. In the gloom I walked, telling the voice-memo app on my iPhone what it might have looked like when those wharves hummed with ship's chandlers and suppliers, with brass founders, stove manufacturers and repairers, with auctioneers and dealers in West Indian and American produce, dry and pickled fish, tea, anthracite and bituminous coal.

Elsewhere in the twenty-first-century world, at that very moment, I knew bombs fell, a pandemic raged and justice was meted out to the guilty, so it felt good to think about a time when someone walking these streets during business hours could buy some fancy millinery, a glimmering watch or a patent medicine that would cure whatever ailed them. They could shop for a piano at Huestis & Moulton, which also doubled as an undertaker's parlour and, on the side, sold sewing machines and offered fine cabinetmaking. If mortality truly seemed to beckon, they could engage Sandford H. Pelton, barrister and attorney-at-law, to draw up a will, and just a few doors away hire S.F. Raymond to make them a gravestone in Italian or American marble or granite.

The great shipping families and partnerships were responsible for Yarmouth's infrastructure, its public companies, its wharves and its telegraph. Merchant money was behind the Bank of Yarmouth, the Yarmouth Steam Navigation Company and the Acadian Insurance Company. Loran Baker, the aforementioned shipbuilder and entrepreneur, is indicative of how important merchant money was to the town's development. It is not, perhaps, surprising that such a man— an Anglican and Freemason, a fellow, according to the *Dictionary of Canadian Biography*, of "industry and high moral character"— would hold a long list of corporate directorships in a variety of local commercial concerns in Yarmouth. But Baker was also a school committeeman for the Yarmouth Seminary, vice-president of the Yarmouth Agricultural Society and president of a local cemetery company. Baker and his partners built Yarmouth's first brick mercantile building. They installed its first plank sidewalk. When it came time to complete the rail link from Halifax to Yarmouth, Baker was installed as its first president. "That's his library," Ruff had said, pointing to a building in a three-acre park.

Yarmouth, decades before Slocum made port there, had a fire department with three fire engines as well as a "hook and ladder company." Yarmouth had newspapers—the *Herald*, a weekly, and the *Tribune*, which came out semi-weekly—a theatre and its own a literary society. If someone back then happened to go on a nighttime stroll like mine and kept walking past the buildings of industry and enterprise—a machine shop turning out steam engines, the pair of foundries, the three ship's-block factories, the pair of sash and door factories, the steam salt mill, the several smaller manufacturers of furniture, buckets, brooms and farm utensils—they would eventually pass schools that a chronicler of the time called "noble and harmonious in design."

Yarmouth and environs, where the vast majority of folks were Baptists and Roman Catholics, boasted forty-eight places of worship at that time. On foot I can see some of them still, just like I can meander past the Cape Forchu Meeting House, the site of many a discussion of matters of import, and its upper graveyard, where I now know that a man named Zachariah Corning was the first person interred.

By the last years of the nineteenth century Yarmouth wasn't the only shipbuilding centre in Nova Scotia. In Pictou County, on the province's northwest shore, barques of nearly 1,200 tons came from the Carmichael yard in New Glasgow, but also the lumbering village of Tatamagouche. Ships emerged from the slips of Pugwash and also the tiny town of River John, where the vessels built there were enough to support a stagecoach company and a pair of newspapers. I have walked in many of those places trying to conjure up those old ghosts. I have nosed around farthest Cape Breton, looking for signs of the brigs and brigantines that came rolling out of yards for the English market, and along the province's southeast shore in Shelburne, Bridgewater, Liverpool, LaHave, Port Medway, Lunenburg, Mahone Bay and other places where copper-fastened and iron-keeled square-riggers of hack-matack and oak were fashioned. I've wandered farther along the coastline in the boomtowns where the Acadians had resettled, where shipbuilding also had its day, as it did in places where English was the predominate language.

All up and down the Bay of Fundy, where the world's greatest tides could float some of the largest wooden ships ever seen, I searched for those sleepy little spots that suddenly enjoyed an unexpected burst of prosperity during the Great Age of Sail. Some of the places that benefited from the Fundy tides continue to thrive now, like Windsor—"with all its beautiful undulations of hill and dale," wrote Howe, "its upland fields." In others, the days of sail are gone with the wind: a plaque far above an inaccessible beach reminds passersby that a thriving shipyard and sawmill once stood in a place called Eatonville; the remains of a wooden wharf next to a trailer park are all that is all that is left of the nineteenth-century Spencer's Island yard that built the legendary ghost ship *Mary Celeste*, found intact but deserted, floating midway between the Azores and Portugal.

Maitland had eleven shingled houses in 1831, four of them taverns, at a time when the mail arrived once a month by horseback, carried by a mailman who could fit every single letter he had to deliver in his pockets. Shipbuilding changed all of that. During the great summers of the 1860s and '70s some one thousand men would be working the Roy family yards on the estuary of the tidal creek right in the small village, at the Monteith yard a mile south, across the river at Norris and Sanderson, and further upriver where

Cameron, McDougall and Adams built ships. From the Putnam, a fleet of barques set forth. In Selma, a few miles from Maitland, Alexander A. McDougall also launched barque after barque. Near there, Sydney Smith built the *Peerless*, which was a great ship, although not as great as the 263-foot *W.D. Lawrence*—the largest wooden sailing ship ever built in this country—fashioned in William Dawson Lawrence's shipyard, across from his Maitland home.

His home is now a museum that I like to visit. I never stay too long. Outside I can focus on the words of a long-ago Maitlander who recalled the "never-to-be-forgotten sounds of those lovely summer mornings." I can almost hear "the sharp 'click' of the fastener's mall as the bolts were secured, the loud and cheery ring of the calker's mailer, the 'thub ' of the dubber's adze, the muffled blows on tree-nails, the swishing of broad-axes." Ship launch days were big events for the village of Maitland. There was usually a sale and a tea, "and always a crowd." I like to picture the farm horses arriving, drawing wagons filled with visitors, great bundles of fragrant hay and little girls in their white dresses and flower-trimmed Leghorn hats. Sometimes, due to the huge tide changes, there had to be a nighttime launch. The ship's mast and rigging would be silhouetted against the full summer moon. I know from the same long-ago correspondent that immense bonfires and workmen carrying torches would illuminate the goings-on. The whole village, kids and all, would be gathered there, such was the spectacle.

Slocum's thirties had been peripatetic: in Honolulu he sold the *Pato* to a local planter for five thousand dollars in gold pieces, then bought a four-hundred-ton barque, the *Amethyst*, aboard which he spent the next three years trading in Manila, Guam and other ports

throughout the Pacific. Somehow he bought a one-third interest in
the *Northern Light*, at the time said to be one of the most magnificent ships afloat. Aboard that vessel, leaving New York bound for
Yokohama, Japan, guns were drawn and the mutiny flag was
raised. As they were putting the crew's ringleader in irons, he managed to stab the first mate multiple times. The "embers of mutiny,"
as his biographer Wolfe elegantly put it, "continued to smolder as
the Northern Light made her way South."

Along the way, in the unaccountable manner Slocum had of finding himself in abnormal situations, he picked up a boatload of
Gilbert Islanders who had sailed through the aftermath of the erup-
tion of Krakatoa. Accounts of what ensued during the rest of the
voyage varied according to the teller of the tale. What is undeniable
is that when the *Northern Light* made New York, the new mate
was in irons and a few days later Slocum was charged with "cruelly
and inhumanly treating his prisoner." In due course he was vindi-
cated. But the editorial page of the *New York Times* had branded
him a "brute." While he was busy defending himself against the
criminal accusations, the *Northern Light* sailed from New York
with a new master.

At an auction Slocum spent the last of his gold coins on a three-
masted barque named *Aquidneck* and then set a course for Buenos
Aires. A thousand miles northeast of their destination, his wife,
Virginia, suddenly grew gravely ill and died at just thirty-four. I'm
going to jump forward now. He remarried—a first cousin who went
by Hettie and was said to be more suited to life on land than that of
being a mariner's wife. En route to Rio de Janeiro he faced mutiny
again, shooting a fellow named "Bloody Tommy" dead and wound-
ing the just as colourfully named "Dangerous Jack." Arrested and
charged with murder, Slocum spent a month in a Brazilian jail. He

was acquitted, but during the legal proceedings nine members of his remaining crew died from smallpox.

Slocum's trials were not done. The *Aquidneck* ran into bad weather and broke up on the coast of Brazil. A practical man, Slocum sold what was left of the ship and paid the crew its wages. Then he fashioned a boat, a cross between a Cape Ann dory and Japanese sampan that was all that he, his wife and their two sons needed to make the fifty-five-day journey from Brazil to South Carolina.

Back in the United States, Slocum discovered that work captaining freighters had dried up. At loose ends, he self-published a book about the voyage home, which sold little. Slocum found work on the Boston waterfront but didn't like paying union dues, so one day he just up and quit. Then, for the first time in a long time, he experienced a small bit of luck. "One midwinter day in 1892, in Boston, where I had been cast up from old ocean, so to speak, a year or two before, I was cogitating whether I should apply for a command and again eat my bread and butter on the sea, or go to work at a ship-yard, when I met an old acquaintance, a whaling-captain who said: 'Come to Fairhaven and I'll give you a ship.'" The ship was an antiquated sloop called the *Spray*, which Slocum found under a canvas "affectionately propped up in a field, some distance from salt water." An old salt asked Slocum whether he intended to break her up. No, he replied, he intended to rebuild her. "Great was the amazement," Slocum wrote. "'Will it pay?' was the question which for a year or more I answered by declaring that I would make it pay."

This is how you met him some pages ago. He would have known by then that the time of sail and the time of all the great Nova Scotian mariners had passed. In the years between 1850 and 1880 the fleets of the Atlantic provinces grew rapidly and almost continuously until they accounted for nearly three-quarters of the shipping tonnage in

British North America. By then, Canada could claim the fourth-largest merchant marine in the world. A good portion of it was from Yarmouth County, which, some enterprising soul had calculated, was the port with the most registered tonnage per capita in the world. When he published his history of Yarmouth around that time, John Roy Campbell deduced that if the same torrid pace were to continue, the township's fleet would quadruple by 1961. As it turned out, wooden sailing ships couldn't compete against iron- and steel-hulled schooners. Freight rates fell and trade patterns changed. Increasingly the old Yarmouth merchants and their sons put their money into railways, textiles, sugar refineries and iron and steel, because in the new Industrial Age that is where they thought their future lay.

In 1895, where we met Slocum, the world elsewhere was aflame with the new: X-rays had been discovered in Germany, the first radio waves had transmitted information in Italy, the first moving picture show was underway in Paris, the first steam engine clanked and hissed its way down railway tracks in Niagara Falls. A country since 1867, Canada had hit some early rough patches. Sir John Thompson, premier of Nova Scotia before becoming prime minister, had unexpectedly died. The country was being run by Sir Charles Tupper, a doctor from Amherst, Nova Scotia, who would hold the title of prime minister for barely two months before being defeated. In the Halifax legislature the management of Nova Scotia continued at its usual languid pace, although during the 1895 session the governing Liberals did make one significant announcement: the signing of contracts to subsidize three new railroads around the province. Two of them were in Cape Breton, where the age of coal was underway. The other was the narrow-gauge Coast Railway, running from Yarmouth to the fishing village of Lockport.

Chances are that the labourers from the American South who were imported to lay the rail line that delineated the before-and-after point in Yarmouth's fortunes were busy as Slocum waited. It was as if this moment had been preordained. Now past sixty, his mental faculties seemed to be failing him: a twelve-year-old girl alleged that Slocum had raped her on a tour of the *Spray*, a charge that was later reduced to "indecent action," which one of Slocum's biographers had attributed to an old man's tendency to be "negligently unbuttoned." Beyond that, how could twentieth-century Canada still find room for the quintessential Nova Scotian—the free spirit, the lone sailor—from the century before? How could the belch of the locomotive compete with the unfettered ocean, where great adventure awaited? I have a little fantasy about Slocum, who would disappear fourteen years later after leaving Martha's Vineyard to explore Venezuela's Orinoco River and the headwaters of the Amazon. In my story, he wasn't actually lost at sea. Instead, tired and old, he somehow made it to some island where the weather was warm and no one had ever heard of a man who was born in the breezes in a place called Nova Scotia.

In my reverie, he lived out his life there, unknown and happy. But this is a book rooted in facts. So I will say that in Yarmouth, the shining principality in the province's most exalted era, Slocum waited in the month of April in the year 1895 for a run of bad weather to pass. He stowed his goods "for the boisterous Atlantic." He took down the topmast, knowing that his ship, the *Spray*, "would be the wholesomer with it on deck." Then, on July 1, after a nasty short gale, "the wind came out nor'west and clear, propitious for a good run." The next morning when Slocum rose, he discovered that the head sea had gone down. So he did what sailors do. His logbook for that morning read: "9:30 a.m. sailed from Yarmouth."

The author's grandfather, Clarence (Flash) Demont,
back in the days when he was fastest man in Canada,
as well as a production supervisor for the *Glace Bay Gazette*,
when its pages were filled with stories of the coal mining
wars of Cape Breton.

# SEVEN

# Way Down in the Hole

*Subterranean Cities—The Deeps—Eleven—The Gilded Age—Coal Is King—*
*Filling in the Map—Jack Briers—Sifting Through the Ruins—Flash—*
*The Big Pays—The Wolf—Blood on the Coal—Inverness Then*
*and Now—The Unaccustomed Smell of Prosperity*

A couple of years ago I read in the papers that the town of Dominion had to demolish its high school and hockey rink after both buildings started to sink into the crumbling mine shaft that runs underneath them. I learned that parts of one of the main streets in Glace Bay would periodically collapse into an old abandoned mine shaft just below the surface. I learned that a hole, a metre or so wide and a couple of metres deep, one day just materialized in the front yard of a house owned by a man named Robert Currie in the town of Donkin. After its appearance, a seventy-five-year-old woman who lived nearby was never quite the same. She couldn't sleep at night for fear that the crater was going to keep widening until it claimed not just Currie's house but hers as well, and for all she knew the rest of their hometown.

All throughout the coal lands of Cape Breton, it is my understanding that the ground will just open up. When that happens, a truck full of municipal employees in hard hats and work boots will materialize and a couple of them will get out and throw a few shovelfuls of concrete into the hollowed-out area. Then, a few months later, it will all happen again. Even if the ground doesn't entirely give way it can still seem alive, rasping and groaning, not just in Glace Bay and Dominion and Donkin, but in the other mining communities on Cape Breton—New Waterford, Florence, Birch Grove, Sydney Mines and Port Morien, west across the island in Inverness and Mabou—and even across the causeway to the mainland of Nova Scotia, in Westville, Stellarton and Springhill, where disconcerting popping and cracking can still be heard way down underground even though coal mining ended in those places a long time ago.

I can't get that image out of my head, maybe because it harkens back to those horror movies I would watch as a kid where some innocent soul would be in a cemetery and a skeletal hand from beyond the grave would burst through the soil. More hands emerged from the ground, then whole bodies, the dead returning, usually because they had some unfinished business with the living. It's an infantile notion, I know, but that can be how I feel walking over this land, where the industrialized past haunts this province still. Not far from where my grandparents lived and my dad and his two brothers grew up is a place called Senator's Corner, one of the cardinal points of the aforementioned town of Glace Bay. I used to just walk by it with barely a thought. Now I understand that when a person stands on that spot they are directly over a bed of coal called the Harbour Seam as well as the Phalen and Emery Seams. If a person with Superman's X-ray vision could look straight down from Senator's Corner they would see three football fields' worth of alternating layers of mine workings and rock. If I somehow saw such a thing I might genuflect right there, might fall to my knees as the pedestrians and traffic passed, and press my forehead to the sidewalk.

Way down in those tunnels, I know, having crunched the numbers, more men from this province have died than met their maker in the Great War. In nearly every coal town in this province I've visited, and I've visited them all, there's a monument to the dead, many of the names matching bodies never recovered from the "deeps." They're down there still, or at least their spirits are, buried beneath millions of tons of rock, miles from blue sky and air that smells of cut hay and ocean brine. Some of them, I suspect, are my kin. Don't ask me for the names because the folks who could supply such information are long gone now. I do know with absolute certainty that, one day in 1906, one of my forebears took a lunch pail and a miner's helmet and walked out into the pre-dawn dark in the town of Sydney Mines. His people were colliers back to the 1750s, in the flat farmland, ancient hedges and stone walls of England's Lancashire County. Perhaps his own father and mother saw no future in their country's depressed coal industry and no way to change the family's trajectory in class- and tradition-bound England. Or maybe they just dreamed of something better than the coal company shacks of Chorley.

At some point, they somehow learned that in Canada, a place they wouldn't have known much about beyond that it still pledged allegiance to Britain's monarch, there was a jurisdiction called Nova Scotia. This place, according to the promotional literature of the time, "surpasses every country of the same extent in the world in the variety and supply of material resources." There, an English enterprise that wanted to harvest the province's vast coal reserves needed colliers and needed them now. Four years later my grandfather followed his own father out into the muddy rutted streets of Sydney Mines. It would have taken some time to reach the Florence Colliery. At the last minute, perhaps, he tilted his head back—in every picture I've seen, his blue eyes, whether because of the life he led or the hard things he would see, were achingly sad—and took one last look up at the sky. The rake, which carried the men along the mine workings running miles out under the Atlantic Ocean, waited. Then Jack Briers, age eleven, went down into the hole.

I remember being eleven, which would have been about the time of the yarn with which I began this book. I've got some old black-and-white snapshots from that era: me in a Davy Crockett coonskin cap; me wearing the pinstripes from my little league baseball team; me lying on the floor, looking back at the camera, turning the rods on one of those tabletop NHL hockey games. There's one that I keep on my desk to this day. It's a school picture. I'm far left in the last row: crew cut, head tilted at what only could be called a jaunty angle, hands clasped behind my back. I'm sporting, along with a plaid shirt, an expression that said that I had not one trouble in the world, which was the case.

I bring this up for the sake of context. As my grandfather sat in the Florence Colliery, listening to rats scurry by in darkness, it was a scant sixty years from when I, at the same age, would sleep in pyjamas adorned with rocket ships and laugh, until the corn flakes flew out of my mouth, at the antics of Max Smart. Everywhere a person looked in 1906, they could see progress. The Dow Jones Industrial Average topped 100 for the first time. Canada's first movie theatre opened in Montreal and the first public library in Ottawa lent out books. Not far from where Jack Briers went into the pit, a young Italian named Guglielmo Marconi had somehow linked together the world's wireless radio network.

The thing is, though, that in 1906, when my grandfather entered the mines, he wasn't alone. That year nearly a thousand boys, 4 per cent of the province's population, toiled in Nova Scotia's collieries.

Before you judge, know that their parents weren't inhuman. This was just the time in which they found themselves. It was the life that you knew if you were a male, not yet into your teens, living in large parts of this province.

What was happening in Nova Scotia at the start of the twentieth century was no different than what had happened in so many other places a long time earlier. Stuff that used to be made by hand, not to mention new things never made before, was now being fashioned by machines—the Industrial Age, they called it. Coal, which was more powerful and much cheaper than wood and which fuelled the mills, forges and factories, was the key to this new world. Coal meant that one day, with a poof, a new place would materialize in this province that remained only partly formed, as if the tectonic plates were still shifting, colliding together and wrenching apart.

I chose that analogy carefully. The story of coal in this province and everywhere else goes way back: big rocks moved around, causing great slices of the earth's crust to rise and fall. As some sections of the earth sunk, sediment quickly (by geological standards) accumulated over top, trapping ferns, trees, mosses and other detritus in between. When the conditions were right—enough heat and pressure over a long enough time, enough moisture to keep the peat from drying out—a shiny black rock formed that, for better or worse, changed the world. Scientists figure this happened somewhere between 280 million and 360 million years ago. No one really cared about Nova Scotia's coal until the start of the 1800s, when a British conglomerate discovered it here in enough quantities to trigger a rush akin to the one soon to overtake California after gold was found there.

I'll spare you the story of coal's rise in Nova Scotia, other than to say that when Howe was rambling around the province near the town of New Glasgow, he found a foundry that resembled "Vulcan's workshop" and coal pits that made him feel like "Captain Symmes traveling through the opening at the Poles" and that, by the time of Confederation, the province had more than two dozen operating coal mines and a weave of rail lines that connected them to wharves for loading onto ships and to the Intercolonial Railroad, which took the coal to bigger markets in the rest of Canada. Trains brought men. Eventually, the trains arriving and leaving meant that if the mines were big enough or there were enough of them congregated loosely together, a rough village materialized.

The map was being filled in. Not in a huge way, mind you. Fewer than half a million people lived in Nova Scotia at the turn of the twentieth century. Broad swaths of this place were as empty then as they were a century before and would be a century later. New layers, though, were being overlaid across the original Mi'kmaq settlements, the Acadian homelands and the places where the dispossessed from the Thirteen Colonies and British Isles and the Swiss and German adventurers built lives.

After coal was discovered, the pace of immigration picked up in Sydney Mines, one of those small collections of humanity that had suddenly, with a poof, materialized around Sydney Harbour. Workers came from Italy, Poland, Germany, Lithuania and Austria. They arrived from England, like my great-great-grandfather, his wife and three children. From the gravestones at Sydney Mines' Shore Road Cemetery—where I like to walk because of the view of the old part of town on one side and out to sea on the other—I know that they also came from Scotland, Ireland and Wales, as well as Newfoundland, then still a separate British colony. The population of Sydney Mines doubled between 1901 and 1911 as men also arrived from France, Spain, the Netherlands and even Sweden, Norway and Germany. A good number of them are buried there in the Shore Road Cemetery, which overlooks the ocean from whence they came with ambition in their eyes and trembling hearts.

No one, on the other hand, is quite sure how Henry Melville Whitney, who shot like a comet across the sky, came to be here. Whitneys invented both the cotton gin and the notion of the assembly line. One of them would become undersecretary of the U.S. Navy. Being a Whitney, you get the sense, meant entitlement and comfort. When Henry Whitney left prep school to work in his father's Massachusetts store it was the late 1800s, America's Gilded Age, when every man was a potential Andrew Carnegie, when rich New Yorkers threw dinner parties for dogs, when Mark Twain would raise no eyebrows by writing of the times, "What is the chief end of man?—to get rich. In what way?—dishonestly if we can; honestly if we must."

Henry Whitney, who was worth next to nothing at thirty-three, had that epochal drive. Three years later his net worth topped half a million dollars, in part because his endeavours usually carried the whiff of scandal. Such was the case in Nova Scotia, where he just seemed to appear one day, like so many others who arrived during this period, brandishing some idea that would make everyone rich. Soon Whitney and the members of a shadowy cadre known as "The Boston Syndicate" controlled most every coal mine in Cape Breton, even though they hadn't spent a dime of their own money. In Sydney they opened an integrated steel mill hailed by the *New York Times* as "A Pittsburgh in Canada."

When I think of the time when industrialization took hold in Nova Scotia, it is unlike the other epochs in this book, where I'm just nosing around a little and letting my imagination fill in the blanks. When I think about this period, I think about my maternal grandfather, Jack Briers, a taciturn old widower by the time he took the train down to Halifax to stay with his daughter and her family. Silence seemed to envelop him as he sat in a chair in our living room, reading about the past and then heading off in midafternoon for a pint in a local near our house. It is odd, given that I now talk to strangers for a living, that I didn't think to ask him much back then. He could have told me about the horrors of the Somme and Passchendaele. He could have told me thing or two about what it was like to blow the clarinet at Saturday night dances at the North Sydney Yacht Club, to thump the organ during Sunday church services and coax sad sounds from the tuba and French horn returning from cemeteries with the rest of the Sydney Mines colliery band. Mostly he could have told me about what it was like to go down into the coal mines at a pitifully young age and spend half a century, in one form or another, underground.

I think about him a lot down there in the dark, far under the ocean floor where most of the Cape Breton collieries extend. Just as I think about Ned Demont, my father's grandfather, who in the early part of the twentieth century was living his own Industrial Age life in nearby Sydney. The DeMonts—the spellings are all over the place, but this is the one I use—didn't range far after Franz Timon got off the *Gale* in Lunenburg in 1751. They put down roots along the coast, becoming farmers and small businessmen. I don't know how long Ned and his wife and kids had been living in Windsor when the great fire of 1897 roared through the town. I just know that at that point my people were also swept along by the great economic forces then transforming the developed world: a brother of Ned's found work in the rolling mills of Pictou County, the province's other industrial hub. Ned, at this point, was forty-one. That didn't stop my great-grandfather from deciding to take his wife and four kids to Sydney, where he understood that the Whitney steel mill, soon to be consuming about half of the coal that Jack Briers and every other Cape Breton collier could harvest, was hiring.

I've driven a lot around the north end of Sydney, looking for the old house where they settled, the place where my father and his brothers would visit as little kids and lie in bed, peering out the window at the flames from the steel mill's stacks that flash-lit the night sky. It's not surprising that I've never found it. Over the years, I've watched the remnants of the age of steel and coal disappear around here. Gone the dark satanic steel mills and coke ovens. Gone the urban badlands—the ground once polluted to a depth of seven stories, the landfill bigger than a hundred football fields—so emblematic of the horrors of industrialization. Gone the tidal estuary so thick with poisons that it was said that a grown man could stand atop it.

I still walk through the coal towns of Cape Breton and Pictou and Cumberland counties the same way I explore the bucolic lands where the Acadians, before the *Grand Dérangement*, thrived: like an archaeologist, searching for the remains of some ancient culture. It's still easy here, where the roll of a village green hides the entrance to some long-abandoned mine entrance and the names of the neighbourhoods and streets can so often be traced back to a colliery, or the man who managed it.

Nova Scotia has many defining architectural features: the dormers of Lunenburg, the salt box houses in the fishing villages, Halifax's stately brick buildings, but most of all the rough little two-storey, semi-detached, wood-framed boxes arranged in the same linear fashion throughout the colliery towns. One spring day I spent an entire afternoon travelling through the old industrial towns of Cape Breton looking for company homes. Hundreds, maybe even thousands of them are in great shape, spruced up and full of life. But in some cases the other half of the duplex was boarded up, abandoned by its owners, or demolished altogether. Not surprising, I suppose, in a place then midway through a multi-million dollar program to demolish hundreds of abandoned and derelict homes in the Cape Breton Regional Municipality, as the collective of industrial towns there are known.

As I wheeled around I discovered that parts of Glace Bay, Dominion and New Victoria looked like Detroit—the lawns of the untended old residences overgrown with neglect, the structures sagging and unstable after having being stripped of saleable metals. I knew from asking around that nothing standing on two legs lived in there. I have to tell you, I love this part of Cape Breton more than a man who lived there for just a year as a child and a few months as an adult has a right to. But in one town that day I looked around to see if a pack of coyotes was roving the streets behind me, on the hunt for human prey.

When those shacks were new they hummed with life. The boggy streets teemed with men carrying their lunch-buckets and pit helmets. By the end of World War I, Halifax, with a population of 58,000, was the epicentre of the province. But the 1921 census showed that Sydney then boasted 22,000 people. If you added in the island's other colliery towns, the population of industrial part of Cape Breton approached 48,000. Over on the mainland—in the steel and colliery centres of Pictou County, along with the far-off coal towns of Springhill, Joggins and others, many of them nonexistent half a century before—lived another 67,000 people who made their daily bread with the pickaxe and blast furnace. All told, one in five Nova Scotians had coal dust beneath their eyes.

These weren't the kinds of lives you or I would envy. My heart, after all this time, still sinks to know that by the 1920s the coal miners and steel workers in my family existed in the same state of servitude as their parents and grandparents: living in houses built, heated and powered by the coal company, drinking coal company water, eating food and wearing clothes that came from the coal company store. The store's credit system kept the miners and their families in perpetual enslavement: when a miner got his weekly pay packet it would include a long list of deductions: rent, coal, electricity, water and anything bought on credit at the company store. I've been dining out for a long time on the story of a miner who lived on my grandparents' street in Glace Bay. His last name was MacDonald and one day, when he picked up his pay envelope and tore it open he discovered, after all the deductions, two copper pennies inside. In Cape Breton, where they'd carried over the old Highland custom of using nicknames to differentiate people with surnames in common, and where a sense of irony is not unheard of, his people were known forevermore simply as the "Big Pay" MacDonalds.

That yarn is sure to get a sad little laugh. The table always goes quiet when I tell people who don't know much about life in the colliery towns about the deaths that multiplied as the Nova Scotia mines grew busier. It has cost more than 2,500 lives to harvest the five hundred million long tons of coal that has been brought to the surface in the history of Nova Scotia. These men died alone, hurtling down shafts, being struck by falling timbers and rocks and earth when ceilings caved in. They were crushed by runaway wagons, coal tubs and the rake that took them back and forth from the mine face. Misfiring explosives took their lives. They got tied up in a piece of machinery or it blew up, sending parts hurtling through the mine shaft. They burned to death, choked on poisonous gas or drowned when the ocean poured in. During the worst disasters—the seventy who died in Westville's Drummond Colliery in 1873, the 125 in Springhill's No. 1 and 2 mines in a single incident in 1891, the eighty-eight miners in Stellarton's Albion mine in 1918—a spark from a pickaxe or some other source ignited coal dust, triggering an explosion that obliterated the mine shaft.

When you look at the list of fatalities it is easy to be overwhelmed by the sheer numbers, to forget that each of those names was a man whose life ended like a lit match going out in a sudden gust of wind. By my reckoning, thirty-one men lost their lives in the Florence Colliery, which my grandfather entered as an eleven-year-old in 1906. Jack Briers could well have known Patrick Clarke, Ingraham Collins and John Riley, who died from falling stone in the same mine eleven years later. Just as there is a good chance that, at some point, he worked next to Albert Smith (according to official records, "burned at the boiler doors") and Bonnar Alexander and Daniel Jobs, who died at the same time as the result of a fall of coal. Or that he put in a shift with John Snow, Arthur Blinkhorn, Charles Penny, James Devoe and Alex Steele, who also died in the Florence Colliery while he toiled there.

A few people were doing okay in the coal and steel towns. In the newspapers of the day you see them in photographs, in their suits with their stiff, high-collared shirts and their shaggy moustaches, the serious men from Boston, Montreal, London and other places far away who owned the mines and mills. You can still see hints of the old money around there if you know where to look. The last time I looked on King's Road, which is a rather grand name for an ordinary commercial street in Sydney, there stood a funny little wooden house with a variety of peaked roofs and windows pointing off in all directions. At the turn of the nineteenth century an Ohioan named Arthur Moxham bought into Whitney's Dominion Iron and Steel Company and was asked to run it. Moxham's wife refused to leave Ohio for the wilds of Cape Breton unless some of their house in Ohio came with them. So her husband had some tradesmen carefully remove the interior walls and staircases from the old chateau. They took down the chandeliers and packed up the furniture and shipped it all by rail to Sydney to fill the thirty-room mansion—complete with a wine cellar, a ballroom and a solarium—that he had built there.

There's a metaphor in this story somewhere, for nothing really good happened to the Moxhams in Cape Breton. A son slipped onto the tracks in the steel plant, was hit by a rail car and nearly beheaded. Months later the son's wife died, along with her stillborn child. Heartbroken, the parents were gone within a year. For a time, a local shipping magnate owned their mansion. By the 1920s, Moxham Castle—now nothing but the old gatehouse—was being used as a convalescent home for returning soldiers from the First World War. By then Whitney, who would end his roller-coaster life penniless back in the United States, was also long gone. Control of his Cape Breton coal-and-coke enterprise—made possible by a series of laughably beneficial royalty agreements granted by job-hungry Nova Scotia governments—had passed to the hands of some smooth operators from Montreal. In time, a British syndicate controlled the collieries, blast furnaces, forges, machine shops and steel mills of not only Cape Breton but Pictou County as well.

Today there would be a Royal Commission if foreigners exercised that much economic clout: by the end of the First World War, Cape Breton's coal mines supplied more than 44 per cent of Canada's annual coal production, while the iron and steel industry produced more than one-third of the country's pig iron. That kind of monopolistic arrangement, it has been argued, established a pattern of economic development that has seldom varied since: foreign capital wringing every last cent out of local resources while the folks who risked their lives working them just never get any traction. It is as Francis W. Gray, a Yorkshire mining engineer who landed here around that time, wrote: "Nova Scotia has achieved the status of a mining camp, whereas its full stature should be that of a metropolis of industry."

On the first day on my very first job as a reporter, I was led into the composing room of the *Cape Breton Post* in Sydney, where newspapers were still put together the old way with the letters cast in hot metal type before they were laid out in words, sentences and paragraphs on the page. The *Post* was a small paper, but the composing room, as composing rooms tend to be, was loud, dank and, because I didn't have to toil in there, wonderful. I was being introduced around. When one of the men heard my name he put down what he was doing, looked me appraisingly in the face and said, "Demont." Then he asked me if I was some relation of a man he had worked with in a composing room just like that one, whose name was Clarie Demont.

My grandfather was known as "Flash" because by the time he died, as his obituary in the *Toronto Star* noted, he had run the fastest hundred-yard dash ever by a Canadian. He didn't work in the pit, making him a semi-rarity in Glace Bay where most people went into the mines or lived off the crumbs that fell from them. As the pressman and later production supervisor of the *Glace Bay Gazette*, then owned by the United Mine Workers of America, he worked in his way for the miners and steel workers. When Flash Demont was learning his trade at the *Gazette* in the early '20s he would have been laying out stories about fires, tavern dustups and the rare automobile accident at a time when few people owned a car. Under his green eye-shade he would have proofed the ads for the movie house, from which his sons would gallop home, slapping their backsides like cow-boys, after the latest Tom Mix duster, and the boxscore for the Glace Bay Miners, the colliery league baseball team for whom he once made fifteen putouts in a single game, dashing around the outfield on those magnificent legs.

Often, in that practised way that composing room supervisors have, Clarie Demont ran a finger down front-page stories that made his town and the rest of industrial Cape Breton sound like their very foundations were breaking apart. Around the kitchen table, at the drugstore soda fountain and in church halls, the people of Glace Bay talked in those days about how the relationship between labour and capitalism was recalibrating itself everywhere. The Bolshevik Revolution near the end of World War I made workers across North America and Europe realize that they could ask for better lives. With the postwar economy mired in depression, returning veterans discovered that the reward for all their sacrifice was a world of massive unemployment and soaring inflation. Displeasure reigned throughout the land: in Winnipeg, where Ottawa unleashed the Mounties after thirty thousand workers left their jobs, triggering sympathy strikes throughout the country, but also in Nova Scotia, where the outrages seemed to grow daily.

The one thing trying to protect the workers from the villainy of the colliery owners in those days was District 26 of the United Mine Workers of America, for whom my grandmother Mabel and later my great-aunt Eva MacKeigan worked as union secretary. Aunt Eva was a lady of refinement, a great cook who at family gatherings would convene sing-alongs around the organ, which she played with flair. I have some trouble, therefore, visualizing her in the union office, where the air would have been thick with talk of class warfare, worker's rights and Joe Hill. There her boss, James Bryson McLachlan, sat in his office, painted symbolically red, typing his letters to the editor about child labour, the way that the companies kept the miners and their families in everlasting slavery and the dangers in the inhuman deeps.

When McLachlan typed the name of Roy Wolvin, the owlish Montrealer who had emerged as the head of the British conglomerate that enjoyed near absolute control over Cape Breton's coal and steel industry, he would have pounded the keys as if they were the bones of Wolvin himself. The Wolf paid dividends to himself and his cronies rather than spending the money on badly needed upgrades for the mines. Though the miners could barely pay for rent and food, he cut their pay packets. When the miners struck, Wolvin's influence ensured that a special thousand-man provincial army was formed to return order to the coalfields. At his request, Canadian destroyers were diverted to Sydney and a request was made to deploy the Royal Canadian Air Force, along with some British battleships, to Cape Breton.

It seemed like such a one-sided fight, this campaign between working folk and the rapacious men of industry, but the proletariat of Cape Breton fought on because there was nothing else they could do. Between 1920 and 1925, Cape Breton's coal miners struck, on average, once a month. I don't know for certain that my people were there as "Armstrong's army," the provincial police force mobilized by Premier Ernest Armstrong, rumbled down the track from Halifax, their machine guns at the ready on a troop train piled high with sandbags, or whether any of my predecessors were hospitalized after the mounted police charged the striking miners and steel workers. Chances are good that my great-aunt Eva was present when Sydney's chief of police and a deputy walked up the stairs into the UMWA offices on Union Street in Glace Bay and arrested McLachlan. During his trial in Halifax, she smuggled union correspondence in with his supper, then snuck his responses out again when she came for the dishes. After his release from prison, thousands waited in the slushy streets for McLachlan's return to Glace Bay. Eva MacKeigan would have been there for him then too.

I grew up hearing about what happened next—not in some seamless narrative, but in dribs and drabs. How Wolvin demanded another wage cut. How, even before the "100 percent strike," so-called because the miners didn't know what else under the circumstances to do, colliers' wives were reduced to using flour bags to clothe their children and feed bags for bedding. Throughout the island, the hungry lined up in food depots that had sprung up in church basements and soup kitchens. The despair was such that a Glace Bay health official sent a report to Prime Minister William Lyon Mackenzie King, stating baldy that thousands of Cape Breton miners and their families were "on the verge of starvation."

Then the British Empire Steel Company cut off the coal to the miners' homes. As the temperatures dropped and the strike of 1925 lengthened, the company police and the strikers fought, lost and retook the mines like two armies fighting for terrain. It was, in the eyes of Aunt Eva and virtually every other family member I've talked to, a battle between good and evil as starkly black and white as Nurse Ratched vs. Randle McMurphy. I've done my best to separate fact from fiction over the years. I've read old newspaper microfiche until my eyes crossed. I've sifted through the impressive collection of historical writing on the subject, both academic and popular in nature. Even with the pretense of journalistic impartiality it is hard to find my way to any version of the facts that doesn't bring my aqueous humour to a rolling boil. Truthfully, it took me a long time to write this paragraph because I'm so wound up that the words just came out in a way that was unsuitable for a book meant to be read by the kind of courtly folk I hope will pick this up. So I just went back and started again.

Because I want you to imagine what it was like during the worst days in the colliery towns, when the latest union contract had expired and the Wolf had cut off every bit of credit at the company stores to the already starving miners and their families. Now people were left to pick through the garbage for half-spoiled food and entire families had to subsist on black tea, molasses and soup bones. Children, left to sleep seven to a bed fully clothed in their hovels, couldn't go outdoors because they didn't have boots or socks and suffered from rickets and malnutrition. I've never eyeballed a picture of the New Waterford miners on the June day in 1925 that I have in mind. I can see them anyway in their cloth caps, their thick pants held up by suspenders or cinched by belts, their shirts opened at the neck with the sleeves rolled up over muscle-corded forearms. The sharpness of the cheekbones and jawlines, the loose way their heavy clothes hung, would have hinted at their hunger. If there were grins on any of the faces, they would have resembled the nervous smile of the soldier before going into battle. At that point more than five thousand Great War servicemen were on the coal company payroll on Cape Breton Island. Some of them were surely here, getting ready to march on a power station that the company's constables had recently recaptured to keep its mines from flooding.

It would have taken some time for the crowd, thought to be in the thousands, to gather. Someone, at a certain point, must have said something. Or perhaps a couple of the men just started walking and the rest, casting "I guess this is it" glances at each other, followed. I imagine them moving haltingly at first along the path, running along the rail line heading west from New Waterford and slowing down again as they hit the woods. But their collective heart would have been beating faster when they emerged from the forest. By then some of them might even have broken into a small jog, the thousands of boots making a sound that seemed to issue from the deep in the summer earth. They weren't necessarily hardcore unionists, or even really political. The nuances of profit margins and dividend-payout ratios were almost certainly far beyond their elementary school educations and their nineteenth-century lives. They just knew that there was injustice in this world. That when a man worked as hard as they did, his children shouldn't be left to starve in the cold. It was the dream of their ancestors. It was their dream too as they stepped from the woods into the opening, where the men with the guns waited, trigger fingers ready.

You know how this story is going to end. Nothing withstands the great forces of history. The Second World War brought an end to the grinding poverty of the Great Depression. Halifax became a staging area for the Allies' efforts in Europe; railcar and steel plants boomed; the coal industry briefly ramped up again. But after the war only subsidies and government ownership kept the mines limping along through ups and downs until one by one they closed. It was bad news from end to end in this province. But, Nova Scotia's Industrial Age, any way you looked at it, was over.

One day in 2014 I went to the village of Inverness, on Cape Breton's west coast. It's a heartbreakingly beautiful place when the weather is decent. This was March; the harbour was choked with chunks of ice the size of smart cars. I was there, weirdly, to talk about a golf course by the name of Cabot Links, which is one of those Scottish-style courses where one starkly stunning hole leads to the next, in this case in a beguiling enough fashion that Hollywood celebrities were flying in by private plane just to play there. Golf had changed the area, no doubt about it. One of the old A-frame coal company homes that couldn't be given away elsewhere on the island had recently fetched a quarter of a million dollars. I knew something was up the previous summer when I had driven down the village's main drag past a young guy in a ball cap—at just the age when his grandfather would have been down in the pit around there—standing on the lawn in front of one of those colliery houses, practising his golf swing. Dreaming, for all I know, of Augusta.

I was there to see if this village, with another world-class course on the way and a smattering of small technology-oriented companies suddenly popping up, could be model for the revitalization of rural Nova Scotia.

"Golf's the future around here," a man named John MacIsaac told me as we stood on the edge of the snow-covered course.

As the village historian, MacIsaac understood the past as well as the future. Our vantage point provided a view of the walls of rock that gave Cabot Links' companion course, Cabot Cliffs, its name. One day during the heyday of coal and steel, a glorious flimflam man from the Boston States, who had somehow found his way here, painted those walls black. He had a plan. His fervent hope was that some men in a boat some distance out in the ocean would think they were looking at immense coal reserves and that they would then give him their money.

MacIsaac was telling me how the men in the boat must have been convinced, because the money came in and the mines were developed. Within a few short years, Inverness—nicknamed Belgium Town for the four hundred Flemish people who arrived here to work the seams—ballooned to three thousand people. Some forty saloons could be found along the road I had just driven down, which back then led to the No. 2 mine, for a time the biggest in the area. Inverness had a trio of hotels, a pair of barbershops, a movie theatre and a railroad station. It had six schools for its children. It had bands and sports fields. It even had a cricket pitch.

Only for a while, of course. The mines there, like everywhere else, started to close. The miners and their families drifted away, and so did the young. By the mid-1950s the train only stopped in Inverness once a week, and then not at all. Inverness's business section, by then, had shrunk to twenty establishments. Now the exodus has stopped. There are about 1,500 people in Inverness, where in 2014 you could get a cappuccino or a flagon of fat, oaky chardonnay. I asked MacIsaac where that old No. 2 was located.

"Right here," he said with a sweeping gesture. "Underneath our feet."

Which meant underneath Cabot Links' swanky hotel and first-rate restaurant. Beneath the golf course. Down in the hole.

A family wedding for the Campbell clan of Weymouth
before they were devastated by World War One.

# EIGHT

# Angle of Repose

*Dennisville—The Carlyle—Clara—Barely Legible Scrawl—The Quaint and the*
*Colourful—Poorest in the Land—Margaret—Memories of Weymouth—*
*Duncan, Glidden and the Debonair One—Ribs or Gas—*
*Haunted by Photographs—Boston Tar Baby—Ghost*
*Towns—Russ and Joan—Horizon of Possibility*

A block from our house in Halifax is a condo development—ten stories high, subdued stone exterior, name written in nice, understated script—that wasn't there when I grew up in this neighbourhood. I had no idea what preceded it until one day when I was looking at some old photographs from the Public Archives of Nova Scotia and saw a black-and-white shot of a roomy, rectangular wooden house with big dormer windows, a pair of chimneys and an airy west-facing veranda. On either side, providing shelter from the street, enough maples and aspens loomed to blot out the sun during the dog days of summer. A driveway—I couldn't tell if it was dirt, gravel or pavement—circled in front of the house. Back by the flower gardens stood a grass tennis court that had to be one of the few in Halifax in the early 1900s, where men in fedoras, vests and ties and women in neck-to-ankle dresses stood stiffly with wooden racquets in hand. Enclosing the entire property was a wrought-iron fence ending in a pair of stone, armpit-high gateposts, which, to this day, stands sentinel for the Carlyle condo residences which, in the year 2016, I walked past most days in my neighbourhood.

Clara Dennis took a lot of photographs of "Dennisville," the house where she grew up with her brothers and sisters, her mother, Agnes, and her father, William, an abstemious workaholic who, at seventeen, emigrated from the British Isles to Halifax where he got a job as a reporter for the city's *Morning Herald*. William Dennis worked his way up to news editor there. In time he bought a controlling interest in the paper, where he became editor-in-chief and president of not only the morning *Herald*, but also its companion, the afternoon *Mail Star*. He once described his philosophy as a newspaper proprietor this way: "It is my wish that *The Halifax Herald* and *The Evening Mail* shall be conducted as public utilities for all the people, and absolutely independent and fearless, offering no unkind or unjust criticism, treating opponents fairly on all questions, giving vigorous and hearty support to movements for the public good." Most of the pictures of the old Dennis family home that found their way into the Nova Scotia Archives were taken in the early years of the twentieth century. By that time William had passed the operations of the paper on to his nephew. In the everything-is-connected way things seem to work around here—Halifax, as is often said, is big enough for a symphony but too small for adultery—that part of the Dennis family still owned Canada's last remaining independent daily newspaper when I signed up for another tour of duty there in 2011.

From the looks of Clara Dennis's pictures, a nice, respectable life was had in this house that, if not a mansion, still had the air of Victorian prosperity about it, right down to the cocker spaniel lounging on the front steps and the black domestic, named Sam, who looked after the grounds and generally added to the comfort of Dennis lives. Yet indications are that she chafed against the restrictions of an upper-crust life in this small, provincial city in the early part of the twentieth century.

I say this because she could have just been content with those progressive after-dinner chats, led by her mother, about how to improve the lot of the disadvantaged women and children of Nova Scotia. She could have found fulfilment working as her father's assistant at the *Halifax Herald* office, which was regarded as appropriate employment then for a young woman who had attended two universities and studied stenography and typing at my old alma mater the Halifax Business College. Let's face it, she could have whiled away her weekends picnicking on the Halifax Arm and her summer vacations at the family farm.

Instead, one day, in an apartment in London, England, she looked at a map of Nova Scotia, apparently for the first time in a while. "What a warm glow came over me at the sight of the familiar odd-shaped little Province by the sea—my own, my native land," she later wrote. At some point Dennis returned to that little province by the sea. She bought some pens and notebooks. She acquired a camera, perhaps one of the popular box models then made by the Eastman Kodak Company. Then she jumped in a jalopy with friends or family, or maybe alone, and headed for the Halifax city limits. Her plan was straightforward. "I would travel over her highways and byways," she wrote in the first of her books about her native province. "I would know her cities, her towns, her villages. I would visit the remote and but little frequented islands of her coast. I would talk with the men, women and children I would meet. In their lives would be unfolded the soul of Nova Scotia." As she travelled, Dennis recorded her observations in what an archivist would later describe as a "barely legible scrawl." Critic V.B. Rhodenizer called her literary efforts, which appeared in books as well as newspaper and magazine articles, "delightful accounts of motor travel." The pictures she took stick with you in a different way.

Among the 2,500 or so photographs of hers in the archives' possession, I could only find one of Dennis as an adult, taken in a small fishing community outside of Halifax. In it she sits side-saddle, her right arm extended for balance, on what appears to be the stern of a small rowboat. Barefoot, in a dark dress, her brunette hair flying in the wind, she squints into the sunlight, slightly embarrassed to be taking a 1930s selfie. She preferred turning the camera on others as she roved Nova Scotia during the Great Depression and the interwar years. In her books she's mostly a chronicler of the quaint and the colourful. Her pictures, I often find disquieting. For the most part, as promised, she steered clear of the few cities and bigger towns. The countryside she chose looks mostly prehistoric, the islands uninhabitable, the rocks spectral. Something about the cameras of the day, or at least the camera she used, made it impossible to translate light. So if the sun didn't glint off the ocean, everything looked washed out, even ashen. The overall impression, despite the close quarters in a province hemmed in by ocean on one side and wild forest on the other, is one of emptiness.

When framing an image, Dennis didn't always follow the rule of thirds, the notion of breaking a photograph down into three horizontal and vertical sections and then placing points of interest at the junction where these sections intersect. Instead, stuff is off to the left or right, or your eye is drawn to something at the bottom of the frame. She seems, in so many cases, to have been attracted to the melancholy: empty houses already being retaken by the wilderness; hotels where no one has stayed in a very long time; the remnants of a shipwreck peeking out from the waterline, like the bones of a sea monster. With a few exceptions—William Martell and his wife and child from Flint

Island, Alex Campbell of Gabarus, the members of the Borden family in Dominion—few folks smile in the pictures I've seen. Her people look as if their presence, as they prepare to go into the mines, out in a dory onto rough seas or just to milk a cow, is a bewildering surprise to them.

It is hard not to impose some kind of narrative as you move through the gallery of unknown faces. In one shot, identified as the home of Dan MacMaster of Craignish (by which she must have meant Creignish), Cape Breton, a man in a light-coloured jacket, his face shadowed by the wide brim of a western-style hat, crouches in front of a single-storey house where stone shows through the worn-away plaster. He stares down at the photographer, as does the child in the narrow doorway. Behind the youngster, a long man in a dark suit, tall enough that the top of his head is cut off by the doorway, lingers like an undertaker. Where exactly did she find the ancient dowser, Walter Thomas of Port Clyde, clutching a twig from a sour apple tree? Did she just come across the organ grinder on the snowy road, bent forlornly under the hand organ strapped to his back? Were the Greek peanut man and the scissor grinder man just there, making their way on foot across the dusty lanes of this province? How much convincing did it take to talk Mrs. Enos Germain and Mrs. Alonzo Minard, great-great-granddaughters of Sylvannus Cobb, the fabled privateer, to stand primly in front of the monument to their forebear? And just who, in the same photograph, is that unidentified seated woman with the enigmatic smile whom you cannot take your eyes off of?

People see what they want to see in photographs. Sometimes it is something that is not even visible, but still is somehow there, frozen in the frame. The mere act of looking at Clara Dennis's photos invites a whole other world to flood in, a world that, to me, evokes people on farms and fishing boats, in the woods and on empty Nova Scotian roads. Lean, hungry folk right out of a Woody Guthrie lyric, they're off the main thoroughfares, these people. They could be there still, haunting the vales and coves, like artifacts from some lost world that hasn't really passed. When the Great Depression hit, Nova Scotia had less of a distance to fall than other provinces. But a Nova Scotian household barely made more than the folks in one of those sod prairie huts when the dust of the Dirty Thirties blew around them. In Sydney Mines only one in twenty miners was working full time. In Sydney some 1,500 young men between the ages of eighteen and twenty-three had never worked, a 1931 government report on the coal industry said, and the way things were going, perhaps never would. When it came to federal relief programs, Atlantic Canadians got barely a third of the national average. The upshot, according to the historian Ernest Forbes: "Elderly and destitute refused assistance, deaf and blind cut off from schools, seriously ill denied hospitalization and moral offenders savagely punished." One of the richest provinces in Canada on a per capita basis before joining Confederation, Nova Scotia became one of the poorest in the land during the Great Depression.

Everywhere there was misery, but particularly in the countryside. You can glimpse the hardness of their lives in Dennis's pictures, which weren't meant to be a social document of the time but end up being just that. People didn't smile much in photographs in those days. But her people stare back in Chebogue, Barney's River and Bay St. Lawrence, on Tancook Island, at Marshy Hope, from Isle Madame and Merigomish. In the latter case, 60 per cent of ordinary working men couldn't find work during the Depression. Some of her subjects seem broken, unable to meet the camera's gaze; others glare, hollow-eyed and defiant. Her photographs are more than a moment in time. Some of the people in them had never known anything other than hardship and penury, and never would. Others were momentarily undone by circumstance and would somehow, through true grit, rise again. Many Nova Scotians just did what had to be done.

Many of the people in Dennis's photos were never the same after returning from the Great War, their lungs flayed by mustard gas, their dreams haunted by the horrors they had seen. Some thirty thousand Nova Scotian men donned uniforms. My maternal grandfather had, for some reason, decided against enlisting in any of the Cape Breton units. Instead he signed on in Truro, where I imagine the recruitment pitch mirrored the one for the Pictou County Unit:

The boys in the trenches are waiting for the guns to smash their way through.

Won't you come with the Pictou County Unit?

Won't you come now? Won't you come along with us?

Come along!

The day he became a member of the 106th Infantry Battalion of the Canadian Expeditionary Force, Jack Briers was twenty-two years old, a practising Anglican with a Grade 5 education and a complexion that his attestation papers described as "fresh." His hair in the one photograph I have from around this period is khaki brown, his eyes cobalt, his lips a thin slit. My grandfather was just over five feet-eight-inches tall when he signed up. His chest when fully expanded was thirty-eight and a half inches, two inches broader than during its resting state. An attentive medical officer noted that he bore two vaccination marks on his left arm. "He can see at the required distance with either eye," added the nameless captain. "His heart and lungs are healthy; he has the free use of his joints and limbs and he declares that he is not subject to fits of any description."

My grandfather and the other members of the 106th—its motto "None So Reliable," its commanding officer, Lieutenant-Colonel Robert Innes, its machine-gun officer a lieutenant named Fleming—received less than three months' training before boarding the *Empress of Britain* and departing for England. The voyage to Liverpool took eleven days. A day later they were in a camp in Shorncliffe. Jack Briers spent just eleven days with his unit before joining another unit, bound for France, where he spent the entire war as part of the 14th Infantry Battalion, part of the 3rd Brigade of the 1st Infantry Division. There he saw the kind of action that a letter from the Canadian Department of National Defence, accompanying his war records, described as "difficult." The world has seldom seen battles as bloody and pointless as the Somme Offensive in which, for five months, Britain and its allies threw themselves futilely and repeatedly at the German lines. On the first day alone, the British lost more than fifty-seven thousand men, while almost all of the eight-hundred-man First Newfoundland Regiment perished. Unlike the more than twenty-four thousand Canadian troops who died there, Jack Briers made it out of the corpse-strewn mud. He was still standing after the Battle of Mount Sorrel (eight thousand Canadian casualties). At Vimy Ridge, where Canada is said to have become a country, nearly four thousand Canadians fell and seven thousand were injured. Once more, Jack Briers escaped the bullets, bombs and bayonettes.

A man named Duncan Campbell, on the other hand, did not. Three months before my grandfather, he walked through the same door into the same Truro recruitment office to join the same battalion.

At Vimy Ridge, the newly married Campbell was wounded in the hand and thigh. I don't know if he had a choice about whether to return to the front, but he reappeared there anyway, a event that left him befuddled and helpless—shell-shocked, as they then called it— when he made it back to his home in the village of Weymouth, Nova Scotia. Few Nova Scotia households escaped sacrifice during this war. Fewer still gave as much as the Campbells, a family of twelve who lived in a rambling house called Riverside on the tidal Sissiboo River before the War to End all Wars changed everything.

On my laptop I have a photograph from Duncan's wedding, taken in front of the Campbell house before he left for duty. It's a wonderful, animated shot: the father in a top hat, the pleased-as-punch mother, the gaggle of men with carnations in their lapels and women clutching bouquets, all struggling to maintain the proper deportment. Nothing is quite in sync, making the photo of these happy people on this memorable day somehow iconic. "It looks like a portrait of social order in a society that was about to be completely devastated," Elissa Barnard, a descendent of those men and women told me one day as we looked at the picture together. "And it was."

I knew about the Campbell boys, but somehow tucked that knowledge away in the back of my mind until I was thumbing through a beaten-up copy of a book called *Nova Scotia's Part in the Great War*, written by a captain named M.S. Hunt and published by the Nova Scotia Veteran Publishing Company two years after the last gun was fired. In it I read about the 185th Battalion, the Cape Breton Highlanders, who wore the Argyll and Sutherland tartans into battle, where some 136 of them fell, and learned of the 25th Battalion, which lost 718 officers and ordinary soldiers as they assaulted Vimy

Ridge, went over the top at the Battle of Hill 70, fought at the Somme and helped capture Passchendaele Ridge. There, in spidery, old-style type, were the exploits of the Nova Scotia Highlanders, whose list of engagements seemed agonizingly long, and the saga of the 36th Battery, raised in Sydney, which upon arriving in France was immediately deployed to Ypres, and from there on endured unrelenting hardship.

I read with particular interest a series of sketches of Nova Scotians who had served with bravery and honour: nurses and airmen, soldiers who led doomed charges on German machine-gun nests, officers dead from an errant piece of shrapnel. A lot of the names, if you've been around Nova Scotia for a while, are still recognizable. The six sons of Douglas and Kate Campbell, each born in Weymouth, each volunteering in August 1914, are singled out for special attention by Hunt. For some reason, though, in all the times we ran into each other on the street, not far from Clara Dennis's old place, I never thought to ask Douglas and Kate's granddaughter a single thing about her brave uncles. We talked about lots of stuff: our neighborhood, the state of journalism—Margaret Barnard had worked at the *Halifax Herald* during the Second World War and could recall seeing the war brides come off the *Queen Mary* and glass on the floor of the Birks jewellery store after the infamous V-E Day riots—and her daughter, Elissa, who wrote for the same Dennis-owned paper as I. Not once did I bring up her people and the tragedy that had befallen them, even though it's the kind of story that, once you hear it, you never forget it.

I had missed my chance in the summer of 2016 when I walked over to Marg's house, where Elissa was tidying up now that her mother had just passed away, at ninety-four. We had company; the ghosts of Weymouth were also there that rainy afternoon, as we sat a few feet from a desk once owned by James Moody, a hero among Nova Scotia loyalists for his swashbuckling raids against the Americans in the Revolutionary War before he settled in the Weymouth area. After visiting Weymouth on his rambles, Joe Howe had predicted that it would grow from a village into a town. By the time the story of the Campbells was unfolding, it had. Elissa told me that the boys' grandfather owned twenty-two ships that roved the world. Their uncle owned sawmills, a pulp and paper business and vast tracts of land. The mills in the area brought the Englishmen with their cricket bats, warm beer and love of the Union Jack, just as the fishery made work for the Acadians who lived just outside of town and the descendants of the black loyalists, living in predictable poverty, across the Sissiboo River.

"When it came to Weymouth, Mom's perspective was very idyllic," Elissa said.

Marg spent her childhood there at a time when the lumber mills still operated, ships regularly docked at the town's wharves and Weymouth's population numbered in the thousands. In those days the unmarried Campbell great aunts still lived in the ancestral home surrounded by apple trees and meadows, which started out small and then grew as rooms were added for the members of the perpetually growing clan. Her mother told Elissa about Cuthbert Taylor, an admiral in real life but "Uncle Cuppy" to her, and his signature riverside martinis, and how the kids rowed back and forth across the river during the summer.

"There was a lot of socializing. In Mom's teenaged diary they were always going," Elissa said. "Everything just seemed grand."

Much as it seemed in Duncan Campbell's wedding day photograph. In it, Marg's father, Glidden, stands on the grass, staring off into the middle distance. He was already a captain in the militia when the war broke out, but with no inkling yet that he would soon lead his company into the Battle of Passchendaele. Or that by the time the war had ended he would have helped wipe out a dozen machine-gun nests and be awarded the Military Cross after single-handedly capturing a German pillbox. In the process, Glidden was wounded twice and gassed. Even then he delayed his return to take command of the 79th Company of the Forestry Corps before heading back to Nova Scotia, the only Campbell boy to return intact in mind and body, except for the lingering laryngitis from the mustard gas attack.

In the same picture, the youngest brother, Colin, stands in the very last row, hair parted as neatly as a small-town cleric's. A graduate of the University of King's College, he was just eighteen when this picture was taken. His letters home showed that Colin craved action. Just weeks after landing in France, he was injured by shrapnel. Before the month was out he was severely wounded at the Battle of La Bassée, for which he received the Military Cross from King George V. After leaving the hospital he returned to the front, where he passed the exams to become a pilot. Colin was scheduled to be transferred to the Royal Flying Corps, but his artillery commander asked him to perform one last mission before he left, which he did, joining the Canadian assault on Passchendaele, where a German shell took his life.

The tallest person in the photo is Kenneth, whom Marg called "the debonair one." He wears an expression that looks pensive, even grave, when you know that five months after arriving in France he would be in the trenches in Vimy, where he would be shot between the eyes while trying to locate the position of an enemy sniper. On the top step of the veranda, his hand clutching the railing, stands Albert, who volunteered with the rest of the brothers but didn't immediately join the fighting because his father needed him for the family store.

When his dad relented, Albert enlisted and headed to the front. His honourable discharge papers read "medically unfit."

Instead of returning to Weymouth, Albert headed to Montreal, where his nervous disposition prevented him from ever holding a job for long and he died in a Department of Veterans Affairs hospital. That, alas, was an almost identical fate to that of his twin brother, Tom, the northwestern-most figure in the picture. Somehow he got lost in no-man's-land at Vimy Ridge. The Allies found him wandering in a German trench, dressed in tatters, bedecked in tin cans by the Germans. Back in Canada the doctors declared Tom physically fine, but emotionally and mentally damaged. He lived a long time after he returned from Europe, all of it inside a DVA hospital, where, like his brother, he died.

In the one picture I've seen of her, Clara Dennis has the glow of the optimist. But as she wandered around Nova Scotia she would have seen close up that pure, unadulterated hope was hard to find in the 1930s. From there on in, when immigrants landed in Canada, it might have been by ship in Halifax, but they quickly hopped on a train and headed west, jumping off in the heart of the country in Ontario or Quebec or continuing on to the new lands in the Prairies, Alberta and British Columbia that were filling up. In Nova Scotia, industrialization divided places into haves and have-nots. During the spirit-sapping Great Depression, people moved and moved again in search of work and an ascendant narrative. Many of them came from towns in the old country and, after a brief interval in the wilderness, aspired to return to towns and villages once again. For some places, it was a gradual upwards or downwards spiral. For others the change was more precipitous, as these things tend to be.

Any way I look at it, I can't think of these as the good years: the men on both sides of our family toiling miles under the ground or in the fiery hell of the steel mills before heading off to fight for our freedom on faraway soil and the shipping laneways of the North Atlantic. My father mercifully avoided service in World War II, but only because, like 40 per cent of young Nova Scotian males, he and his brother had contracted tuberculosis, a disease that particularly afflicted the coal and steel towns of Cape Breton, which had more than their share of malnourished folk living in small, poorly ventilated, overcrowded homes.

I've seen a picture of where he spent eighteen months of his life when he should have been out playing basketball at the Knox Church Hall in Glace Bay, bird-dogging chicks down at Senator's Corner or throwing rocks at the Catholics from Saint Mike's. Bathed in sunlight, the Glace Bay sanatorium looks like a school—two storeys, with a white, wooden exterior, sloping roof and brick chimney, a church steeple off in the background. But I think I can see faces in the windows, the ghosts of kids like my father and his brother who endured a procedure in which inert air was injected into the area around the diseased lung, but which sounded far better than the other common TB treatment of the day, commonly known as "ribs" because it involved having several ribs surgically removed in order to collapse the stricken lung in the hope it would recover.

I don't think I'm drawn to gloom, but I'm haunted by the pictures that I've seen from these years, when photographic studios seemed to be opening up in every small town throughout the province. I don't know where Lawson Hardy, who was first a cooper and then a merchant before opening a photographic studio above a former candy store in Kentville, got his training or even what Georgia Harriet Cunningham, a daughter of a saddler and justice of the peace, did before she bought a studio in Bridgetown. My guess is that Helen Creighton, the great folklorist who travelled the province through these years, capturing the old people and ways in photographs, sound recordings and moving pictures, was self-taught. I do know that our most famous photographer from this period, Wallace MacAskill, studied in New York. In his studios in Glace Bay and later Halifax, he learned to produce the soft-focus impressionism that was the hallmark of his marine and landscape images, his well-known pictures of the fabled racing schooner *Bluenose* and the province's coastal fishing villages already fading into the romanticized past.

I see no such sentimentality in a picture of the most famous citizen from Weymouth Falls, photographer unknown, which sits in the Nova Scotia Archives alongside a huge collection of MacAskill's work and Clara Dennis's pictures. The Campbell boys would have been just kids when Sam Langford, at twelve, left the hardscrabble black community just outside of Weymouth for Boston. One day Langford walked into a drugstore owned by a hustler named Sam Woodman, who also operated a small fight gym. Before long the broad, round face of the "Boston Tar Baby," as Langford was known in those enlightened times, was plastered on kids' trading cards, matchboxes, cigarette packages, American sports pages and the covers of French magazines. The fight writers of the time said there was never a better fighter pound-for-pound than the five-foot, eight-inch Langford. I take as gospel the word of the brawler Jack Dempsey, who said he feared no man but was afraid of Sam Langford, who, in his prime, was nearly fifty pounds lighter than the world heavyweight champion.

There is a predictable arc to fighters' lives. Langford's, because of what might have been, was sadder than most. When he took on the most punishing prize fighter on the planet, the bigger, stronger

Jack Johnson, Langford lost. But the fight was close enough that the great Johnson saw no money to be made in two black boxers pummelling each other and refused to give Langford a rematch. So he spent the rest of his career wandering, fighting for lesser titles and smaller purses, throughout Europe and South America. He was fat and legally blind when he won the heavyweight championship of Spain in Mexico City in 1923, at age 40. No one knew precisely how many hundreds of bouts Langford had fought when he retired, penniless.

Everything I'd read led me to believe that he had disappeared during the rest of the '20s and '30s. Then I saw this photograph in the Nova Scotia Archives from the collection of a sportsman named Tom Connors, thought to be taken sometime between 1929 and 1935. In it you can see Langford's cauliflower left ear and his blind-man's squint. The great fighter had grandmotherly arms. His ass, as they say in some places in Nova Scotia, is eight axe handles wide. It must have been cold when the picture was taken, because he's sporting an unflattering dark leotard. So is the white guy crouched across from him, a leaner, younger specimen named Joe Hartnet. Work was scarce for everyone in 1930s Nova Scotia, yet I still find it so achingly sad to think of a warrior like Langford, broke and blind, travelling the Maritimes as part of the Bill Lynch Carnival show. Every day or two they went from Depression-era town to Depression-era town. There, wearing gloves as big as pillows, Langford would move his fat, broken body—the account from the *Halifax Herald* said he looked like a huge rubber ball—around the makeshift ring.

As the calliope played and the locals, trying to forget their own woes, stomped and whistled, he would slip Hartnet's punches, occasionally throwing one of two of his own. The *Herald*'s reporter noted that he paid close attention to the timer. When a bell rang the great

Sam Langford, who had fought in the ring with as much skill and bravery as any man before or since, would trudge to his corner. He would
sit down on his stool, look out into the crowd that to his eyes would be
nothing but shapes and shades, and wait for the bell to ring again.

Like the carnies from the Bill Lynch shows, I've meandered all across
this province, stopping when I felt like it, turning in here or there for
no good reason at all, going down some old back road just because.
When you do that it's easy to imagine a time when hand-cranked
cars still clanked and wheezed down Nova Scotia's twenty miles of
paved roads and when most travellers here, like most people everywhere, got around on passenger trains, which stopped not just in
bigger spots like Windsor, Weymouth, Digby, Kentville and Sydney,
but brought men in hats and women in their Sunday best to and from
stations in tiny places like Paradise, Plympton, Saulnierville and
Wilmot that had already begun to recede into history.

It's even easy to see the landscape near the midpoint of the twentieth century, when almost half of the province's 640,000 people still
lived somewhere outside of an urban area, which then meant a thriving metropolis of one thousand people. Nova Scotia in the postwar
years was already starting to resemble the Nova Scotia I drive
through in 2016. If you looked hard, deserted homesteads could be
glimpsed slowly going down the road to ruin. Empty window frames
bulged, roofs sagged, barns returned to the earth at a glacial pace. In
some cases, whole hamlets seemed to be here one day and gone the
next when timber prices collapsed or every last bit of wealth had
been extracted from a mine.

I've gone searching for some of these places, because I'm
inclined that way, but also because ghost towns are testaments to

the spirit of the folks who once lived somewhere as much as to their dashed dreams. You marvel, head bowed before some gravestones out in the middle of nowhere, at the mettle of people who could make lives in such a place, even if just for a short time in the twentieth century. You stand on top of a cliff, staring down at a beach that seems inaccessible by man, but where sawmills, lumber camps and a large shipyard stood, and realize that Nova Scotia's pioneering ethos was as alive at the end of the Second World War as it was in the seventeenth century.

People by then were starting to pack their bags for Ontario and the Canadian West as well as the "Boston States." They were heading to the provincial capital, Halifax, where one-third of everyone in the province lived in mid-century and where, at a dance one night, Russell Demont, born and bred in Glace Bay, met Joan Briers, a coal miner's daughter from Sydney Mines, thereby ensuring my presence on this earth. When I go sifting through my old black-and-white pictures from this period—the start of the baby boom and the advent of many of the country's social welfare policies, when every Canadian suddenly could dream of a house, possibly in some new suburb—it is hard not to feel the giddy excitement of the people peering back. The woman who would be my mother in a group shot of the 1947–48 Sydney Mines High School Glee Club, in which the girls outnumber the war-decimated ranks of boys four to one. Joan Briers standing at the old car ferry, soon to be replaced by a causeway forevermore connecting Cape Breton to mainland Nova Scotia, perhaps returning home, or maybe leaving the island for good. Then there is Russ Demont, boater atop his head and cane clutched in his hands, performing a soft-shoe act at Acadia University, a tiny school in the Annapolis Valley, where, I believe, he became the first Demont ever to enter a college classroom. The same man in another picture, the ravages of TB no longer evident on his happy, healthy face, in front of what I'm assuming was the first automobile ever owned by a member of my clan. Clad in a white T-shirt, his foot on the guardrail on some elevated roadside, my father shields his eyes as he looks out. He could have been staring at a ship in the distance or an eagle circling in the sky, or maybe just a horizon of possibility bigger and broader than anything anyone in his family had ever seen before.

So much about Nova Scotia was different and so much the
same when the author returned in the late 1980s.

# Back Home

Midway around a dinky little curve, my bald all-weather tires lost purchase on the snowy highway. Mercifully, I had been creeping along, the ice-rucked waters of the Gulf of St. Lawrence on one side of the road, the deep, dark woods of Cape Breton on the other, the winter storm of the century, according to CBC Radio, bearing down on me. Already the snow was blowing horizontally, flaring past my windshield like the blur of planets when Han Solo snapped his starship into light speed. On the black ice, my car didn't so much skid as glide implacably towards the ditch and, beyond that, the second-growth evergreens, where I would never perhaps be heard of again. It still happened too fast for the essential irony to register. A few days earlier John Morris Rankin, the renowned fiddler and songwriter, the oldest member of the Rankin Family musical group from the tiny village of Mabou, had been driving his fifteen-year-old son and two friends north to a kids' hockey game in the Acadian village of Cheticamp. Not long before they came around the same bend, a municipal truck had dumped a pile of excess road salt. Rankin swerved his Toyota 4-Runner, but hit the mound of salt anyway, sending the car across the road and over an eighty-foot embankment into the water. His son and the other two boys escaped through one of the car windows. The father, at forty, was dead, probably killed by the impact.

"A fiddler dies on the way to a hockey game," said an editor in Toronto. "What could be more Nova Scotian than that?"

Newsroom gallows humour, but he had a point. Mabou, with its arbour and mountain meadows, its Gaelic street signs, its music that soared just as it did when Bonnie Prince Charlie marched through the Highlands of Scotland, seemed an otherworldly place in the first days of the twenty-first century. When I arrived, I found a village in mourning for a musician whose image, along with those of his siblings, were the first things you saw on the broad side of a building entering the town limits. Mabou had watched John Morris grow up. Playing the music of their forebears, he and his brother and sisters had sold millions of records, helped spark a continental renaissance in Celtic music, and, I suppose, put Mabou on the map.

"In John Morris, perhaps more than the other members of the group, the villagers seemed to glimpse something of themselves," I wrote in my *Maclean's* story about his death. "He, after all, was the shy Rankin who shunned the spotlight despite his virtuosity on the fiddle and piano. He was the one who stayed closest to the area's proud, three-hundred-year-old musical tradition. He was also the Rankin who came home, moving to nearby Judique when the group announced its amicable split."

I checked into an inn on the outskirts of town, but didn't even try to get into the Rankin family house, where John Morris's body lay in state, the mourners lined up two deep down the village's main road.

Instead I made for the Red Shoe Pub, my favourite watering hole in all of Nova Scotia, normally a raucous joint, but one where the atmosphere tonight resembled a wake. I hung around for a while, listening to a fiddler in a tie, dress shirt and suspenders and a piano player sporting coveralls play John Morris's tunes, but on so sombre a night, I couldn't bring myself to ask the usual journalistic questions about what a person's life had meant. When I'd seen and heard enough I trudged back to my inn through snowy streets beneath an illuminated white cross atop the village's Roman Catholic church, which stood on a hill above the village.

Around noon the next day I was inside St. Michael's church, up in the balcony with the other reporters, because there was no room in the pews below. I counted seventeen clergy at the front of the church. Tradition dictates that when a Cape Breton violinist dies, every fiddler who can make it shows up to play them into the next world. Instead of choir members, the rows in the sanctuary were filled with musicians carrying their instruments. Some had played before presidents and monarchs, others had never put bow to strings in a venue bigger than a village church, like this one, but they all greeted each other like family as they arrived.

I don't remember anything the clergymen said or even whether there was some kind of eulogy, such things requiring papal approval at a Catholic funeral. What I do recall is the way each of John Morris's siblings touched the polished wood of his casket as it was carried down the aisle of the church, and how the hearse drove slowly down the main street, past the general store with the sign in its front window that read, "Closed from 1 to 3 p.m. because of a death in the family." I can, if I listen hard, still hear the soaring notes of "The Glencoe March," the final tune at the funeral of any Cape Breton fiddler, which is enough to make me weep on the best of days and did its job in Mabou. It was written by Dan R. MacDonald, the Duke Ellington of Cape Breton Celtic music, who had a special connection to John Morris: in the closing shot of *The Vanishing Cape Breton Fiddler*, a CBC documentary credited with bringing the island's traditional music back from the dead, John Morris, then thirteen, and fat, four-eyed Dan R., with only three years to live, walk down a Mabou back road. When the older man places his paw on the young fiddler's shoulder, it's like a literal laying on of hands.

I was thinking about all of that—the sadness of a man gone too early, a place and a tribe on the Canadian margin that refuses to budge, a landscape that has shaped the people and upon which the people have shaped themselves—as I lined up in the church hall beside the long tables of triangular sandwiches, hearty Scottish oatcakes, the frosted squares, sugary enough to make a diner's teeth ache. A person doesn't have to believe in God to see the value of ritual in soothing grief. Inside the hall, the sorrow seemed somehow less raw. I stood around for a while, nodding at the few people I knew, watching the church-auxiliary ladies dispense strong tea, observing the formal way that even old friends greet each other on mournful occasions such as this. Then I walked outside and climbed into my rental car.

I had one last duty before trying to outrace the blizzard to Halifax: I wanted to see the place where John Morris died, because that is what reporters do. Clouds sped across the darkening sky as I made north up Route 19, the woods on either side of the road yawning and malevolent. Once there, I pulled over on the left side of the highway and walked across land rutted by wheels and human feet to the place where his car had gone over the cliff. I spread my legs wide against the wind, and stared down at the rocks and the water, black as a banker's heart, wishing that when my moment came it would happen in a gentler way than it had for John Morris. Back inside the car I cranked the heat all the way up. I snapped in a CD that I had purchased especially for this trip: *Fare Thee Well Love*, the Rankin Family's second recording. Then I turned it up as loud as I could stand and started singing.

As a nine-year-old I had a good enough voice to earn the lead in the Christmas concert at the only church that I have ever called home. My voice is a tuneless croak now, discordant enough to make the dog slink from the room. Through places with old-country names I sang anyway. Making up words when I didn't know the lyrics, I filled the car with noise to keep the dark and the sadness of the day at bay. As my car neared the lights of Mabou I was singing, as I was when my treadless, studless tires lost all traction. For all I know, I was singing still as my car listed into the drainage ditch, coming to a jolt-free rest at a forty-five-degree angle from which the world looked off-kilter, yet in no way alien.

Not much had changed in the seven years we had been away. Frozen bodies of young men were still being fished from the North Atlantic. Warships were still leaving Halifax Harbour to go to battle—in this case not against Hitler and Stalin, but in support of an American effort against a new despot named Saddam Hussein. We were still fighting to hold on to what we had, whether language (Gaelic) or culture (Acadian), the transfer payments from Ottawa which accounted for a disproportionate percentage of provincial revenues, or the sweet rural life, which more Nova Scotians enjoyed than anywhere else in Canada. As my wife and I returned after stints in Calgary and then Toronto it was impossible not to notice the young and ambitious heading in the other direction. Life seemed as good as we remembered in Halifax, where we rented a funny little yellow house amongst rambling old Georgian homes on a street where nurses, university students and government bureaucrats walked to and from work. When I got in a car and set out for places I'd never visited before, or at least not in a while, it was a different story. I suppose that it always has been.

After some early fits and starts, I had found something suitable for a man with wandering powers of concentration and Grade 11 math, who could not fix an engine, build a shelf that was flat or sell something that somebody wanted to buy. A short stint rewriting slow-pitch softball scores at the *Cape Breton Post* was followed by nine months learning the five Ws at the University of King's College and a gig as an all-round reporter at the Halifax paper. When I took a job in Calgary for a financial newspaper, it was because I wanted to learn my craft writing stories that I hadn't been hearing all of my life, but also because my wife and I had to go and try things somewhere else for a while, before we ended up here for good.

My title, when we did, was Halifax bureau chief for *Maclean's*, the country's national news magazine. It was a dream job—I held the phone away from my ear and yelled, "Fuck yessssss!" when the magazine's national editor called me at home to say the gig was mine— even if the bureau was just me, and I was supposed to write about all four Atlantic provinces. That meant a story every couple of months in New Brunswick and even less often in Prince Edward Island, with the population of Toronto's smallest boroughs. Newfoundland, because I was so smitten by it, I visited as often as the bureau budget could manage it. Mostly I stayed in Nova Scotia, a place where editors in Toronto had few preconceived notions about what needed to be covered, leaving me to write pretty much about what I wanted.

It was harder—way harder—than I thought it would be. It always is for any reporter who ever has to write about their home, particularly when it is a place they love, even if it is with a righteous indignation. I wanted Nova Scotia to match the vision I had of it when I lived thousands of miles away and made my daily bread writing about businessmen who wore suits that were worth more than the used Toyota Corolla we'd bought from a dodgy dealer in the Halifax suburbs. Back then, I used to literally dream of Nova Scotia, its mouldering sea-stink and incessant damp, its buildings hunched like a linebacker's shoulders against the elements, its people with their mishmash of enterprise, humanity and grit. My kind of people, I would tell myself, sitting across from a bond trader with a pinky ring in an eatery in Toronto's financial district. People who managed, who did what had to be done.

The first time I hit the road as a big-shot magazine writer in my home province, it was January and I was bound for a fishing village that boomed back when it had multiple plants to process cod and lobster and big ships docked there to take lumber and salt cod to the West Indies. Then, the fish that first brought John Cabot to these parts disappeared due to overfishing, the warming oceans and regulatory incompetence. Ottawa stepped in to save the big seafood companies from failure, but there was only so much a government could do.

Eventually, one of those big fishing concerns shuttered its only plant in Lockeport, where it was far and away the town's biggest employer. A woman named Patricia Ferguson, the first person I talked to in the town of eight hundred, was one of the 250 plant workers pink-slipped when the plant closed. At nineteen thousand dollars a year, she said it was no one's idea of a dream gig, but there wasn't much else in her town, where people started to hit the bottle, prescription drugs and, increasingly, each other as the money ran out. Ferguson, who was solid and straightforward, told me about how her marriage failed and how, after her ten weeks of severance pay came to an end, she sank into depression. Then, somehow, the funding materialized to open a community support centre. No one argued when she was hired to run it. Ferguson called herself a "former fish-plant worker who wanted to do her part," as I wrote those words down in a stenographer's notepad. On the way to the door a guy grabbed my arm and pulled me over to the side. He told me that around Lockeport they called Ferguson the "fairy godmother" for everything she did for people. I wrote that down too, as the curtain of winter night fell.

The economy was the story when I returned. It usually is in Nova Scotia, where the good times are just around the corner, a place that is always Tomorrowland. The latest new saviour had arrived: offshore energy. Before I was a reporter, a Nova Scotia premier once held a small vial of black sludge on the front page of the Halifax paper under a double-deck headline declaring, "It's Oil." The mid-'80s slump in petroleum prices took care of that. Instead, the cheapest natural gas on North America's entire eastern seaboard—trillions of cubic feet of it, in reservoirs beneath the shipwreck-filled waters near Sable Island, was going to create jobs and erase the province's mounting debt. Natural gas was going to make everything all right. The kids would come back. The hard times we knew so well would disappear forever.

Headed northeast from Halifax one day, I drove and drove until I could no longer find a station on my radio dial. A century earlier a man named Howard Richardson discovered gold in the place where I was headed, putting Goldboro on the white man's map. Production of that precious metal only continued for a couple of decades before things went back to being the way they mostly were there. I made the trip, on a day that was mild by Nova Scotia standards, because luck had struck again: the two-billion-dollar pipeline that would take the offshore natural gas to its customers in Nova Scotia, New Brunswick and New England needed to make land somewhere. Goldboro, with just three hundred residents but a mere two hundred miles from Sable Island, was the natural place not just for a processing plant, but for power-generating stations, petrochemical plants and all of the other spinoff businesses that attached like pilot fish to megaprojects of this sort.

The village worthies were understandably jazzed about the future, which for the first time in generations seemed bright indeed. The mood, I recall, was more subdued inside the five-table Venture Coffee Stop, even though the owner had named his business after the source of the area's hope for the future, the Venture natural gas field. "Let's face it," said Richie Burns, early fifties, a grey half-beard and backcombed hair. "We've been hearing the energy boom is coming for a long, long time."

Out in the borderlands I interviewed the latest generations of Nova Scotia families who had been making their living on the ocean for centuries. Now, with the cod gone and the federal government closing the fishery, it seemed like the gods had turned against them. It was iffy too in the mill, mine and plant towns where deindustrialization was picking up steam. One day in a lot at the end of a back road in Cape Breton, I parked my car in the afternoon sunlight, took a seat on the hood of my car and waited outside a coal mine for the men to come out.

"The last shift, when it comes sometime in the next couple of months, will likely end the way they always did in the Prince Colliery, in Point Aconi, N.S.," I later wrote in the magazine. "After eight hours the black-faced men will be bushed. Thank God that's over, some will think. But Cape Breton miners don't make it a habit of whining. They don't complain about the damp cold that penetrates arthritic joints, for the same reason they're willing to inhale the same coal dust that killed their fathers and grandfathers, and for the same reason they endure the possibility that at any moment a methane gas explosion could send a fireball streaking down the mine shaft; it goes with the job. As does having to grab a sandwich at the coalface for lunch. Or moving your bowels in the open in the pit, with a piece of newspaper or an empty bag as toilet paper."

As the last miners from Cape Breton's last underground coal mine walked out into the parking lot, I unfurled my notebook and walked towards them. I didn't know any of these pale, solemn men— the father of two who had spent twenty-five years underground, the fifth-generation miner whose grandfather, like mine, had emigrated from Lancashire, England, to try his luck in the Cape Breton pits, the quiet guy whose blue eyes told of the long journey a grandfather made here from Poland—but I took their pain personally. For nearly two hundred years coal had ruled these parts, bringing their people here just as it had mine. But the coal beneath the Cape Breton soil wasn't the right kind in these environmentally focused days; Ottawa was done with keeping the money-losing mines alive.

A little bit later I sat inside one of the old company homes, the kind, as the novelist Hugh MacLennan wrote, "crowded so close together they looked like a single downward-slanting building with a single downward-slanting roof." Billy Ludlow, his face pale and lined from a working life spent underground, his eyebrows teepeed with concern over his question mark of a future, can't have weighed much more than when he was a skinny nineteen-year-old going underground for the first time. His father died in the pit. Now here he was, a middle-aged man with a Grade 8 education, the achy joints of a pensioner and the kind of cough that does not speak to a long future. "When my grandchildren ask me what it was like in the pit, I'll say, 'Those were the good old days.' That's what I'll tell them," he said to me.

Eight years later I saw in the paper that he died. Ludlow was only fifty-five, by my reckoning. But going by the information in his obituary, the last day he left the Prince mine was the last day that William Ludlow—who enjoyed "playing darts, shooting pool, reading and most of all, spending time with his grandson"—collected a regular workingman's paycheque on this earth.

Nova Scotia wasn't one of those places that had been on a glorious roll and then fell on hard times, where people wandered around in once-fine clothes gone to seed, dazed by the dramatic turn of events. What prosperity we had experienced was mostly short-lived. In most of the last century and a half, struggle has been more the norm. So we pushed on, because that is what we did. In the last years of the twentieth century it seemed like everyone was making TV shows and movies in Nova Scotia, drawn here by the generous tax incentives that allowed the old port town of Shelburne to stand in for seventeenth-century New England in a forty-million-dollar adaptation of Hawthorne's *The Scarlet Letter* that scores a rousing 14 per cent on *Rotten Tomatoes*. We tried telephone call centres, because they'd worked in New Brunswick. Fishermen turned to whale watching and in some places began to wonder about growing fish in cages instead of going out and catching them in boats in the wintery North Atlantic. We just kept throwing stuff at the wall to see if something would stick.

Halifax was different. Big American magazines were raving about our homegrown music scene, our art college, our cool colonial buildings and even our interesting mix of humanity that now included hundreds of Buddhists who had followed their Tibetan leader here. Due to the slumping provincial economy, Halifax lost two thousand people during the first two years we were back. But when I stood on a street corner a block from my house one evening and watched Bill Clinton ogle a mom from the neighbourhood as he drove by on the way to an economic summit of the G-7 countries, I felt safe in writing this:

> Certainly, the Plains of Abraham contain all the drama, sadness and triumph of the national psyche. But in Halifax, with its 250 years of rollicking, myth-laden life, the past so overlays the present that history seems alive. "It had always looked like an old town," the novelist Hugh MacLennan once wrote about his hometown. "It had a genius for looking old and for acting as though nothing could possibly happen to surprise it."
>
> Well, maybe in 1941 when those words were written. But what would MacLennan think about Halifax today? Would he see the old garrison town to which Rudyard Kipling once gave the stodgy handle "Warden of the Honour of the North"? Or would he see a boisterous, good-time city of the moment—a place with an inspiring landscape, a distinct culture and a relaxed mindset, but humming with more edgy energy than it has in years?

I don't know if I actually interviewed anyone for that story or just transcribed my feelings, the viewpoint of someone who realized he was living at a charmed moment in his hometown's history. I do know that there was so much to write about in the late days of the last millennium. For long decades Nova Scotia had been governed by solid, savvy men named Macdonald, Stanfield and Smith—men who paved the province's highways, put in electrical transmission lines, improved the public schools and modernized the hospitals. Men who knew that deck was stacked against us from the moment Ottawa decided to protect the manufacturers of Ontario and Quebec and let our industries stagnate, but men who pushed on anyway, making incremental progress.

I returned to Nova Scotia at a time when rapscallions seemed to be in charge. From Calgary and Toronto, I watched the premiership of John Buchanan unfold, even if I met him for the first time in a hotel room in New Orleans, where I had gone to cover his speech before the world's biggest offshore energy conference. The word "avuncular" is habitually used to describe Buchanan, who was known back home for standing with his wife at a Halifax traffic roundabout after election victories, waving thank-yous to the passing cars. He made an immediate impression on me with his scholarly recall of my family's voting patterns—my dad and Uncle Earl were good Tories, Buchanan said approvingly, but my Liberal-supporting Uncle Eric, he said, shaking his head, "What, oh what, happened to Eric?"—and the impudent way he entered the prestigious energy show, clapping away to the skirl of bagpipes as the international oil men sat there as flat-faced as flounder.

But by 1991 Buchanan was on his way to Ottawa to sit in the Canadian senate after Prime Minister Brian Mulroney, desperate for help pushing through a controversial tax change, extricated him from one of those distinctly Maritime political scandals. This one had an accuser, who thought himself the reincarnation of St. Thomas Aquinas, and claimed that his bosses, doing the premier's bidding, had him institutionalized in a psychiatric clinic. In Buchanan's absence, a sweet-natured caretaker sat in the premier's chair speaking to the province in the cornpone malapropisms of a Down East

Yogi Berra. For a reporter, let alone the average Nova Scotian, it was hard to keep track of all the alleged skulduggery and the dramatis personae of party capos, influence peddlers and shakedown artists from all points on the political spectrum.

I doubt Nova Scotia was any different from any other jurisdiction in Canada then. This was how things got done in this time and place, even if the culture was starting to change. After the free-spending Buchanan years the province opted for an austere, teetotalling farmer named Donald Cameron as premier. A fiscal reformer who wanted to slash government spending, he also promised Nova Scotians a government free of patronage. I was in Cameron's riding when that dream died: May 9, 1992, the day an explosion erupted in the Westray coal mine in the village of Plymouth, trapping twenty-six men underground. Westray was my first big Nova Scotia story for *Maclean's.* In the months and years that followed I wrote a lot about the aftermath and political fallout of the twenty-six deaths. For a time, there was talk of jail for the chairman of the mine developer, but no charges were ever laid. The reputation of the premier, who had always denied that the mine received any special treatment by a Nova Scotia government, suffered too. When I went to see him in his Halifax office a year after the disaster, Cameron, a stony Pictou County Scot, was as unrepentant as ever. "I have never seen a tragedy exploited for political benefit the way this one has," he said, adding that in the end the people would decide who was to blame for the disaster—which they did, eleven months later, dumping Cameron and his Conservative Party.

I was there the night that happened, too: in the roomy ballroom of a Holiday Inn where the Liberals, giddy with anticipation after fifteen years in opposition, waited for their newly minted MLAs to arrive. The biggest cheers that night went to John Savage, a prickly

Welsh-born reformer from the left, who campaigned on his own promise to end all forms of patronage. Once in power, he did precisely that, eschewing the time-honoured practice of firing every card-carrying member of the Tory party from any government jobs and replacing them with Liberals. But Nova Scotia, it is often said, is full of people who are resolutely in favour of change—just as long as nothing changes. The anti-patronage stance went over badly. A bout of cutbacks in health care and education and a string of municipal amalgamations sparked a revolt within Savage's own party. When he resigned it marked the last time in my memory that a government dared to try to do anything truly bold in this province.

Some other things I noticed rambling around this place looking for news as the twentieth century gave way to the twenty-first. Not much had changed: the landscape was still magnificent, the villages still proud, the people, myself included, as tribal as ever. The folk from elsewhere still viewed us as colourful and quaint or as drags on the national economic engine. In many ways we didn't do much to change the narrative: it was still a man's world; whenever some national reporter brought up Africville, the marginalized black community that was allowed to endure in squalour on the outskirts of Halifax until the land was needed for development, we became again synonymous with backwoods racism. Everybody seemed to work for the bureaucracy, or a business that depended upon government, despite all the talk about becoming less reliant upon the public purse.

Yet "everything" had changed. The place sounded different. New accents could be heard amongst Halifax's merchants and developers, for so long a class dominated by pasty-faced men whose ancestors hailed from the damp of the British Isles. A new sound emanated from the musicians and singers who merged the new with the old, and the writers, part of a tradition now deep enough to include descendants of Scottish Highlanders but also outliers with black loyalist and Mi'kmaq blood, who told stories with themes that have been around since Homer.

It looked different too: golf courses dotted the open country, taking over long-vacant farmland. Traditional Nova Scotian homes—the old ship owners' residences or the newer places with perfectly weathered shingles and docks from which no fishing boat ever left—were now owned by summer vacationers, or other folks with no real connection to the local economy. The weft of the place was surely changing: more back-to-the-landers and big-city downshifters, Germans happy for a little elbow room, Americans searching for something more authentic than what they left behind. For those from here, Nova Scotia's pull seemed strong as ever. The economic exigencies of the province meant that people had to leave, but when they did they pined to return. Or, because they couldn't bear to leave for good, they settled for some kind of shadow life, shuttling back and forth between work in Alberta's tar sands and a life and family in some Nova Scotian village. Or they just stayed put, in towns and villages where the land had shaped them, like pebbles worn smooth by the tide and deposited on a beach.

Death still came to a person from funny angles here: underground and out on the ocean, even from the sky. I swear that I have never approached a scene as grim as the grey, primordial rocks of the iconic tourist destination of Peggy's Cove, under a rainy, graphite-coloured sky with the lights of the television vans casting shadows on cloud so low and thick it seemed like nothing got out or in. Out on the water, rescue crews searched vainly for survivors from among the 229 passengers and crew members of Swissair Flight 111, which left New

York one September day bound for Geneva but instead plunged into the waters of St. Margaret's Bay. I had arrived the night before from Ottawa, where I'd been moved by my magazine. But this was Westray all over again: the eternal waiting, the awful official updates, the terrible sight of the family members clinging to each other as they mourned their losses.

I noticed as I wandered around that people in Nova Scotia would still talk to anybody. So I talked to gas station attendants, who often did other things like tend the ice at the local curling rink, and waitresses in diners, whom I made a point of calling by their first name whenever it appeared on a badge on their chest. I walked up to the doors of people I had never seen before and, chances were, would never see again, and found myself still there forty-five minutes later, sleepy from the tea and cookies and the cranked-up parlour thermostats. I talked to a blacksmith who forged odd iron contraptions and then pounded them until they made strange, scary noises, men who had given up everything to move here in search for Captain Kidd's treasure, and a gentle fellow with thighs as big as my waist who had devoted his life to becoming the world's strongest man. I stepped into funny little museums that didn't seem to have had a visitor in weeks, crammed some money in the donations boxes and talked to the people on duty, surrounded by old pictures of men and women with faces creased by time and sorrow.

With notebook or tape recorder in hand, I talked to moonshiners in the backwoods and a really rich guy who had erected an expensive golf course where U.S. presidents liked to play, next to the little community where he grew up poor as a church mouse, and an actor, once a star at the Stratford Festival, who now took money in a booth at a Halifax parking lot. One of the last men to work in a Nova Scotia lighthouse told me his story. So did a pre-teen with a voice like an angel who dreamt of stardom at the Grand Ole Opry and a black Baptist pastor who felt he had been put on this earth to preach at the very church, founded by freed black slaves, where he granted me an audience.

One day, in a Halifax apartment building that was mostly home to senior citizens and university students, I went to talk to a man who had never made much money or had much luck. Donald Marshall Jr. was just seventeen, a tough, street-smart punk living in Membertou, the Mi'kmaq first nation located inside the Sydney town limits, who happened to be in a local park one night in 1971 when a black teen was stabbed to death. Marshall did eleven years of hard time before being cleared of the murder. The anger over the miscarriage of justice—a white drunk with a fetish for knives was eventually convicted for the death, but served just a year in jail—along with the pitiful financial compensation he received was written all over Marshall's face when I saw him sipping draught beer in a dingy watering hole across from the *Chronicle Herald*. I hope he took some solace with one thing: the Royal Commission into his wrongful conviction helped clean out the rot in Nova Scotia's criminal justice system.

Junior, as he was known, fell out of the public eye after that. Then he got caught fishing for eels without a licence. When the Supreme Court of Canada upheld a centuries-old treaty between the Mi'kmaq and the British Crown in acquitting Marshall of the charges, First Nations people throughout the region rejoiced. When I went to see him, Marshall wasn't quite fifty, his hair thin, his clothes flapping loosely over his once-fearsome frame. A few years away from a double lung transplant for the respiratory disease that would take his life, he looked worn out by his eventful life. "I'm just a normal guy," he insisted. But he kept his door open as we chatted. He didn't park his car in the underground parking lot, either. Marshall had spent too much time indoors, surrounded by four walls. Now all the man who was one of the greatest Nova Scotians of my generation desired was room to breathe and to know that he could come and go as he wanted.

On another day, this one in winter and bitterly cold, I sat in a chauffeur-driven Mercedes-Benz beside a rich man who seemed to long for the days when his name still mattered around here. He lived in the Carlyle, the condo on the site of the old Dennis compound, which was only blocks from Marshall's apartment. On the way downtown his driver spun past Camp Hill Cemetery, where Joe Howe was buried and where this book began. At the Halifax Club, the city's sleepy old bastion of male privilege, a waiter set a dry martini in front of my host as soon as we sat down. We talked about all kinds of things over lunch that day. Afterwards, he told the driver to take the long way home. Which is how we came to park, motor running, facing the harbour and an island in the middle of it, which had been home to Mi'kmaq shell middens, English fortresses and Victorian gardens.

My host had lived there for a while. He was just a kid in 1917 when the *Imo* and the *Mont Blanc* collided in the harbour, triggering the biggest manmade explosion the world had ever seen. But what I remember, what I will never forget, is how this old man, who was now completely blind, still recalled the wreckage he saw from McNabs Island, looking back towards Halifax. The smoke was billowing way back then—as, unbeknownst to him, it was today, the air being colder than the water. For all this man who had not seen a tree or a flower in a very long time knew, the flames from the Halifax Explosion were out there still, rising into the sky.

———

Another day around that time I sat in a farmhouse atop a bare hill in Grand Etang, a little Cape Breton hamlet settled by Acadians after they returned from their years of wandering. I was talking to an oldtimer named Elie-Joe Chiasson, who was telling me about *les suêtes*, the vicious winds that terrorize that French-speaking stretch of Cape Breton between Margaree Harbour and Bay St. Lawrence. When those winds come roaring down from the highlands they wreck homes, trash fishing boats, lift buildings off their moorings, and flatten trees and telephone poles. Over the years, *suêtes* had smashed Chiasson's windows and destroyed the insides of his fourth-generation farmhouse. Once, he told me, his heating-oil tank just disappeared in a bad wind, presumably blown into the Atlantic. Another time, when the winds topped 120 miles an hour, he had to crawl along the ground in the hope of reaching his barn. When a particularly strong gust hit, Elie-Joe grabbed for a fence post. He just kept holding on as his body was lifted off the ground, blown horizontal by winds that began somewhere on the Atlantic and might not sputter to a stop until they hit Anticosti Island.

On bad days, that seemed to be how it was for us here in Nova Scotia. We were all, I feared, like old Elie-Joe, hanging on, buffeted by things beyond our control: geography, lack of political clout, the big forces of global economics, just plain bad luck. Hard as we tried, nothing much changed. The old patterns—anticipation fol-lowed by disappointment, new groups of immigrants trying their luck, the perpetual exodus, the inevitable rural-urban divide—just keep repeating themselves. Perhaps because change wasn't really what was wanted in a place that so treasures the past. Possibly because most of the big events in Nova Scotia's story, like the sto-ries of most every other places in the developed world, have by now been largely written.

Within the slipstream of that greater narrative, smaller stories were being written. Kids were born, houses bought, jobs came and went. When I rejoined the *Chronicle Herald*—after *Maclean's*, no longer feeling the economic imperative to employ an Atlantic Canadian correspondent, closed the bureau—things looked as bedevilling as ever: in the two decades since we moved back from Toronto, Nova Scotia possessed the worst-performing economy in the country. More than ever before there were two Nova Scotias: prosperous Halifax and everywhere else. Around the edges things seemed to be fraying. The young everywhere, our kids included, wondered whether they had a future here, as they wondered the same thing in any small place in this increasingly centralized world.

It was something I thought and wrote a lot about. I thought about it for sure one summer day, sunset approaching, as I prepared to wade out up to my knees in a Cape Breton river where generations of Demonts had swum and cast for trout. There wasn't the hint of a breeze as I deposited my mother's and father's ashes, which had been standing for a long time on a shelf in my house in Halifax, into the water. At first, the grey dust just floated there, on the surface. After a couple of minutes what was left of Russell and Joan Demont slowly converged, as had their lives and the long narratives of their two families, in this unlikely place that they never lost faith in.

Another day, I went for a drive in the countryside, far from the Mira River. I hadn't read a word he had written in a long time, but that didn't mean Joe Howe was ever really far from my mind. I used to imagine his horse clip-clopping into a clearing as I stood on a hill, looking down on some town that was probably on the rise in his day. I see him slapping the front of his jacket after dismounting so that the dust from his travels floated upwards, and then running a hand through his finger-in-the-light-socket hair. Howe would have had no qualms about offering a hand, fingers ink-stained from the previous night's writing, to a stranger and then just seeing where the conversation went. There would be no awkward pauses with a man willing to debate for eight straight hours if the subject interested him. He would have spoken, as he usually did, in speeches, beginning slowly by making some reference to local history or tradition, about which his knowledge seemed inexhaustible, and then subtly elevating the discussion to some loftier plane.

As he did in the very first address before the Halifax Mechanics' Institute, he might have given voice to his dream: that in time "the contrast between Nova Scotia and her neighbors will be less striking; the evidences of their superiority less disheartening and distinct." He might have expressed his firm belief that if every Nova Scotian worked together, this province "shall be a synonym for high mental and moral cultivation," that the sound of its name "in a Briton's ears shall be followed by the reflection that the good seed which he had sowed had fallen upon genial soil" and that an American casting his eye over the map of this mighty continent "shall recognize in the little peninsula jutting out upon the bosom of the Atlantic, the home of a race superior to many and second to none of the countless tribes by whose gigantic territories they are embraced."

In this scene I imagine, Howe would have stood there, knowing full well that what he had hoped for in 1834, when Nova Scotia was still in what he called "the infant hour," hadn't come to pass. There were sad places to see as I wandered around as his surrogate, along with scenes that I would never in a hundred years understand. Yet poems also unfolded, right there before my very eyes. Like a man who probably wouldn't get this chance again, I looked hard at the people I saw as I travelled: the horny-handed men and women working close to the land; the politicians with hope in their hearts; the effervescent small-town merchants; the young men lingering at the service station way out in the country; the old woman, hair as immovable as porcelain, walking out to the road to get her paper from the mail box in the place where she had lived her entire life. My admiration is deep for them, as it is for the Acadians fighting for cultural survival, the Mi'kmaq and black people just battling for a chance, the pasty-faced Celts, like myself, who have also hung in, making this place what it is.

Sometimes people from away, usually free-marketers who like to look at things as lines in a balance sheet, ask me what the future is for Nova Scotia. The truth is that after all of this reading and travelling and interviewing, I don't know whether we will find some fresh way forward, or whether the new story will be a lot like the old. History has never been particularly good to this place, where the defining myths and stories are mostly about loss, fortitude and sheer determination. But something good has come out of that, for as a people our spirits have been hardened by our times, but our hearts have not. There's a Madame La Tour-ness to the place, a Junior Marshall grit. We're a Dan R. fiddle tune, heard over a car radio, heading down a stretch of lonely midnight road. We're still here. We're ready for a tomorrow that might be worse than today; we will deal with that when we get there, I tell the people from elsewhere, as we somehow always have.

Sometimes when I travelled around this province it seemed like I could hear some voice from long ago, calling from the dark, telling me these things. At least so it has always seemed to me, someone more comfortable journeying into the past than the future. I never felt alone on this trip, because ghosts and memories have always haunted the pathways that I have walked. I know what you mean, Howe would reply. I hear them too, I see him saying, then, with a flick of the reins, easing his horse back into the woods, from where he came.

The pull of Nova Scotia has always been strong for the
author, pictured here with his mother and brother as they
look out on it from the Prince Edward Island Ferry.

# Epilogue

I haven't gone far in life. I live across the street from an elementary school where I was an underperforming student, a couple of blocks from the field where I played touch football with friends who are now dead, a few minutes away from the house where I kissed a girl for the very first time. When I was a young boy, before I really knew anything about Nova Scotia, its story and my people's place in it, I used to like to wander around, much as I do today. Even then, I had a sense that my small bit of this small city had multiple worlds and that I had company as I travelled. I've felt this way as long as I remember, even though, after all this time, I still struggle to explain what exactly I feel, let alone why. I can recall, for example, a winter back in the days when the snowdrifts seemed so much higher than they are now—even though I know that wasn't the case—I guess because we were so small. After supper some accomplices and I would crawl into a partially built house blocks from my house on the wonderfully named Bliss Street. We didn't do much in there, just hammered a few nails and stole the occasional piece of lumber to reinforce the boards in a backyard hockey rink. When I walk by the house that stands there now—two storeys high, brick below and wood above, often with a gleaming white Mercedes-Benz in the driveway—it is enough to know that here once stood Sam Wah's laundry, started by Ngoon Lee, who arrived in Halifax after paying the five-hundred-dollar head tax to immigrate from China. Before that a boat shed stood on the same land. Before that there wasn't enough on Bliss Street to even warrant it being called a street.

If the child I was then could have just walked backwards in time, I would have seen tramcars and the first automobiles rattling by. Had the decades continued to dissolve around me, fine gentlemen and ladies would have sauntered past, and then soldiers from various wars and bowlegged mariners on muddy roadways. If I had then walked across one of those avenues into Camp Hill Cemetery, where the ghosts spoke to me, and just kept walking, on adolescent legs, I eventually could have climbed the hill, with the commanding view of the harbour that a century earlier had been chosen to fortify the new city. From there I would have seen the old buildings—the sinful Waterloo Tavern, the legislature where Howe held court, Enos Collins's counting houses—today barely detectable amid the glass and concrete.

When the first of my people laid the bricks for the fortress, Halifax was a few hundred ramshackle houses where newcomers coughed, spat and shivered against the New World damp as the coals in their fireplaces glowed red-hot with hope. Before that, if I kept travelling along those pathways on which time seems to double back on itself, it was only the First Peoples there, the ones who called the area Jipugtug, which was anglicized as Chebucto, meaning "largest port."

Evidence points to them summering on the shores of the basin in the interior of the harbour before heading inland when the harsh Atlantic winter set in. But Mi'kmaq lived and died all throughout the mainland in those parts, long before the tall buildings rose like canyons around the harbour and the city lights spread until they were visible from a jet plane thirty thousand feet up in the sky. In those days, the time-travelling me would have seen how the land rolled over the hills and plateaued down to the water in sheets of forest that Edward Cornwallis, upon viewing the terrain for the first time, declared "one continual wood" with "no clear spot to be heard of." In those days, before the wilderness was known to the Europeans, the First Peoples made their way among woods that were black, red and white spruce, sugar maple, eastern hemlock, balsam fir, tamarack and white pine.

Through birch, beach and red oak I would walk and climb as they did. Looking high overhead I would see gulls wheeling and yellow-eyed osprey preparing to dive. Eventually, if I heard a noise, it could only be a deer, or even a moose or bear crashing through the woods. No one knows exactly when, but at some point there wasn't the sound or sight of man anywhere in this province. I would be alone then, on land that is perpetually a work in progress, forever being carved by the ocean and reconfigured by the winds.

# Notes on Sources

PROLOGUE: Up in the Old Cemetery

Biographical information on Howe, generally speaking, comes from
J. Murray Beck, *Joseph Howe: Volume 1, Conservative Reformer, 1804–1848*,
(Montreal and Kingston, ON: McGill-Queen's University Press, 1982)
and D.C. Harvey, *The Heart of Howe: Selections from the Letters and
Speeches of Joseph Howe* (Toronto: Oxford University Press, 1939).

5      *His hair—which one historian*   Thomas H. Raddall, *Halifax:
       Warden of the North* (Toronto: McClelland & Stewart, 1974), 170.

6      *"when his face glowed with the inspiration . . ."*   Beck, *Joseph
       Howe*, 17.

6      *plunge into the harbour for a starlit swim*   Raddall, *Halifax:
       Warden of the North*, 170.

6      *a "restless, agitating uncertainty"*   This description comes from
       *Joseph Howe: Voice of Nova Scotia*, ed. and with an introduction
       by J. Murray Beck (Toronto: McClelland & Stewart, 1964), 7.

7      *His very words about the journalist's trade*   Howe's words come
       from his libel defence, the text of which can be viewed on the
       Nova Scotia legislature's website: http://nslegislature.ca/index
       .php/about/joe-howe/howedefense.

8      *The old Demont hacienda*   My family spells its surname several
       different ways. I stick with the capital M.

9        *"the Birmingham of the Country"*    This quote is found in
         T.W. Acheson, "The National Policy and the Industrialization of the
         Maritimes, 1890–1910," *Acadiensis* 1, no. 2 (Spring 1972): 20–21.

10       *The Mi'kmaq have an old story*    The migration of humans
         to what would become North America comes from Harold
         Franklin McGee Jr., "Mi'kmaq," *The Canadian Encyclopedia,*
         http://www.thecanadianencyclopedia.ca/en/article/micmac
         -mikmaq/. The Mi'kmaq legend is retold by Stephen Augustine—
         based on a version originally by Silas Rand found in *Legends of*
         *the Micmacs (London: Longmans, Green,* 1894)—on the website
         of the Canadian Museum of History in "Arrival of Strangers:
         The Last 500 Years," *Civilization.ca*, http://www.history
         museum.ca/cmc/exhibitions/aborig/fp/fpz4inte.shtml.

12       *Time, my twin, take me*    Ilya Kaminsky, "Praise," in *Dancing*
         *in Odessa* (Dorset, VT: Tupelo Press, 2004).

ONE: **Creation Song**

Biographical information about Champlain and Port Royal, and the
information about Pierre du Bosc-Douyn, comes from David Hackett
Fischer, *Champlain's Dream* (Simon & Schuster, 2009). The description of
the rituals and appearances of the members of the Order of Good Cheer
comes from Marc Lescarbot, *Nova Francia: A Description of Acadia,*
*1606* (London: RoutledgeCurzon, 2005), 118–19. Some biographical
information about Poutrincourt comes from page 7 of the same volume.

Information about Lescarbot, including the quote about "his desire
to flee a corrupt world," comes from the introduction, on page 10.

18       *"My shirts are all torn"*    Henri IV's lament can be found on the
         CBC's *Canada: A People's History* website at http://www.cbc.ca
         /history/EPCONTENTSE1EP2CH4LE.html.

20      *to whom the king had granted a charter*   The original
        charter granted to de Mons can be found on the website
        of the Avalon Project of Yale Law School's Lillian Goldman
        Law Library at http://avalon.law.yale.edu/17th_century
        /charter_001.asp.

22      *Cabot left Bristol in the spring*   "John Cabot: Biography,"
        *Bio*, http://www.biography.com/people/john-cabot-9234057
        #north-american-voyages.

24      *a Basque whaler he encountered*   The information on Savalette,
        the adventurous Basque fishing captain, comes from Appendix B
        of Henry David Thoreau's 1865 book, *Cape Cod*, available online
        at http://thoreau.eserver.org/capecdoo.html.

24      *a Portuguese explorer*   James H. Marsh, "Joao Alvares
        Fagundes," *The Canadian Encyclopedia*, http://www.thecanadian
        encyclopedia.ca/en/article/joao-alvares-fagundes/.

27      *Before long the scurvy set in*   Champlain's account of the
        scurvy outbreak at the St. Croix settlement is found on Parks
        Canada's website on a page called "Champlain's Description
        of Scurvy" at http://www.pc.gc.ca/eng/lhn-nhs/nb/stcroix/natcul
        /natcul8.aspx.

29      *a new governor, Poutrincourt*   "Jean de Biencourt de
        Poutrincourt et de Saint-Juste," *Dictionary of Canadian
        Biography*, http://www.biographi.ca/en/bio/biencourt_de
        _poutrincourt_et_de_saint_just_jean_de_1E.html.

30      *Staged completely on water*   Information about the first play
        comes from René Baudry's entry on Lescarbot for the *Dictionary
        of Canadian Biography*, found at http://www.biographi.ca/en
        /bio/lescarbot_marc_1E.html, and Martin Banham, *The
        Cambridge Guide to Theatre* (Cambridge, UK: Cambridge
        University Press, 1995), 641.

31    *an English ship approached a shaloop*    John A. Poor and
      Laura Elizabeth Poor, *The First International Railway and
      the Colonization of New England: Life and Writings of John
      Alfred Poor* (New York: G.P. Putnam's Sons, 1892), 303.

31    *"as thickly planted there"*    Paul Chiasson, *The Island of Seven
      Cities: Where the Chinese Settled When They Discovered
      America* (Toronto: Random House, 2010).

31    *The Mi'kmaq they met moved around*    The information about
      the Mi'kmaq comes from a variety of sources, including: the
      Nova Scotia Museum; Daniel Paul, *We Were Not the Savages:
      A Mi'kmaq Perspective on the Collision Between European and
      Native American Civilizations* (Halifax: Fernwood, 2000);
      Geoffrey Plank, *An Unsettled Conquest: The British Campaign
      Against the Peoples of Acadia* (Philadelphia: University of
      Pennsylvania Press, 2003); and *The Canadian Encyclopedia*.

32    *Lescarbot's view that the First Peoples*    William A. Haviland,
      *Canoe Indians of Down East Maine* (Charleston, SC: History
      Press), 120.

32    *Their wide-bottomed birchbark canoes*    Some of the informa-
      tion about the Mi'kmaq canoes comes from Alan McMillan and
      Eldon Yellowhorn, *First Peoples in Canada* (Vancouver: Douglas
      & McIntyre, 2004), 59, and the author's email exchange with
      Roger Lewis, ethnology curator of the Nova Scotia Museum.

33    *Glooscap, a giant warrior hero*    The legend of Glooscap comes
      from a variety of sources, including the Mi'kmaq Spirit website
      (http://www.muiniskw.org/).

34    *Like many Aboriginal nations*    The information about Mi'kmaq
      spirituality comes from Cape Breton University's *Mi'kmaq
      Resource Guide* (http://www.cbu.ca/indigenous-affairs/unamaki
      -college/mikmaq-resource-centre/mikmaq-resource-guide/).

35    *"The greatest, most renowned"*    The description of Membertou
is from a letter written by Father Pierre Biard, in H.F. McGee,
*Native Peoples of Atlantic Canada: A History of Indian–
European Relations* (Montreal and Kingston, ON: McGill-
Queen's University Press, 1974), 26 and 27. Biographical
information on Membertou comes from Lucien Campeau,
"Membertou," *Dictionary of Canadian Biography*,
http://www.biographi.ca/en/bio/membertou_1E.html.

36    *He had lost his trade monopoly*    Lescarbot, *Nova Francia*,
125–127.

37    *when a grudging Biencourt*    From Jean de Biencourt de
Poutrincourt's *Dictionary of Canadian Biography* entry and
the article "Port-Royal National Historic Site of Canada"
on the Parks Canada website at http://www.pc.gc.ca/eng
/lhn-nhs/ns/portroyal/natcul/histor/Hard%20Times.aspx.

37    *Captain Samuel Argall, recently appointed admiral.* Argall's
biographic info comes from W. Austin Squires, "Sir Samuel
Argall (Argoll)," *Dictionary of Canadian Biography*,
http://www.biographi.ca/en/bio/argall_samuel_1E.html.

37    *what happened next is conjecture* The controversy about
whether or not Father Biard led Argall to Port Royal is referred
to in George Folsom, *Collections of the New-York Historical
Society, Volume 1: Second Series* (New York: H. Ludwig,
1841), 341.

TWO: **Ruins**

41    *My atlas of Nova Scotia*    The atlas I refer to is Nova Scotia
Surveys and Mapping Division, *A Map of the Province of
Nova Scotia* (Halifax: Formac, 1992).

41    *Mi'kmaq referred to the place*    The Mi'kmaq place names
come from the Ta'n Weji-sqalia'tiek Mi'kmaw Place
Names Digital Atlas and Website Project, viewable at
http://mikmawplacenames.ca.

43    *Howe skipped it altogether on his rambles*    The quotes and
information about Howe's rambles come from *Western and
Eastern Rambles: Travel Sketches of Nova Scotia: Joseph Howe*,
ed. M.G. Parks (Toronto: University of Toronto Press, 1973).

43    *one, true, real location*    The attempt to get to the bottom of the
actual location of Charles La Tour's fort comes from Father
Clarence d'Entremont, "Fort Saint Louis," *Yarmouth Vanguard*,
October 24, 1989; Henri Leander d'Entremont, *The Baronnie de
Pombcoup and the Acadians: A History of the Ancient "Department
of Cape Sable," Now Known as Yarmouth and Shelburne Counties,
Nova Scotia* (Yarmouth, NS: Herald-Telegram Press, 1931), 82;
Henri Leander d'Entremont, *The Forts of Cape Sable of the
Seventeenth Century* (Centre East Pubnico, NS: R.H. Davis &
Co., 1938).

45    *When William the Conqueror's claim*    My information on the old-
time French-English animus comes from a variety of sources,
including the Biography.com entry on William the Conqueror at
http://www.biography.com/people/william-the-conqueror-9542227.

46    *each resented the claims of each other*    Francis Parkman and
David Levin, *France and England in North America* (New York:
Library of America, 1983), 1071.

46    *roving existence like "people of the country"*    John Mack
Faragher, *A Great and Noble Scheme: The Tragic Story of the
Expulsion of the French Acadians from Their American
Homeland* (W.W. Norton, 2005), 38. The early information about
Charles La Tour and his father, Claude, comes from "Charles de

Saint-Étienne de La Tour," *Dictionary of Canadian Biography*, http://www.biographi.ca/en/bio/saint_etienne_de_la_tour _charles_de_1593_1666_1E.html.

47   *We cherish the crumbling barn*  The quote comes from the introduction to Rose Macaulay, *Pleasure of Ruins* (New York: Thames and Hudson, 1964).

49   *Sir William Alexander of Menstrie*  The biographical information on Sir William Alexander the Elder is from "William Alexander, 1st Earl of Stirling," *Encyclopaedia Britannica*, https://www.britannica.com/biography/William-Alexander-1st -Earl-of-Stirling, and "William Alexander, Earl of Stirling," *Dictionary of Canadian Biography*, where the quote about his dreams of making a name for himself is found—as well as *The Biographical Dictionary of the Society for the Diffusion of Useful Knowledge, Volume 2, Part 1* (London: Longman, Brown, Green and Longmans, 1843).

50   *a forty-seven page pamphlet*  Alexander's work of propaganda, *An Encouragement to Colonies*, can be glimpsed at https://archive .org/stream/cihm_13904

51   *new species of nobleman*  Information about the knights baronet of Nova Scotia comes from "A Short History," *The Standing Council of the Baronetage*, http://www.baronetage. org/a-short-history/.

52   *In his 1673 book*  Nicholas Denys's description of the meeting of Claude and Charles La Tour is found in his book *The Description and Natural History of the Coasts of North America (Acadia)*, trans. and ed. William F. Ganong (Toronto: Champlain Society, 1908).

54   *at eighteen a knight*  Biographical information on Isaac de Razilly, Charles d'Aulnay and Françoise-Marie Jacquelin can be

found in their respective entries in the *Dictionary of Canadian Biography*, available online at http://www.biographi.ca/en/bio /razilly_isaac_de_1E.html, http://www.biographi.ca/en/bio /menou_d_aulnay_charles_de_1E.html and http://www.biographi. ca/en/bio/jacquelin_francoise_marie_1E.html, respectively.

56     *no more than sixty nautical miles apart*   My main source on the great rivalry between La Tour and d'Aulnay is M.A. MacDonald, *Fortune & La Tour: The Civil War in Acadia* (Nimbus, 2000). Also N.E.S. Griffiths, *From Migrant to Acadian: A North American Border People, 1604–1755* (Montreal and Kingston, ON: McGill-Queen's University Press, 2014).

THREE: **Scheen of Sorrow**

My main sources on the historic backdrop to the expulsion of the Acadians were: Naomi E.S. Griffiths, *From Migrant to Acadian: A North American Border People, 1604–1755* (Moncton, NB: Canadian Research Institute for Public Policy and Public Administration, 2005); Plank, *An Unsettled Conquest*; and Dean W. Jobb, *The Cajuns: A People's Story of Exile and Triumph* (New York: Wiley, 2005).

69     *some 250,000 English settlers*   My figure on the number of English in North America comes from *North America: The Historical Geography of a Changing Continent*, ed. Thomas F. McIlwraith and Edward K. Muller (Lanham, MD: Rowman & Littlefield, 2001), 98. The figures on the French population of the continent at that point come from Statistics Canada, "Early French Settlements (1605 to 1691)," http://www.statcan.gc.ca /pub/98-187-x/4064812-eng.htm.

70     *larger-than-life men like Pierre Maisonnat*   Information on Maisonnat and Broussard comes from their entries in the

*Dictionary of Canadian Biography*, at http://www.biographi.ca
/en/bio/maisonnat_pierre_2E.html and http://www.biographi.ca
/en/bio/brossard_joseph_3E.html. The Broussard–Beyoncé connection was noted in Megan Smolenyak, "A Peek into Blue Ivy
Carter's Past," *Huffington Post*, January 12, 2012 (updated
March 13, 2012).

71    *the Deerfield Massacre in Massachusetts*   "The Deerfield Raid,"
*The Canadian Encyclopedia*, http://www.thecanadianencyclopedia
.ca/en/article/the-deerfield-raid-feature/.

71    *Naomi Griffiths has calculated*   Griffiths, *From Migrant to
Acadian*, 162.

71    *Nicholson and some Mohawk and Iroquois chiefs*   Donald A.
Grinde and Bruce Elliott Johansen, *Exemplar of Liberty: Native
America and the Evolution of Democracy* (Los Angeles:
American Indian Studies Center, 1991).

72    *a fleet of five warships*   The 1710 siege of Port Royal is detailed in
Harold Horwood, *Plunder and Pillage: Atlantic Canada's Brutal and
Bloodthirsty Pirates and Privateers* (Halifax: Formac, 2011), 68.

74    *Like most things I know about them*   The information about
the Acadian habits and character comes from a variety of sources,
including: Plank, *An Unsettled Conquest*, mainly on pages 23
and 24; Gisa I. Hynes, "Some Aspects of the Demography of
Port Royal, 1650–1755," *Acadiensis* 3, no. 1 (August 1973);
"Acadian Society," *Canada: A Country by Consent*,
http://www.canadahistoryproject.ca/1755/1755-03-acadian
-society.html; and the *Acadian Genealogy Homepage: Life
in Acadia Before the Deportation*, https://www.acadian.org
/acadlife.html.

75    *Their relationships with the First Peoples*   Information about
the relationship between the Acadians and Mi'kmaq comes from

Mi'kmaq historian Dan Paul's writings on the subject, which can be seen online at http://www.danielnpaul.com/Col/1997 /Mi'kmaqAcadianRelationship-Respectful.html

77     *The census of 1671*   The number of Acadian surnames comes from the Acadian-Cajun Genealogy and History website, viewable at http://www.acadian-cajun.com/genac5.htm.

77     *"One sees no drunkenness"*   This nice quote about the Acadians comes from the Acadian Genealogy Homepage. The less flattering quotes are from "Population Growth Becomes a Worry to the British," *Les Doucet du Monde* (the Doucet Family website), http://www.doucetfamily.org/heritage/Growth.htm.

77     *earthen, sod-covered dykes*   The explanation of how the Acadian dykes worked is from Nova Scotia Department of Agriculture and Marketing, *Maritime Dykelands: The 350-Year Struggle* (Halifax: Province of Nova Scotia, 1987).

78     *"those who reclaim land from the sea"* A.J.B. Johnston, "*Défricheurs d'eau:* An Introduction to Acadian Land Reclamation in a Comparative Context," *Material Culture Review*, https://journals.lib.unb.ca/index.php/MCR/article /view/18101/19438.

78     *"make you sigh for the possession"*   Howe's line about the dyke lands comes from Howe, *Western and Eastern Rambles*, 76.

78     *a reviewer of one of her books noted*   Sheila Andrew, "Exploring the Acadian Identity: A Review of Naomi Griffiths' *From Migrant to Acadian,*" *Acadiensis* 35, no. 1 (Autumn 2005).

79     *Louisbourg would in the 1720s*   Louisbourg's importance is noted in Francis Parkman, *Montcalm and Wolf: France and England in North America* (Boston: Little, Brown, 1916).

79     *"If France were to lose this island . . ."*   The quote from Louisbourg's governor is found in Lesley Choyce, *Nova Scotia*

*Shaped by the Sea: A Living History* (Toronto: Viking, 1996), 62.

80  *In May of 1745 four British ships*   The information about the siege of Louisbourg—plus the quote about the impact of its fall on American morale—is from Luther C. Leavitt, "The Siege of Louisbourg," *The Order of the Founders and Patriots of America*, http://www.founderspatriots.org/articles/louisbourg.php.

81  *severed heads impaled on spikes*   Plank, *An Unsettled Conquest*, 78.

81  *Chebucto, where a humble English stockade*   Information about the founding of Halifax comes from Raddall, *Halifax: Warden of the North*, 17–20.

82  *the liberal daily grog ration*   C.W. Jefferys, "The Founding of Halifax," in *Dramatic Episodes in Canada's Story* (Toronto: Ryerson Press, 1930).

83  *Four times, the Mi'kmaq raided Halifax*   The information about the Mi'kmaq raids and the British retaliation comes from Jon Tattrie, *Cornwallis: The Violent Birth of Halifax* (East Lawrencetown, NS: Pottersfield Press, 2013).

84  *more than a century ago a poet*   The information about the Grand-Pré reclamation comes from a variety of sources, including Gwendolyn Davies, "John Frederic Herbin," *Dictionary of Canadian Biography*, http://www.biographi.ca/en/bio/herbin _john_frederic_15E.html.

84  *Their population had swelled to just under fifteen thousand*   The population figures from the early eighteenth century came from Plank, *An Unsettled Conquest*, 87–88.

85  *Yet the beginning of the Seven Years' War*   The information about the lead-up to the Acadian internment at Grand-Pré comes from Plank, *An Unsettled Conquest*, 140–47, and Jobb, *The Cajuns*, 118–20.

85    *John Winslow, a member*    Quotes from John Winslow are found
      in *Collections of the Nova Scotia Historical Society*, Volume 3
      (1883), 109–10.

88    *they prayed and sang hymns*    The information about the
      hymns the Acadians would have sung on their way to the
      British ships—along with the words for "Tout Passe"—
      comes from Sally Ross, "Hymns Sung at Grand-Pré in
      1755," *Acadian and French-Canadian Ancestral Home*,
      http://www.acadian-home.org/1755-Hymns-Grand-
      Pre.html. Suzie LeBlanc sings the song on her 2007
      CD *Tout Passe.*

90    *How deep was the despair*    The names of the Acadians who
      would have left on the first British ships can be found at "Acadians
      Deported at Grand Pré 1755," *Acadian-Cajun Genealogy and
      History*, http://www.acadian-cajun.com/deportgp.htm.

91    *the innocently named vessels* The information on the ships carry-
      ing the Acadians, and their destinations, comes from Jobb, *The
      Cajuns*, 153, and "The Exile," *Acadian-Cajun Genealogy and
      History*, http://www.acadian-cajun.com/exile.htm.

FOUR: **Someplace, Somewhere**

Information on the early days of Shelburne comes from Sarah Acker and
Lewis Jackson, *Historic Shelburne*, (Halifax: Nimbus Publishing, 2001)
and Marion Robertson, *King's Bounty: A History of Early Shelburne,
Nova Scotia* (Halifax: Nova Scotia Museum, 1983).

93    *Back when the privies of Halifax*    Walter Stewart, *True Blue:
      The Loyalist Legend* (Toronto: Collins, 1985), 122.

93    *the Grand Banks fishery off of Newfoundland* I learned about
      the Irish in the Newfoundland fishery from "Holy Cross

Cemetery," *Saint Mary's University*, http://www.smu.ca
/history/holy-cross/.

94 *if Franz Joseph Timming* All of the Demont/DeMont family
material comes from Frank V. Demont of Vermont and Allen
DeMont of New Glasgow, Nova Scotia.

94 *to compensate for Halifax's cockney rabble* Edward
Cornwallis's view of the original settlers in Halifax is noted in
Raddall, *Halifax: Warden of the North*, 36.

94 *The handbills and posters that appeared* The information on
the European recruitment of the Foreign Protestants to Nova
Scotia comes from Winthrop Pickard Bell, *Register of the Foreign
Protestants of Nova Scotia (ca. 1749–1770), Volume I*, ed.
J. Christopher Young (Guelph, ON: self-published, 2003), 5–9.

95 *the overcrowded tween decks* My main source on the shipboard
conditions on the *Gale* and the other ships, plus the early history
of Lunenburg including the Mi'kmaq raids, is Winthrop Pickard
Bell, *The "Foreign Protestants" and the Settlement of Nova
Scotia: The History of a Piece of Arrested British Colonial Policy
in the Eighteenth Century* (Toronto: University of Toronto Press,
1961; Sackville, NB: Acadiensis Press, 1990).

95 *the* Sally *would lose forty passengers* The fatality rates on the
voyages from Europe to Nova Scotia come from Bell, *Register of
the Foreign Protestants*, 10. The passenger list for the *Gale* can
be found on the *Olive Tree Genealogy* blog, where it has been
transcribed by Catherine DiPietro from Ruth E. Kaulback's
self-published 1970 book *Historic Saga of LeHeve*, at
http://www.olivetreegenealogy.com/ships/nsship07.shtml.

95 *This was no triumphant arrival* The hard first days for the
Foreign Protestants in Halifax are detailed in Raddall, *Halifax:
Warden of the North*, 37.

96    *Lunenburg was sectioned off into divisions*   Information on the settlement and grant system for Lunenburg comes from Bell, *Register of the Foreign Protestants.*

96    *Timming . . . drew lot B-9*   My ancestor's original grant, and the land he later acquired along with his livestock, is noted in Bell, *Register of the Foreign Protestants of Nova Scotia,* 569, with additional information from the South Shore Genealogical Society.

97    *A Temperance Hall used to be*   The information about the Temperance Hall came from genealogist Terrance Punch.

97    *Sam Slick, the Yankee trader*   Sam Slick's line about the New England Planters comes from T.C. Haliburton, *The Clockmaker; or The Sayings and Doings of Samuel Slick, of Slickville* (London: Routledge, 1884), 15. The information about the Planters is from R.S. Longley, *The Coming of the New England Planters to the Annapolis Valley,* a paper read before the Nova Scotia Historical Society in April 1960.

100   *Howe, visiting the Planter village of Bridgetown*   Howe's description of Bridgetown is from *Western and Eastern Rambles,* 98–100.

102   *Henry Alline grew up*   The biographical information about Henry Alline comes from J.M. Bumsted, *Henry Alline 1748–1784* (Toronto: University of Toronto Press, 1971). The quotes from Henry Alline can be found in *Henry Alline: Selected Writings,* ed. George A. Rawlyk (New York: Paulist Press, 1987), 65, 78, 86 and 88.

102   *What a sight he must have been*   The description of Alline's appearance comes from George A. Rawlyk, *Wrapped Up in God: A Study of Several Canadian Revivals and Revivalists* (Montreal and Kingston, ON: McGill-Queen's University Press, 1993), 84.

The description of Alline's complexion, hair and eyes comes from Bumsted, *Henry Alline 1748–1784,* chapter 3.

103    *his "New Light" theology*    Information comes from a wide variety of sources, including Gordon Thomas Stewart and George A. Rawlyk, *A People Highly Favoured of God: The Nova Scotia Yankees and the American Revolution* (Hamden, CT: Anchor Books, 1972). The "people highly favoured of God" quote comes from Rawlyk, *Henry Alline: Selected Writings,* 126.

104    *the best estimate is 19 per cent*    General information about the Loyalist influx into Canada, how many of them there were and why they came is from Stewart, *True Blue.* The quote from Stewart comes from page 2 of the same book.

105    *Nowhere was this truer*    The estimate of the number of British loyalists who immigrated to Nova Scotia comes from Brian McConnell, president of the Nova Scotia branch of the United Empire Loyalists' Association of Canada.

105    *Others, said the provincial surveyor*    The quote from William Morris comes from Stewart, *True Blue,* 131.

105    *Aboard the* Apollo    The *Apollo's* passenger list is viewable online on the Global Genealogy website at http://globalgenealogy. com/news/articles/00100.htm. Biographical information about Wilkins and McIntyre is viewable at http://globalgenealogy.com /news/articles/00098.htm.

105    *Charles Roubalet's smoky tavern*    Information about the doings at the tavern near the Paulus Hook ferry is from Stephen Kimber, *Loyalists and Layabouts: The Rapid Rise and Faster Fall of Shelburne, Nova Scotia, 1783–1792* (Toronto: Doubleday Canada, 2008), 8–9. The thought process of the loyalists when it came to choosing a new home is from page 10 of the same book, while Shelburne's various names are detailed on p. 134.

106    *a deep-seated hate of the Americans*    This anger is noted in William Baker, "The Anti-American Ingredient in Canadian History," *Dalhousie Review* 53, no. 1 (1973): 57–77.

106    *speculator and adventurer Alexander McNutt*    McNutt's background is from *The Chronicles of Canada: Volume IV, The Beginnings of British Canada*, ed. George M. Wrong and H. H. Langton (Tucson, AZ: Fireship Press, 2009), 129.

106    *Mostly they headed to Port Roseway*    The Shelburne area post-McNutt, along with the information about Shelburne's population at its peak, is detailed in Acker and Jackson, *Historic Shelburne*, vi–vii. Parr's description of Shelburne at its peak comes from Kimber, *Loyalists and Layabouts*, 160–61.

107    *I met a man named Richard Gallion*    My time with Richard Gallion is detailed in John DeMont, "Reclaiming a Hard Past," *Maclean's*, February 14, 2000. The story of Birchtown comes from a wide variety of sources.

108    *Lydia Jackson was pressured* Lydia Jackson's story comes from the website *Black Loyalists: Our History, Our People*, as do the stories of "frolicking" and brutal whippings. The site can be found at http://web.archive.org/web/20050402021037 /http://collections.ic.gc.ca/blackloyalists/wireframe.htm.

109    *black loyalist leader Boston King*    Boston King's story can be found in Peter C. Newman, *Hostages to Fortune: The United Empire Loyalists and the Making of Canada* (Toronto: Simon and Schuster, 2016), as can King William IV's quote about the wretchedness of the residents of Birchtown.

109    *Despite all of their misery*    "The Shelburne Race Riots," *The Canadian Encyclopedia*, http://www.thecanadianencyclopedia .ca/en/article/the-shelburne-race-riots/.

109    *"anxious anticipation of what the future"*    Kimber, *Loyalists and Layabouts*, 108–9. The anecdote about female arrivals sitting down and weeping comes from page 119 of the same book.

110    *the newcomers' stubborn belief*    The information about the early days of Shelburne comes mainly from Kimber, *Loyalists and Layabouts* and Acker and Jackson, *Historic Shelburne*.

111    *Lorenzo Sabine sent me*    Information on Lorenzo Sabine comes from William L. Welch, "Lorenzo Sabine and His Critics," *The New England Quarterly* 78, no. 3 (September 2005): 448–52. The sketches of the Shelburne settlers came from Sabine's *The American Loyalists: or, Biographical Sketches of Adherents to the British Crown in the War of the Revolution, Alphabetically Arranged, with a Preliminary Historical Essay* (Boston: Little, Brown, 1847).

114    *a here today, gone tomorrow place*    Shelburne's breathtaking decline is detailed in Kimber, *Loyalists and Layabouts*. The quote about the Halifax situation is found on page 179.

115    *"a pestiferous charnel house"*    Josiah Conder, *The Modern Traveller: A Popular Description, Geographical, Historical and Topographical of the Various Countries of the Globe, Volume 22* (London: James Duncan, 1830), 157.

115    *Valentine Strasser, a twenty-five-year-old*    Valentine Strasser's woeful later years are detailed in Simon Akam, "The Vagabond King," *The New Statesman*, February 2, 2012.

115    *summit of black Canadian political leaders*    I wrote about the congress of black political leaders gathering in John DeMont, "Black political leaders meet in historic Birchtown," Halifax *Chronicle Herald*, June 8, 2015.

116    *in front of a stone cairn*    You can read all about the Moidart cairn and what happens there in Bill McVicar's privately produced document *Battle of Culloden Remembered in Nova Scotia*.

118     *the "cutting and slicing" began*   Donald Mackay, "Eye Witness Account from Frost's Anatomy of Scotland: The Battle of Culloden," *Scottish Tartans Authority*, http://www.tartans authority.com/tartan/the-growth-of-tartan/the-battle-of-culloden /eye-witness-account/. Information also comes from "The Battle of Culloden—1746," *Scotland's History*, http://www.bbc.co.uk /scotland/history/union_and_jacobites/the_battle_of_culloden / and "Battle of Culloden," *New World Encyclopedia*, http: //www.newworldencyclopedia.org/entry/Battle_of_Culloden.

119     *virtually doubled Pictou's population*   Donald MacKay, *Scotland Farewell: The People of the Hector* (Toronto: Dundurn, 2006), 182. The way they spread throughout the province is explained on the next page in the same book.

121     *the first shipload of ragged settlers*   My information on the Scottish migration to Cape Breton comes from Stephen Hornsby, *Nineteenth-Century Cape Breton: A Historical Geography* (Montreal and Kingston, ON: McGill-Queen's University Press, 1992).

122     *among them people named McKeigan*   The information about the MacKeigans comes from Bill Lawson, "From the Outer Hebrides to Cape Breton," *Electric Scotland*, http://www.electricscotland.com/ history/canada/hebrides_breton.htm and Lark B. Szick, *MacKeigans: North Uist to Cape Breton* (Montreal: Self-published, 2000).

FIVE: Ace, Joe and Me

All of the quotations and information from Howe's rambles comes from Howe, *Western and Eastern Rambles*. Biographical information on Howe, generally speaking, comes from Beck, *Joseph Howe: Volume 1* and D.C. Harvey, *The Heart of Howe*.

125   *the sports columnist W.J. "Ace" Foley*   For more on Ace Foley
      read his autobiography, *The First Fifty Years: The Life and Times
      of a Sports Writer* (Windsor, NS: Lancelot Press, 1970).

127   *first paper ever published in Canada*   Information on Halifax's
      first newspaper comes from Stephen Kimber, "John Bushell:
      Canadian Newspapering's Unlikely Father," http://stephenkim-
      ber.com/bio/journalism/canadas-first-newspaper/.

127   *Halifax had an even dozen papers*   Judith Fingard, Janet
      Guildford and David Sutherland, *Halifax: The First 250 Years*
      (Halifax: Formac, 1999), 62.

129   *"dullness succeeded enthusiasm, cynicism faith"*   This quote is
      attributed to J.A. Roy and is found in J. Murray Beck's entry on
      Howe in the *Dictionary of Canadian Biography*, http://www.
      biographi.ca/en/bio/howe_joseph_10E.html.

129   *"When I sit down in solitude"*   Howe's famous journalistic
      credo is from his libel defence of March 2, 1835. It can be
      found online at http://nslegislature.ca/index.php/about/joe-howe
      /howedefense/.

130   *"genuine capacity to be with people"*   The anecdotes about
      Howe's affinity for the common folk come from the author's
      interview with Michael Bawtree.

133   *"essentially a New England community"*   C. Bruce Fergusson,
      "Simeon Perkins," *Dictionary of Canadian Biography*,
      http://www.biographi.ca/en/bio/perkins_simeon_5E.html.

134   *his voice from his voluminous diaries*   Simeon Perkins, *The
      Diary of Simeon Perkins, 1766–1780*, ed. with introduction
      and notes by Harold A. Innis (Toronto: Champlain Society,
      1948), viewable online at http://link.library.utoronto.ca
      /champlain/item_record.cfm?Idno=9_96877&lang=eng&
      query=Perkins,%20Simeon,%201735-1812.%20;%20ed.%20

with%20introd.%20and%20notes%20by%20Harold%20A.%20
Innis.&browsetype=Author&startrow=1.

134     *Perkins was a man of enterprise*   Fergusson, "Simeon Perkins,"
        *Dictionary of Canadian Biography.*

134     *a pair of Yankee privateer ships*   Information about the Yankee
        marine raiders comes from Stephen Schneider, *Iced: The Story of
        Organized Crime in Canada* (Mississauga, ON: John Wiley &
        Sons, 2009), 24.

134     *men aboard those Nova Scotian ships*   The wording for a typical
        Nova Scotia privateer's commission is from a commission issued
        in 1777 by Lieutenant Governor Arbuthnot for the commander
        of the *Revenge*. It was quoted in George E.E. Nichols's 1904
        paper for the Nova Scotia Historical Society, *Notes on Nova
        Scotia Privateers.*

136     *"Privateers and their prizes"*   Dan Conlin, "Privateer Entrepot:
        Commercial Militarization in Liverpool, Nova Scotia, 1793–1805,"
        *Northern Mariner* 8, no. 2 (1998): 21–38.

136     *merchants that included Simeon Perkins*   Information about
        Simeon Perkins's privateering exploits is from Schneider, *Iced*, 24,
        and Nichols, *Notes on Nova Scotia Privateers.*

136     *the brig* Rover   Information on the *Rover* is from Horwood,
        *Plunder and Pillage*, 135–38.

137     *the name of the* Liverpool Packet   The *Packet*'s exploits
        were detailed in Edward Butts, "Joseph Barss: The Greatest
        of the Nova Scotia Privateers," *Toronto Star*, September 28,
        2012.

138     *a man named Enos Collins*   The information about Enos Collins
        comes from Diane M. Barker and D.A. Sutherland, "Enos
        Collins," *Dictionary of Biography*, http://www.biographi.ca/en
        /bio/collins_enos_10E.html, and Elizabeth Pacey (text) and

Alvin Comiter (photographs), *Historic Halifax* (Willowdale, ON: Hounslow Press, 1988), 60.

138    *The end of the War of 1812*    The description of Halifax after the War of 1812 is from Raddall, *Halifax: Warden of the North*, 158.

139    *"its streets are laid out with regularity"*    Thomas Chandler Haliburton, quoted in Fingard, Guildford and Sutherland, *Halifax: The First 250 Years*, 50.

139    *"more refinement, more elegance and fashion"*    The Scot was named John MacGregor and is quoted in Fingard, Guildford and Sutherland, *Halifax: The First 250 Years*, 51. On page 37 of the same book is found the information about Collins picking up waterfront properties.

140    *a man in search of elevated thoughts*    Details of the intellectual life of Halifax in those days can be found in Charles Bruce Fergusson, "Laurence (Lawrence) O'Connor Doyle," *Dictionary of Canadian Biography*, http://www.biographi.ca/en/bio/doyle_laurence_o_connor_9E.html.

140    *the Halifax Mechanics' Institute*    Howe's address can be found online at https://archive.org/details/cihm_21391.

140    *editor of the competing* Acadian Recorder    This anecdote can be found in Pacey and Comiter, *Historic Halifax*, 68.

140    *a tiny, congested place*    The information about Halifax's congestion and "The Hill" comes from Fingard, Guildford and Sutherland, *Halifax: The First 250 Years*, 53 and 55.

141    *no decent water supply*    The information about Halifax's lack of sewers comes from the Public Archives of Nova Scotia, while the progression of street lighting is from the collections of Library and Archives Canada.

141    *begun to move from their mansions*    The description of the centre of Halifax comes from the *1830 Plan of the Town of*

*Halifax, Including the North and South Suburbs, Illustrating
the Workhouse, Correction House, the Poor House and the Jail,*
found in Cynthia Simpson, "The Treatment of Halifax's Poor
House Dead During the Nineteenth and Twentieth Centuries"
(master's thesis, Saint Mary's University, 2011), 44.

141   *cholera ran rampant*   The description of fatal maladies in
Halifax in the early nineteenth century and the process for bury-
ing the dead are detailed in Raddall, *Halifax: Warden of the
North,* 177. Information on the smallpox epidemics is also found
in Simpson, "The Treatment of Halifax's Poor House Dead."

142   *groggeries and brothels on Barracks*   The description of Barracks
Street comes from Judith Fingard, *The Dark Side of Life in
Victorian Halifax* (Porters Lake, NS: Pottersfield Press, 1989), 19.

142   *old-time practice of branding criminals*   This practice is referred
to in Pacey and Comiter, *Historic Halifax,* 116.

142   *"squalid and poverty-struck"*   This quote and R.H. Dana's observations comes from Fingard, *The Dark Side of Life in Victorian
Halifax,* 19; the visiting clergyman's comment about Halifax
drinking habits is quoted on page 17 of the same book.

143   *a man named James Bossom*   The woeful saga of the Bossom
clan is found in Dianne Marshall, *True Stories from Nova Scotia's
Past* (Halifax: Formac, 2012).

143   *tar-covered bodies of pirates*   The information about the pirates,
hanging and tar-and-featherings is from Dan Conlin, "Pirates:
A Fact Sheet by Dan Conlin (former Curator, Marine History),"
*Maritime Museum of the Atlantic,* https://maritimemuseum.
novascotia.ca/collections/pirates.

144   *power was the exclusive possession*   The information on
Nova Scotia's oligarchical political situation comes from several
sources, including: Fingard, Guildford and Sutherland, *Halifax:*

*The First 250 Years*, 43 and 52; Catherine Buckie, *Parliamentary Demoracy in Nova Scotia: How It Began, How It Evolved* (Halifax: Communications Nova Scotia, 2009); and "Council of Twelve," *The Canadian Encyclopedia*, http://www.thecanadian encyclopedia.ca/en/article/council-of-twelve/.

146   *tax on foreign brandy*   Information on the brandy tax dispute comes from Beck, *Joseph Howe*, 62; Diane M. Barker and D.A. Sutherland, "Enos Collins," *Dictionary of Biography*, http://www.biographi.ca/en/bio/collins_enos_10E.html; and J.M. Beck, "'A Fool for a Client': The Trial of Joseph Howe," *Acadiensis* 3, no. 2 (spring 1974): 27–44.

147   *The letter that appeared at the bottom*   George Thompson's letter, which sparked Howe's libel trial, can be seen on the Nova Scotia legislature's website at http://nslegislature.ca/index .php/about/joe-howe/howepaper. The libel indictment against him can be found at http://nslegislature.ca/index.php/about /joe-howe/indictment.

147   *"would not bear their banners unsullied from the field"*   Howe's warning comes from Beck, *Joseph Howe: Volume 1, 135*. His preparations before and observations during the trail are found on the same page. The whole of Howe's famous address is viewable on the website of the Nova Scotia legislature at http://nslegislature .ca/index.php/about/joe-howe/howedefense.

153   *"the press of Nova Scotia is free"*   Quoted in Beck, "'A Fool for a Client,'" which also discusses the impact of the trial on Nova Scotia's press and Howe's travels after the trial.

155   *"without a blow struck"*   The quote about peacefully achieving responsible government comes from "Joseph Howe," *The Canadian Encyclopedia*, http://www.thecanadianencyclopedia .ca/en/article/joseph-howe/.

155    *the Charlottetown Conference in September 1864*
"Charlottetown Conference," *The Canadian Encyclopedia*,
http://www.thecanadianencyclopedia.ca/en/article/charlottetown
-conference/.

155    *Howe thought from the start*   Howe's fears about the impact of
Confederation are referred to in Gerald Friesen, "Atlantic
Canada's Historical Writing Today: No Howe?", *Acadiensis* 30
(autumn 2000): 64–72.


SIX: **Making it Pay**

My main sources of biographical information about Slocum and his
voyages were: Geoffrey Wolff, *The Hard Way Around: The Passages of
Joshua Slocum* (New York: Alfred A. Knopf, 2010) and Joshua Slocum,
*Sailing Alone Around the World and the Voyage of the* Liberdade
(London: Readers Union, 1949).

160    *"tough as wrought iron"*   Wolff, *The Hard Way Around*, 83.
The anecdote about the scar over Slocum's eye is from page 30 of
the same book.

160    *"I was born in the breezes"*   Slocum, *Sailing Alone*, 33.
The "I had resolved on a voyage around the world" quote
is found on page 39. That he was born "in a cold spot, on
coldest North Mountain, on a cold February 20" is from
page 31, while his "a thrilling pulse" line is on page 39.

162    *including Captain George Clements Sr.*   The information about
Captain Clements comes from "George W. Clements House,"
*Canada's Historic Places*, http://www.historicplaces.ca/en/rep-
reg/place-lieu.aspx?id=6922.

162    *Slocum's upbringing had been harsh*   Slocum's memories of
Westport come from Slocum, *Sailing Alone*, 47 and 48. On the

latter page is also found his recollection of his pleasant days in Yarmouth and the anecdote about Lowry.

163    *New Englanders joined the Mi'kmaq*    Information on the early history of Yarmouth comes from John Roy Campbell, *A History of the County of Yarmouth, Nova Scotia* (Saint John, NB: J. & A. McMillan, 1876) and David Alexander and Gerry Panting, "The Mercantile Fleet and its Owners: Yarmouth, Nova Scotia, 1840–1889," *Acadiensis* 7, no. 2 (spring 1978): 3–28.

164    *We do know that in 1761*    For much of the section on the history of shipbuilding and ownership in Nova Scotia I am indebted to Eric Sager and Lewis Fischer and their 1986 monograph for the Canadian Historical Association, *Shipping and Shipbuilding in Atlantic Canada, 1820–1914.* The figures on the increase in Yarmouth shipbuilding come from Campbell, *A History of the County of Yarmouth,* 96 and 97; Alexander and Panting, "The Mercantile Fleet"; and Sager and Fischer, *Shipping and Shipbuilding in Atlantic Canada.*

166    *Immigration, new markets for the fish*    The information on Nova Scotia shipbuilding after the American Revolutionary War comes from Sager and Fischer, 4–7, and Alexander and Panting, 5, 18 and 20. The biographical information about the great shipbuilding families of Yarmouth comes from a variety of sources, including Alexander and Panting and *The Canadian Encyclopedia.*

167    *bed and breakfast of unaccustomed splendour*    The information on Lovitt House comes from "Walking Tour of Yarmouth Heritage Properties," *Yarmouth County Museum and Archives,* http://www.yarmouthcountymuseum.ca/index.php/walking-tour.

168    *big picture of Izaak Walton Killam*    "Izaak Walton Killam," *The Canadian Encyclopedia,* http://www.thecanadianencyclopedia.ca /en/article/izaak-walton-killam/.

169    *In his grand, gloomy book*    The quotes about the nature of the
       ocean depths come from James Hamilton-Paterson, *The Great
       Deep: The Sea and Its Thresholds* (New York: Random House,
       1992), 143 and 165.

170    *the desert island genre*    The definition of Robinsonade is from
       the *Encyclopaedia Britannica*, https://www.britannica.com/art
       /robinsonade, while the meaning of nesomania is from the
       *Online English Encyclopedia*, http://www.encyclo.co.uk
       /meaning-of-nesomania.

171    *The Maritime Museum of the Atlantic's database*    The database,
       https://maritimemuseum.novascotia.ca/research/shipwreck
       -database is the best single source of information about
       Nova Scotia shipwrecks.

171    *at least 350 wrecks*    The figure for shipwrecks off of Sable
       Island comes from the Maritime Museum of the Atlantic. The
       information about St. Paul Island comes from an article by
       Terry Dwyer on the *Wreck Hunter* website, http://wreckhunter
       .ca/index.php/st-paul-island/st-paul-island-home.

171    *a grim spring tradition*    The Seal Island anecdote comes from an
       article about the Seal Island Lighthouse found on the Nova Scotia
       Lighthouse Preservation Society's website, http://www.nslps
       .com/dir_AboutLights/LighthouseSingle.aspx?LID=362&M=
       IP&N=3.

171    *saga of Howard Blackburn*    Blackburn's biographical informa-
       tion comes from the article "Captain Howard Blackburn, the Lone
       Voyager" on the website of the Cape Ann Museum in Cape Ann,
       Massachusetts, http://www.capeannmuseum.org/blackburn/.

172    *A great mariner needed*    The information about the prerequisites
       for being a great mariner come from the Penobscot Marine
       Museum in Searsport, Maine.

172    *George Spicer of Spencer's Island*    Information on George
       Spicer comes from Stanley T. Spicer, *Captain from Fundy: The
       Life and Times of George D. Spicer, Master of Square-rigged
       Windjammers* (Hantsport, NS: Lancelot Press, 1988).

173    *In 1870 Bessie Hall*    The information on Bessie Hall and
       her family and adventures comes from the Canada's Historic
       Places entry on Captain Joseph Hall House in Annapolis
       Royal, http://www.historicplaces.ca/en/rep-reg/place-lieu
       .aspx?id=14161&pid=0 as well as a variety of scholarly and
       popular sources.

174    *As his hailing port he chose*    The quote about Slocum's activities
       in San Francisco comes from Wolff, *The Hard Way Around*, 34–35.

176    *the port's registered shipping tonnage*    The information about
       the port of Yarmouth's registered shipping tonnage being equal to
       the whole of British shipping in the time of Henry VII comes from
       Campbell, *A History of the County of Yarmouth*, 133.

176    *when those wharves hummed*    The survey of the kinds of busi-
       nesses on the Yarmouth waterfront in the 1870s comes from
       *McAlpine's Maritime Provinces Directory* for 1870–71 and
       *Lovell's Province of Nova Scotia Directory* for 1871.

177    *Merchant money was behind the Bank*    The observation that
       merchant money was behind the Bank of Yarmouth, the Yarmouth
       Steam Navigation Company and the Acadian Insurance Company
       comes from Eric W. Sager and Gerald E. Panting, *Maritime
       Capital: The Shipping Industry of Atlantic Canada, 1820–1914*
       (Montreal and Kingston, ON: McGill-Queen's University Press,
       1990), 84. Biographical material about Loran Baker is from Eric J.
       Ruff, "Loran Ellis Baker," *Dictionary of Canadian Biography*,
       http://www.biographi.ca/en/bio/baker_loran_ellis_12E.html;
       Alexander and Panting, *Shipping and Shipbuilding*; and Sager,

*Maritime Capital.* The types of companies and buildings around Yarmouth at that time come mostly from Campbell, *A History of the County of Yarmouth,* 109, 172 and 188–90.

178    *wasn't the only shipbuilding centre*    My primary source on the shipyards and shipbuilders of Nova Scotia is Frederick William Wallace, *Wooden Ships and Iron Men: The Story of the Square-rigged Merchant Marine of British North America, the Ships, Their Builders and Owners and the Men who Sailed Them* (New York: George Sully, 1924).

178    *the tiny town of River John*    Information on the River John yards comes from "River John Reinventing Itself," *Charlottetown Guardian,* September 18, 2013.

179    *"with all its beautiful undulations"*    Howe's quote about Windsor comes from Howe, *Western and Eastern Rambles,* 65.

179    *Maitland had eleven shingled houses*    The information about Maitland and its yards comes from the Maitland History section on the Municipality of East Hants website, https://www .easthants.ca/visitors/history-east-hants/villages-of-east-hants /maitland-history/, as well as Frederick William Wallace, *In the Wake of the Wind-Ships: Notes, Records and Biographies Pertaining to the Square-Rigged Merchant Marine of British North America* (Toronto: Musson, 1927).

181    *"embers of mutiny"*    Wolff, *The Hard Way Around,* 93.

181    *had branded him a "brute"*    *New York Times* calling Slocum a "brute" is mentioned in Wolff, *The Hard Way Around,* 144.

182    *"an old acquaintance, a whaling-captain"*    Slocum, *Sailing Alone,* 33. The quote about "making it pay" is from page 34 of the same book.

183    *fourth-largest merchant marine*    Sager and Fischer, *Shipping and Shipbuilding.* The same book provided the information that

Yarmouth's merchants and their sons put their money into railways, textiles, sugar refineries and iron and steel.

183    *the same torrid pace*   Campbell, *A History of the County of Yarmouth*, 133.

183    *the most registered tonnage*   Campbell, *A History of the County of Yarmouth*, 138.

183    *its usual languid pace*   The information about the 1895 session of the Nova Scotia Legislature is from J. Murray Beck, *Politics of Nova Scotia: Volume 1, 1710–1896* (Tantallon, NS: Four East Publications, 1985), 263.

184    *a twelve-year-old girl*   The story of the rape allegations against Slocum comes from Walter Teller's introduction to *The Voyages of Joshua Slocum* (Dobbs Ferry, NY: Sheridan House, 1985), 22.

184    *"the wind came out nor'west"*   Slocum, *Sailing Alone*, 49.

SEVEN: **Way Down in the Hole**

187    *Robert Currie in the town of Donkin*   "Donkin hole blamed on old mine workings," *CBC* News, January 6, 2006, http://www.cbc.ca/news/canada/nova-scotia/donkin -hole-blamed-on-old-mine-workings-1.612473.

189    *"surpasses every country"*   John DeMont, *Coal Black Heart: The Story of Coal and the Lives it Ruled* (Toronto: Doubleday Canada, 2009), 109.

190    *nearly a thousand* boys   Robert McIntosh, "The Boys in the Nova Scotian Coal Mines: 1873–1923," *Acadiensis* 16, no. 2 (spring 1987): 36.

191    *when Howe was rambling*   The quotes from Howe's rambles come from Howe, *Western and Eastern Rambles*, 165.

192    *The population of Sydney Mines*    "Population of Cities and
       Towns Having Over 5,000 Inhabitants in 1911, compared with
       1871–81–91–01," Canada Bureau of Statistics, *Canada Year
       Book: 1919* (Ottawa: King's Printer, 1920), 106. According to the
       1911 census, the population of Sydney Mines had grown to 7,470
       from 3,191 in 1901.

193    *like a comet across the sky*    Don MacGillivray, "Henry Melville
       Whitney Comes to Cape Breton: The Saga of a Gilded Age
       Entrepreneur," *Acadiensis* 9, no. 1 (autumn 1979): 44–70;
       Don MacGillivray, "Henry Melville Whitney," *Dictionary of
       Canadian Biography*, http://www.biographi.ca/en/bio/whitney
       _henry_melville_15E.html; and Thomas W. Lawson, *Frenzied
       Finance: The Crime of Amalgamated* (New York: Greenwood
       Press, 1905, 1968).

193    *"What is the chief end"*    The Mark Twain quote about the
       Gilded Age comes from several sources.

193    *"A Pittsburgh in Canada"*    "A Pittsburgh in Canada: Plant at
       Sydney Could Compete with Carnegie Combine," *New York
       Times*, February 17, 1901: 14.

196    *program to demolish seven hundred*    Author's interview with
       Cape Breton Regional Municipality Mayor Cecil Clarke.

197    *cost more than 2,500 lives*    Information on colliery deaths in Nova
       Scotia comes from "Nova Scotia Mine Fatalities, 1838–1992,"
       Nova Scotia Archives website, https://novascotia.ca/archives
       /meninmines/fatalities.asp.

198    *funny little wooden house*    Lois Legge, "The rise, fall and
       legacy of Sydney's Moxham Castle," *Chronicle Herald*
       (Halifax), July 18, 2014, http://thechronicleherald.ca
       /thenovascotian/1223389-the-rise-fall-and-legacy-of
       -sydney-s-moxham-castle.

199     *Cape Breton's coal mines supplied*    David Frank, "The Cape
        Breton Coal Industry and the Rise and Fall of the British Empire
        Steel Corporation," *Acadiensis* 7, no. 1 (autumn 1977): 6. The
        Francis W. Gray quote comes from page 7 of the same article.

201     *relationship between labour and capitalism*    John Manley,
        "Preaching the Red Stuff: J.B. McLachlan, Communism, and
        the Cape Breton Miners, 1922–1935," *Labour / Le Travail* 30
        (fall 1992).

202     *destroyers were diverted to Sydney*    Don MacGillivray,
        "Military Aid to the Civil Power: The Cape Breton Experience
        in the 1920s," in *Cape Breton Historical Essays*, ed. Don
        MacGillivray and Brian Tennyson (Sydney, NS: College of
        Cape Breton Press, 1980).

202     *Cape Breton's coal miners struck*    Information about the strikes
        comes from coverage of events in the *Sydney Post*.

202     *machine guns at the ready*    MacGillivray, "Military Aid to the
        Civil Power."

203     *the "100 percent strike"*    Details about the destitution during
        the "100 percent strike" come from a number of sources, includ-
        ing the *Sydney Post*, the *Halifax Morning Chronicle* and David
        Frank, *J.B. McLachlan, A Biography: The Story of a Legendary
        Labour Leader and the Cape Breton Coal Miners* (Toronto:
        Lorimer, 1999).

EIGHT: **Angle of Repose**

General biographical information about Clara Dennis can be found
on the Nova Scotia Archives website (https://novascotia.ca/archives
/dennis/). Her photographs can be seen by using the page's search
function or clicking on the Graphic Material tab.

210    *William, an abstemious workaholic*   Information on William
Dennis comes from Stephen Kimber, "What Would Graham Say?"
*Atlantic Business*, January/February 2017 and Kimber, "The
Publisher's Daughter," *Cities*, March 1988. His newspapering credo
comes from *Our Late Chief*, a 1920 publication by the staff of the
Halifax *Herald* memorializing William Dennis. I learned of its existence through Tim Bosuquet's *Halifax Examiner* website, https://
www.halifaxexaminer.ca/featured/william-dennis-the-friend-of-the
-men-morning-file-tuesday-march-1-2016/#Noticed.

211    *"I would travel over her highways"*   Clara Dennis, *d* (Toronto:
Ryerson Press, 1934), 1.

211    *Critic V.B. Rhodenizer*   V.B. Rhodenizer, *At the Sign of the
Hand and Pen: Nova-Scotian Authors* (Nova Scotia Branch,
Canadian Authors Association, n.d.).

214    *a Nova Scotian household barely*   Information about life in the
coal towns during the Great Depression came from Michiel
Horn's essay "The Dirty Thirties" for the McCord Museum,
http://collections.musee-mccord.qc.ca/scripts/projects/CH/
animCH.php?tourID=GE_P4_1_EN.

214    *Elderly and destitute refused*   Ernest Forbes, "Cutting the Pie
into Smaller Pieces: Matching Grants and Relief in the Maritime
Provinces During the 1930s," *Acadiensis* 17, no. 1 (autumn 1987).

214    *60 per cent of ordinary*   Joe Martin, "The Great Depression hit
Canada the hardest," *Kitchener-Waterloo Record*, March 28, 2013.

215    *I imagine the recruitment pitch*   Nova Scotia World War I
recruitment posters can be seen in the online exhibit "An Act
of Remembrance" on the Nova Scotia Archives website at
ttp://novascotia.ca/archives/warposters/archives.asp?ID=54.

215    *a member of the 106th*   John Briers's attestation papers from the
Department of National Defence, http://www.bac-lac.gc.ca/eng

/discover/military-heritage/first-world-war/personnel-records
/Pages/item.aspx?IdNumber=63873. Information on Nova
Scotia's war effort comes from *Nova Scotia's Part in the Great
War* ed. M. Stuart Hunt (Halifax: Nova Scotia Veteran
Publishing Co., 1920). Information on the Campbell clan comes
from Hunt, *Nova Scotia's Part in the Great War* and author's
conversation with Elissa Barnard.

222    *I don't know where Lawson Hardy*    Biographical info about
Hardy comes from Graeme Wynn, "Images of the Acadian Valley:
The Photographs of Amos Lawson Hardy," *Acadiensis* 15, no. 1
(autumn 1985). Information about Georgia Harriet Cunningham
comes from the Annapolis Heritage Society. Information about
Wallace MacAskill comes from the Nova Scotia Archives.

223    *Sam Langford, at twelve*    Biographical information about Sam
Langford comes from Clay Moyle, *Sam Langford: Boxing's
Greatest Uncrowned Champion* (Seattle: Bennett and Hastings,
2006). The quote from the *Chronicle Herald* is mentioned in that
book on page 368.

225    *twenty miles of paved roads*    Stanley Graham, "Pictou County
Reminiscences—Highways," http://www.rootsweb.ancestry
.com/~pictou/hiwaysg.htm.

225    *almost half of the province's*    "Population, urban and rural, by
province and territory," *Statistics Canada*, http://www.statcan
.gc.ca/tables-tableaux/sum-som/l01/cst01/demo62d-eng.htm.

NINE: **Back Home**

229    *A few days earlier John Morris Rankin*    My story about John
Morris Rankin's death was called "A Cape Breton Farewell" and
appeared in the January 31, 2000, edition of *Maclean's*.

233    *transfer payments from Ottawa*    Canadian Centre for Policy
        Alternatives—Nova Scotia, "A Better Way: Putting the Nova
        Scotia Deficit in Perspective," https://www.policyalternatives.ca
        /sites/default/files/uploads/publications/Nova_Scotia_Pubs/NS
        _abetterway.pdf and Jean Soucy and Marion G. Wrobel, "Fiscal
        Policy in Canada: The Changing Role of the Federal and
        Provincial Governments," http://publications.gc.ca/Collection
        -R/LoPBdP/CIR/912-e.htm.

233    *the sweet rural life*    "Population, urban and rural, by province
        and territory," *Statistics Canada*, http://www.statcan.gc.ca
        /tables-tableaux/sum-som/l01/cst01/demo62d-eng.htm.

235    *I was bound for a fishing village*    My story about Lockeport was
        called "Learning to Climb Back" and appeared in the January 21,
        1991, edition of *Maclean's*.

237    *"The last shift, when it comes"*    My story about the closing of
        the Prince Mine was called "One Last Whistle" and appeared in
        the August 6, 2001, edition of *Maclean's*.

238    *Billy Ludlow, his face pale*    Billy Ludlow's death notice can
        be glimpsed at http://www.inmemoriam.ca/view-announcement
        -21362-william-billy-ludlow.html.

239    *Halifax was different*    My story about Halifax's ascendance is
        called "The Last Best Place" and is from the June 19, 1995, edi-
        tion of *Maclean's*.

242    *May 9, 1992*    Those looking for more information on the
        Westray disaster could consult the prologue to my book *Coal
        Black Heart*. My interview with Donald Cameron about Westray
        can be found in "Thunder Out of Westray," in the July 27, 1992,
        issue of *Maclean's*.

246    *Donald Marshall Jr. was just seventeen*    The story of my visit
        with Junior Marshall, "A Long and Winding Road," appeared

in the August 20, 2001, issue of *Maclean's*.

248 *an oldtimer named Elie-Joe* My chat with Elie-Joe Chiasson was part of the story "The Wild Winds of Cape Breton," which ran in *Maclean's* on December 9, 2002.

250 *Howe would have had no qualms* Information on Howe's oratorical style comes from Friesen, "Atlantic Canada's Historical Writing Today: No Howe?" Quotes from Howe's speech to the Mechanics' Institute can be found in Harvey, *Heart of Howe*, starting on page 54.


## Epilogue

254 *started by Ngoon Lee* Ngoon Lee's background comes from his grandson Albert Lee's reminiscence, which appears on the Chinese Canadian National Council's website at https://ccncourstories.wordpress.com/our-stories-features /reflections-of-activists/albert-lee/.

254 *called the area* Jipugtug "Halifax," *The Canadian Encyclopedia*, http://thecanadianencyclopedia.com/en/article /halifax/.

255 *the phantom me would see* This section, about the trees through which a ghostly me would have walked on the way down to Halifax Harbour, is educated speculation based on information in the Halifax Regional Municipality's *Urban Forest Master Plan Digest*, August 2014.

255 *"one continual wood"* Cornwallis is quoted in C.W. Jefferys, "The Founding of Halifax."

# Photography Credits

Pages x, 186, 228, 254 courtesy of the author; page 14 "Order of Good Cheer," Nova Scotia Information Service, photographer, ca. 1959; Nova Scotia Archives, NSIS Photo no. 13005; page 40 Royal Engineers, Nova Scotia Archives 7013; page 62 "Where the Acadians embarked for deportation, Grand-Pré, Kings Co., NS," Clara Dennis, photographer, 1930s; Nova Scotia Archives, Clara Dennis fonds, 1981-541 no. 746; page 92 courtesy of Bill McVicar; page 124 "Province House in winter show-ing statue of Joseph Howe, Halifax, NS," W.R. MacAskill, photographer; Nova Scotia Archives, W.R. MacAskill fonds, 1987-453 no. 4491; page 158 "Yarmouth Waterfront," Enos R. Parker, photographer, 1900; NSA Photograph Collection: Places: Yarmouth: Waterfront; page 208 courtesy of Elissa Barnard.

# Acknowledgements

The most obvious debts of thanks for this book go to every teacher, family member and person who ever tried to explain this province to me. Immense thanks as well to each newspaper, magazine and book publisher that has allowed me to write about Nova Scotia.

Jim Meek, Stephen Kimber, Peter Moreira, Philip DeMont, Chris Lambie, Jonathan Fowler, Roger Lewis, Bill McVicar and Heather Dennis read sections of the book and made invaluable suggestions.

It was Scott Sellers's inspired idea. My sage agent Dean Cooke made the deal happen. Tim Rostron and Lloyd Davis gave coherence to my ramblings. Jennifer Griffiths made the book look great. Valentina Capuani oversaw production. Kimberlee Hesas saw the project through to daylight.

A colossal shout-out to my offspring Belle and Sam for encouraging, grounding and amusing me. Lisa Napier, as always, gets the biggest thanks for too many reasons to list here.

# A Note About the Type

*The Long Way Home* has been set in Sabon, an "old style" serif originally designed by Jan Tschichold in the 1960s.

The roman is based on types by Claude Garamond (c.1480–1561), primarily from a specimen printed by the German printer Konrad Berner. (Berner had married the widow of fellow printer Jacques Sabon, hence the face's name.)